GABRIELLA D'ITALIA

GETTING
DRESSED
IN THE
DARK

AN ARTIST'S WAY HOME

This is a memoir. The author has taken great care in telling her story and representing her experience. No harm was intended in the telling of these experiences.

Attention schools and businesses: for discounted copies on large orders, please contact the publisher directly.

For information contact:
Unsolicited Press
Portland, Oregon
www.unsolicitedpress.com
orders@unsolicitedpress.com
619-354-8005

Cover Designer: Kathryn Gerhardt
Editor: Summer Stewart

ISBN-13: 978-1-963115-42-0

Contents

GABRIELLA D'ITALIA

GETTING DRESSED IN THE DARK

AN ARTIST'S WAY HOME

PART 1: The Turtle

A turtle is characterized by defense. Her main architecture is a bony shell capable of completely obscuring the tender meandering of her cold-blooded body. This cold-bloodedness is often misunderstood because it's not that the blood of a turtle is cold, but rather, it is variable according to her surroundings. Perhaps this makes her an empath of the highest order, absorbing what is outside so that she requires this all-but-consuming carapace. She is hard because she is soft and slow in a world, whose very being, threatens her boundaries, her integrity.

1. Split in Two

The week my parents traveled to St. Martin leaving me alone for the first time in months, I rarely left the bathtub. I lay there until the water turned cold. I stared at the pinkish brown tiles that covered the walls and ceiling, a hard cocoon for an indeterminate and dubious stay. I couldn't cry. I sat in the graying water hoping to thaw. I was hoping to become fluid, commensurate, a part of the world again. If only in texture, that would be a start.

Episodes of *Bored To Death* flickered from a Kindle poised at the edge of the tub. The tub was also pinkish brown, matching the tiles. This improvised cocoon was located neatly at the center of an impervious house, the five-bedroom colonial where I grew up in Morristown, New Jersey. The shine of stainless-steel stockpots, spotless windows, and dustless bureaus alerted even the most casual observer to the spell cast here. Imperviousness ran through each one of six identical pie plates, five frying pans, twenty mixing bowls, four full sets of dishes, ten baking sheets, and countless glasses lined up in neat rows in each of two china cabinets: one yellow chinoiserie and the other, mahogany. There were more still in the kitchen cupboards. If anything was broken or tarnished something would immediately take its place, pristine. There was no soft underbelly, no moment of absence suggesting uncertainty, just a Hydra of *things*. I had no mechanism for grief.

I left Maine in a blur of violence just a handful of fleeting and interminable months earlier. I can't be sure of timelines. I didn't know then that I would never return, only that I wouldn't survive if I stayed. I could tell you stories of things that happened before and after, but inside those stories are only more stories—not reasons, not even truths, just an elaborate network of mirrors and lenses. The way I was looking at it all. The way I saw myself. Everything woven together with the present bearing down on the past just as much as the past bears down on it.

I had no permanent place to live when I left. I had taken the dogs with me, all four of them. Petey, Pony, Buster, and Flash. Pony is a perfect animal. A black, fifteen-pound prancing deer. He's slender like an Italian greyhound, but with huge fruit bat ears, like a chihuahua, and a mysteriously docked tail like someone tried to pass him off as a Min Pin. They'd obviously failed to notice his deeply sweet elegance. He's ferociously fast catching sight of a squirrel or chipmunk, but falls trying to corner, his rudder removed by someone who clearly had no understanding of his purpose, his joy. Mostly we called him Prince Pony once we got to know him. Rob and I ended up with three more dogs. Had we gotten any of the others first, especially Petey, who on the day we brought him home walked straight through the fence that enclosed our acre of Maine garden as if it wasn't there at all, while the others watched as if he'd just walked through a wall, things probably would not have gone that way. Each one created the conditions for the next as is the exigency of specific creatures and objects.

In the predawn darkness, Rob would head downstairs to get in a couple of hours of writing before daybreak. He would rekindle the fire in the woodstove and let Pony, Petey, Buster, and Flash out one of the glass doors I'd carefully selected to flank the white enamel stove heating the one-room schoolhouse we called home. They'd burst from the door and race each other to the outer corners of the fenced portion of two acres, howling and barking fury to announce their territory to anything that may have crept in during the night. Rob would make me a latte and leave it on the yellow pine bedside table next to me.

When everything happened, and despite being in no state to have living creatures depend on me, there was no way I was leaving the dogs behind with Rob. In all the ways that the story of the previous two decades we spent together would alternately unravel and metastasize, that the dogs would remain with me was beyond the grasp of rewritten histories.

A trailer loaded with my belongings (what odd, impulsive curation of them remained) was unceremoniously dropped at a storage facility on the side of a highway in New Jersey. I had only a small window of time to unload it before a truck would come to retrieve the container. It grew dark and the storage facility closed, meaning the lights went out and the doors locked. I propped the doors open with some boxes, which slowly bent and twisted under the pressure of this task they were never intended for. I lay down on the asphalt pavement. I looked at the urban sky, never fully dark enough to reveal the thousands of glittering, massive stars left behind in Maine. I didn't bother to brush away hard bits of gravel that stuck to my face and hands.

Cameron, Rob, and I had been in a relationship for the previous decade, before polyamory became mainstream nomenclature. My relationship with Cameron remained strong, albeit darkened like everything else. After all, Rob and I had traced the arc of more than half our lives together. Our time spanned and resolved an impressionable and formative twenty years; our marriage preceded our time with Cameron. The three of us had always been loath to generalize about what we had, to name it. After all, the impulse to be in this relationship was a challenge to our own internalized versions of convention, even in our most intimate lives. Naming seemed just part of a strategy of justification in which we had little interest. It seemed to stifle and foreclose the expanse we'd intentionally, if not trepidatiously, entered. It was all too personal, not public enough even for words.

When I left Maine, time was lifted out of its line, suspended. I was moving back and forth between my childhood home in New Jersey and Cameron's small fifth floor walk-up in Harlem which he shared with his best friend. I awoke before dawn and took my only pleasure of the day before the rest of life and all its unrelenting routines stirred, foreclosing the space around me. Climbing out of bed, I'd try not to wake Cameron still asleep next to me, and head into the kitchen. There, I sat on the cold stone counter, tucking my knees to my chest, and lighting a cigarette. Smoking alone, inside, in the early morning, was a luxury. That moment, delivered by the metamorphosis of tobacco wrapped in thin paper into a warm cylinder of ash and rising smoke, brought me back into my body, like two identical images resolving into one, focused. I stared out the window, allowing three small potted Rosemary plants on the sill to blur into the periphery, toward the window in the brick wall across the airshaft. Their yellow curtains that framed that window only sometimes obscured the view inside to the mother and daughter that lived there. I lit another cigarette. Clothing was hung all around inside their apartment, in a way that made everything seem maybe not temporary, but at the ready, as if they might always be preparing to go somewhere or just to leave. The curtains themselves felt ad hoc, as if they weren't intended as curtains at all, but were playing that role for a time. I only just fit there, at the edge of the counter in the dim light before anyone else was awake. It felt like escape.

When that same early hour would find me in my parents' home, in a moment I adjusted my eyes, searching out the warmth in the linen white crown molding, that tiny hint of yellow in the ceiling that mitigated against the otherwise cool space. I pushed back the gray blankets on the gray bed in the gray room, my parents still asleep in the next room. I headed downstairs, opened the front door, and sat on the brick steps of the porch. I'd been looking at this view since my childhood almost four decades prior. Some trees were larger now and some had disappeared in the series of increasingly destructive storms that leveled themselves at the mid-Atlantic in more recent years, forever changing the landscape. Although the shapes and orientation of the houses appeared much the same, many of their colors had changed, the textures that clad them changed, too. Certain innovations in siding and roofing over the years each had their way of translating light, even at a distance, some appeared more like plastic and some more like wood. I lit a cigarette, stealing time.

I spent my days making myself invisible, my impact less obtrusive to my hosts. You see, being invisible and frozen go hand-in-hand. It is easier to go unnoticed if you are deathly still. That goal was ever-elusive and exhausting.

My parents' house was clean. My mother would run her finger along the tops of picture frames or door molding and inspect the level of dust. No level was acceptable. She'd often seek out someone else's attention to corroborate any evidence she found. "Look at this," she'd insist, holding out a dust-covered finger or rag as proof. "Filthy," the summation of her case. As a child, I would climb the stairs reaching my elbows toward the walls for balance, fearing my mother's wrath should I get fingerprints on the walls.

Household things that were decades old looked like the day they were purchased. A griddle from my great-grandmother, spotless. Baking pans and baking sheets bore no patina of grease. One would be under the misconception that no one ever cooked in our house. Only certain rooms were permitted regular habitation, the others were to remain fallow except for certain occasions, like holidays. These occasions were rare.

The basement was piled high with contingencies: shelving lined with cans of food, little jars full of mismatched screws, old paperwork, an empty fish tank, boxes of unused dishes and glasses, empty boxes and packing materials, piles of fraying towels and sheets, broken and unbroken pieces of furniture. Everything embodied a desperate striving to hold still. To mitigate against the day when one might encounter lack, or decline, or even change at all. Stacks of canned beans, boxes of pasta, and gallons of neon cleaning solvent felt like a mantra. Excess as a hedge against death. A stillness that, paradoxically, created the feeling of what it most feared.

My mother suffered the dogs on my account. Not a day went by without mention of the ways they represented constant imposition, a transgression of boundaries. The way dog toenails scratched the wood floors kept meticulous through regular refinishing and multiple daily cleanings. The atmosphere was so tightly wound, that a stray hair, of which there were now many, could erupt in violence. I was given instructions for daily vacuuming, which nagged at me as I failed in the simple task. I couldn't bring myself to bear the noise, to wrestle the incumbrance of the heavy machine. The same body that needed to lay down in the middle of a self-storage parking lot was still suffering its own weight.

I had all but ceased animation from within.

2. Love Lessons

"If you actually cry right now, I will lose all respect for you," Rob said, his eyes narrowed as tears ran down my face. In my twenties and thirties, I worked in a studio on the second floor of the Bell School, the 1870s one room schoolhouse Rob and I had painstakingly renovated into our home and workplace. I was putting grommets into some fabric when I slipped, catching my finger between the full force of the hammer and a small length of wood.

Twenty years before, I was eight years old when I'd caught my finger in a car door in the parking lot of a North Jersey furniture store called Huffman Koos. My fingernail blackened and—over the course of several weeks—slowly rotted off, from the bottom up, unhinged. I remember scraping chunks of dark, dried blood out from under the cuticle side of the nail. On the day it happened I had stayed home sick from school. My mother wanted to go furniture shopping and the last thing I wanted was to be dragged along. I begged to stay home, but my mother insisted. There was tension about whether or not I should have stayed home at all and making me go, rather than letting me stay home and watch television, would have to suffice as a kind of punishment lest I come to think staying home was a good alternative to school. We parked in the lot and as I got out of the car, truculently in the manner of one thwarted, I caught my finger as the door slammed and locked solidly.

My mother was livid. Once she freed me from the grip of the car, she dragged me, crying, into the store. She somehow found a salesperson who was able to procure some ice from a warehouse room in the back. There was an employee refrigerator and a couch, which is where she left me to sit while she browsed the store. I remember feeling that she was satisfied at my injury, a punishment for my attitude.

In July of 2017, less than a year after I left Maine forever and now forty years old, I spent ten days in silent Vipassana meditation. Day one of the meditation, I'd entered the room to the neat rows of cushions marking each person's place. As the days went on my mind took snapshots as the rows became increasingly disordered with attempts to quell what was undoubtedly coming up for everyone: pain. For some, this meant cushions or blankets to bolster knees and hips, so-called back jacks to appease strained backs, chairs, and an increasing number of cushions positioned against the perimeter wall. Each place a still life, a memorial, a testament to the truths of each of us, welling up, side by side, equal in all their differences.

My body was overcome with waves of heat so intense that once, I came out of my meditative state, opening my eyes enough to voyeur the other meditators. I could see even through the darkness of the room, each person sitting on their own cushion spread out across the hall in neat rows. To my surprise, they were wrapped in blankets. Not just one, but all. This was the truth of my body. It surely appeared they were not hot at all, but cold. Outside of the sanctuary created in such settings, that heat I was experiencing might easily have been experienced as an emotion of some kind, perhaps anger, and just as easily expressed as such, but sitting there, protected by silence, I could accept the remarkable waves of energy that I experienced. I could separate the sensations in my body from the stories and emotions that would rise and fall throughout the silent days, sitting there in the dark. This was a room full of changing stories, each with different characters and different effects, regardless of the number on the thermostat, the uniformity of our props, or any apparent sameness to our bodies.

My memory of these stories, two injuries to my hand years apart, now appeared to me, a juxtaposition curated by some invisible hand. In those ten days of silence I had expected my mind to wander to my life with Rob and to the still-fresh horrors of its catastrophic end. What I did not expect was how my mind traveled to my childhood.

3. Promises

"Touch my fingers and I'll give you the sled," my uncle held out the scarred tips at the end of his hand. He was actually my grandmother's brother, Pellegrino Desimone; we called him Uncle Billy. He was not very tall, but he was solid, almost mythologically so, his face and jaw impossibly square. His eyes twinkled in a kind of mischief, as if he were always in the middle of a joke that you may or may not be the butt of, not in a particularly malicious way, but in a way that always located the center of control. The power was so obvious in his body, in his deep voice. He seemed always at the ready. Not in the coiled way of anxious and feral people, but in a slow and deliberate way reserved for creatures who fully inhere in their own physicality. Although he seemed like a gentle man, I could sense, if not articulate, that kind of power needing an outlet, the tense and distinct possibility that jokes wouldn't always be enough. This was a trait that ran through that bloodline, that first generation, the children of immigrants, but also in my mother, (although in her it was tempered with subtle inflections of existential concern). This quality appeared equally as humor and violence, ways of pulling the rug out from under, like a willingness to just burn it all down and start again; this an inheritance from their homeland, Avellino, ready to receive, to endure, and to rise from earthquakes, covered in the ashes of Vesuvius. It was not reckless, it was the fierce brand of faith in a people who knew from experience that one can survive on squirrels and bluejays, even in a new land. I was about seven, when we went to his house so that he could give me an old sled, a wooden Radio-Flyer with red, metal blades that once belonged to his children. A carpenter by trade, Uncle Billy had, in a moment that got away, sawed off part of the fingers on his hand.

On my seventeenth birthday, I inherited my mother's ten-year-old Chevy Caprice Classic. On that day, my mother decided to punish me. I don't know why, I certainly don't remember why now, but even then, I think it wasn't terribly clear. I remember her demonstrative anger feeling particularly cruel on a day I'd hoped to celebrate. I also remember I was not allowed to drive the car that day: "You don't deserve anything. Do you think I got a car handed to me when I turned seventeen? You are *spoiled*." That word, *spoiled*, was deployed so frequently and casually that the meaning registered like one's mother tongue, inextricable and so clear as to be inexplicable. It was as if this one way of failing was more grotesque than the rest, in part, because it reflected badly on those doing the so-called spoiling - it was a family shame. Was my mother struggling against the image of herself as the kind of mother that would simply give a child a car? Invoking *spoiledness* was a mantra of unworthiness, but unworthy of something very specific. It was unworthiness of the world, of material things. It was as if my mother wanted to instill in me the feelings of being poor, so that I would know to be afraid. Fear and guilt were as if the only motivating forces for work, for achievement. It was as if the knowledge of pain and lack were the only fertile soil for gratitude.

My father followed me as I tried to escape him into the bathroom. "You don't deserve to go to a good school," he yelled. I'd gotten a D in gym class after refusing to change my clothes in the public locker room, exposing myself to my classmates, revealing everything I hated about myself which was the entirety of my physical existence. Not the least of which was its extension into space via an uncommonly homely and cumbersome, plastic and metal back brace. Of course none of this was I willing to explain. The possibility for vulnerability was long gone at that point. My father was in a rage. Not unlike my mother's feelings about giving me a car, I now believe that he was feeling stress over the cost of college tuition and despite his promises, was using the occasion of my grade, to avoid or displace his own anxiety. He understood the privilege he'd worked so hard to create for his children, for me, yet he hadn't fully metabolized it. It was a tool still awkward in his hands. He feared it made us weak, lazy, or worst of all, stupid. He told me I wouldn't be able to go to some faraway, elite, private school of my choosing as I'd been promised my entire life, but instead, to a local, state school.

At the time, I felt the rug had been pulled out from under me. I felt the image and plan I'd had for my life dissolve. What's worse, I felt afraid and indignant. I did not feel entitled, (a word that tread quite close to spoiled.) I felt he'd betrayed a promise. It wasn't just a personal promise, it was a class promise. I saw disenfranchisement from my peers, and it felt like hopelessness. It was an intergenerational hopelessness that I bore responsibility for in that moment. After all, the promise was not just of school, but the love and pride such an accomplishment would surely garner from my parents. The ivy league seemed uniquely suited to redeem intergenerational striving.

Fear underpinned these dark familial incidents. I was afraid of the instability created in these betrayals, in the volatility. I felt the sense of unworthiness that grows in the face of scarcity, the deep loss or exchange required for gain. My parents felt if they weren't hard on me, I wouldn't become hard enough for the world. Not hard-working enough, not hard-feeling enough, and not hard enough to be independent, like a plant put out into the cold to prepare for a life outside.

The pangs of fear and rage at being told I didn't deserve things, that I could no longer count on a car or a particular college, those pangs became my navigational infrastructure. On the one hand, my parents desperately wanted me to be part of this better world, on the other, they taught me that I was unworthy of it. Maybe, accidentally, even to despise it, as if it were unworthy of decent people, unworthy of me.

4. Beacons and Bonds

"I've known Gabby forever. Since we were in junior high. I remember seeing her for the first time. She was wearing her father's vest and I thought, "I'm going to be friends with her." Monica introduced herself to some friends of mine in New York City, after my life had fallen apart and I'd moved back. And so we have been friends for over thirty years.

My father's vests, like all the other material experiences of my life, honed a path. My attraction to things was part of my knowing. I used them as stories, props, defenses, and lifelines. I saw myself in them and then saw the world through them. They became shaping vessels, molds for how I would know myself. I encountered my own resistance in things. I alternatively betrayed or honored my truth in my relationship to things. Things, most especially clothing, were lighthouses, casting both brightness and shadow. They called in lifelong friends, like Monica. The shadows are vast and complicated. They are a place where people and experiences stay unseen and unknown. Shadows are also beacons, but for those who would unearth great pain.

My adolescence was fraught with deep insecurities and a dysmorphic apprehension of my young and changing body. Every day it was as if a new face and body appeared in the mirror, thwarting attempts for my mind to hold on.

My father was about 6' 3" and 190 pounds in 1989, when I was in junior high. He wore three-piece, wool suits to work then. I would try on the vests, one gray with small, white pin stripes, one navy, one black. The back was made of a shiny fabric, polyester, and had one of those small adjustable belts sewn where the waist would be. Buttons down the front. They hung large and long over my adolescent body. I liked hiding in the oversized shapes and the projection of masculinity. I knew it was more powerful than the alternatives. The idiosyncratic choice satisfied my barely latent subversive streak. I was always seeking a subtle expression of the alienation that seemed my birthright, "I am not like you." I did not feel safe in my difference, but at the same time I was compelled to protect it fiercely.

The vests called Monica into my life. She is an artist, someone who follows the breadcrumb trail of material experiences. She left high school a year early and moved to New York City. She knew when to trade art school in New York for Los Angeles. She knew when to produce a feature film. She knew when to leave her corporate design job to start her own prestigious firm. One clue after the next, followed in faith. Had she not known to follow these smallest inklings, a vest across a crowded schoolyard, she might not have known when to leap when confronted with her larger callings. Her path follows a truth, even when idiosyncratic and out-of-step with other people's expectations. We, to this day, create a safe space for the difference we found in each other.

Years before I met Monica, when I was just five or six years old, I rolled and writhed on the gray carpeted hallway outside of my bedroom as if I were trying to escape my very skin. It was a rainy morning when my mother dressed me in tights and insisted

I carry an umbrella. I cried in utter distress and frustration. I was so young then I don't think I'd mapped the bodily sensations I was experiencing to clear emotions or narratives, but the sensations themselves were so uncomfortable, so dissonant, that I literally felt sick. I was trapped. I headed to school having already learned my lesson: my boundaries did not matter.

I was a notably obedient child. I buried the distress, moved it into the background so that I could get through the rest of the day. School and then homework. In my bedroom a small desk painted yellow with pink flowers and green leaves trailing over the drawers sat against the wall. I sat on the matching chair upholstered with stripes of yellow velvet and I practiced arithmetic and spelling. Writing the same words over and over again on thin sheets of lined paper. My body echoed its faint distress in the distance.

Throughout grade school, my inclination for clothing became quite specific. I had a strong impulse for color-blocking and a kind of ordered arrangement of pieces. For example, I would alternate the color of each item of clothing for the day: turquoise socks, black pants, turquoise shirt, black scrunchie. I was often thwarted from the full incarnation of the image I held in my mind. I would ask my mother for a red T-shirt from a particular place, just the one I wanted, and she'd get me one, from a different store with some wayward pocket on the chest or some embroidered off-brand insignia, "It's the same thing," she'd insist. I wanted the shapes to be right, and a wayward chest pocket was no different from throwing a pebble into my shoe while insisting it wasn't there. I would've loved to have worn black shoes in the outfit of alternating colors, but as a kid, things like that were not fully in my control. At the time, I think I had a pair of pale blue, canvas,

Converse hightops. These sneakers were more masculine than the shoes of many female peers, but I knew, even then, that being male meant having power. I studied who I took seriously, who others took seriously, and I practiced lowering the tone of my voice. When my mother and father would fight, my mother always seemed to lose. I figured it was on account of her voice, always higher, faster, and more frantic.

My first shoes were orthopedic. I entered preschool and then kindergarten and beyond, feeling this difference from my peers. I was ugly, and more importantly, as I grew, these shoes were another impediment to achieving any sartorial images that persisted in my imagination. If I was sensing where power lay, it certainly wasn't with those who appeared different.

In high school, I was prescribed a brace for scoliosis. I was supposed to wear it 23 hours a day. I wore an enormous Champion brand sweatshirt, bright yellow with the small logo insignia on the chest, to cover this bulky and painful appliance that wrapped around my entire body, hips to clavicle. I tried to be diligent for a time, despite feeling utterly humiliated. I had no control over my own body and what was worse, I didn't trust it. It seemed bent on subverting my very chances for survival, always deformed and preventing me from connection; my body was a betrayal. I stopped changing clothes in gym class, which was sadly the primary basis of our grade in that class. The lowest grade I ever got was a D and it was in gym, all owing to the fact that I did not want to change my clothes. Otherwise achieving mostly or all A's. I remember I participated in gym class, playing volleyball or softball, (although never quite getting the spirit of competition that was supposed to motivate the whole thing, another check in the increasing list of dissonances charting my course). I just wouldn't change clothes in the locker room.

My anger kept me alive. Every violent song, every Manic Panic inspired hair color, every pair of ripped jeans, oversized hooded sweatshirt, discarded hospital scrubs found at some thrift store, or Doc Marten boots that kept that anger present, those were my lifelines. As a female, as someone close to the truth of my material experiences, perhaps a more common word is *sensitive*, I was under siege. I was being told not only that my experience didn't matter, but that it made me unworthy. It made me unsuitable. My solution was to be ever ready for battle. The way I looked, piercings, clothes, hair color, posture, and facial expressions, they were a communication inward, a note to self: stay angry, stay alive. I was still fighting to preserve that part of myself that could step back and witness the truth. I was fighting to preserve the part of myself that still trusted that truth, no matter how weary and tattered. No matter how many grown men advised me, unsolicited, to smile.

Soon, I stopped wearing the back brace during the day. I remember sneaking out of the house without it, wearing a heavy coat and ducking out the front door, trying to be unseen. As it turned out, nothing the renowned New York doctor said would turn out to be true for me. My regular x-rays were always fine, never progressing to a more severe stage. My bones did not crush my organs or prevent me from having children. This despite wearing the brace about 30% of the prescribed time.

5. Casting

"Getting pregnant at 40," I typed into Google. I sat at my huge computer crowded onto the new plywood desk Cameron built and fit into the living room. "I should consider myself lucky if I become pregnant at all and even if I did, it would take an average of eight months," Google informed me. I was now living with Cameron full time in New York City. It was only five short months since leaving Maine, since sitting in my parents' bathtub in New Jersey.

Cameron purchased a pregnancy test before I needed one and kept it in a hard, glossy, brown suitcase, worn and peeling, stored under the bed and full of extra toothpaste, soap, and cotton swabs. The package contained two testing wands. While he was at work, I peeled one wand from its package. I'd only seen people use these things on television. The process included a suspenseful waiting period and then confusion, "Is it pink or blue? Do you see one line or two?" I dreaded this kind of uncertainty. (Patience has never been a virtue I could credibly lay claim to. Cameron says I may be the only person who considers having to wait a form of being thwarted.)

I watched my urine hit the little wand and balloons might as well have fallen from the bathroom ceiling. The result was instantaneous and indisputable.

We'd wanted to have a baby. We'd talked about it for years but since I was already married to Rob and since Cameron and I lived in different states for the better part of ten years, we couldn't see that path. Although sad, it was something we were willing to give up for our relationship with one another and our relationship with Rob. The three of us often imagined our dotage, three rocking chairs lined up on the porch.

I never played with baby dolls. I was at best ambivalent about having children and certainly not willing to sacrifice anything for parenthood. That Rob had a sort of antipathy towards the idea never bothered me so much except insofar as I suspected it was another symptom of his fundamental absence which I tried desperately to ignore or imagine away. Despite this, he wouldn't have resisted having children at a certain point. He even went so far as suggesting it himself, albeit in a strange kind of disembodied desperation, at the very end of things, once he admitted what he'd done. But then, it was as if the suggestion came from a death drive rather than a life force. I let myself desire a life for us, for the both of us, my desire was big enough to keep it all moving. I refused, however, to *want* a child by myself. Not out of willfulness, mind you, it was just the state of things, metabolically. Of all the times I was able to ignore myself, to act contrary to my intuition, this time I didn't. I couldn't.

Cameron and I wanted a child together. It was something about the *together* that gave rise to the desire. It was an extension of our desire for one another, of our curiosity, of our commitment. Over the years, we resigned ourselves sadly to our circumstances, confident they couldn't bear the changes wrought by parenthood. We knew that having a child together would destroy the life we were living with Rob. In a contest between queer and convention, we always chose queer. Queer emerged as a kind of terrain. What we knew in our deepest intuition and in our bodies encountered all of the expectations and rules that came from outside. This terrain was where our truth, which sometimes hummed along, unaware and unencumbered by exception, was now set in stark and even violent contrast from the familial, cultural, and political space around us. Queer became an ethical obligation to choose that truth above stories that weren't our own. It was the only ethical choice, even if it meant sacrificing parenthood. When Cameron and I met, I was 28 years old, as I moved into my mid-thirties, and then my late thirties, the grief became more real. The threshold for something to shift and change enough to make children a possibility was closing.

When Cameron returned to the apartment from work that day. I told him the news. He began to cry. We were the kind of happy that exists inside funerals; I think it's called joy, which can admit the absence of happiness. The news compounded the urgency to scrape up all the bits of shattered life and build them into something new. We were also relieved. If I hadn't been able to become pregnant, I didn't imagine myself above succumbing to bitterness and despair. Our relief felt like hope, but perhaps not quite that.

We'd created a North Star, one of many material incarnations we'd cast gently ahead of ourselves, calculated changes that would surely change us. And we wanted to change, to thaw, to become fluid and whole.

6. Ropes

When I fell in love with Cameron it was by the ocean, but not in a warm place. There were trees and moss and gray, weathered decking. I was learning to do simple tasks with my hands like crocheting and making nets at an artist's residency on the coast of Maine. In order to make nets one must tie a series of knots and connect them. Like those walls with images and names, bits of button or cloth pinned up in clear plastic sleeves or bags, old hairnets and cigar boxes, an ashtray from a rest stop in Alabama — all clues that a detective collects and then connects with marker or pieces of red string, connecting until something comes together that can be used to catch other things. Maps, scrapbooks, and sketchbooks. They all hold other things. They hold the shape of time we call our story.

When I fell in love this time, it was not with my husband.

When I fell in love I sensed something invisible, something different from what I sensed before, a different kind of substance. It felt like an illness or perhaps more like deafness or blindness, a diminution of certain senses that allows others, now enhanced, to come to the forefront. This substance, I started to sense it between the other stuff. Between the people and the words and the blue jeans and the chairs. This love was darkness.

Fifteen years later I moved from Maine to New York City and I watched the double Dutch jumpers that had long held a place in my imagination, now come to life on the street outside of my fifth-floor walk-up in Harlem. What I always remembered was the rocking. The focused-eyes, elbows slightly bent, back and forth. As long as it takes, sometimes more, sometimes less. Back and forth. It's the invisible stuff that lets the double Dutch jumpers know the moment to jump into the swinging ropes, it is not only where the ropes are but where they aren't and this is never static. What is it they are waiting for? What are they acclimating themselves to as they rock back and forth? They are falling in love. Sensing the movement of space and substance and accommodating oneself to that rhythm, first inside feeling that particular fullness and lacking that is that other person. It is a rhythm you find before you can jump in. It feels good to be home in that way, to find a movement that is yours, sweeps you up and folds you in, even if it looks different than you thought it might. We hear these words: flow, alignment.

I watch the girls playing double Dutch. Two swing the ropes, connected not through ropes but through rhythm. *But there is no rhythm without the ropes.* And the one girl readying to jump in. She rocks back and forth, one might say waiting for her moment. She is not waiting. She is preparing. She is wiser than the detective. She is not mind, not future, not past. She is human, that inimitable magic of body and spirit, sacred and mundane. An intersection, a movement, a style. She is becoming part of the rhythm, taking on some part of the motion and adding her own. Becoming present. Practicing truth.

I can now see the rhythms that we enter into. The ones that match our own, so we can most easily move with and through them. It feels like agency. Like swimming with the current. It is learning to see what is not visible. It is not simply turning on a light, but instead, learning to see in the dark.

My friend Monica once told me, "Once you settle, that's what you get." The light is like settling for what you already know, laid bare before our most trusted senses. The dark is the truth of being, the truth of our creative dreams. This truth must be approached like a wild animal: sidle up, avert your gaze, and be quiet.

7. Permeable

My new material circumstances, New York City, created their own energetics. People pressed in on all sides, cars, bicycles, and pedestrians alternately whirred quickly and loudly, or sat implacably across a sidewalk, or on steps descending into a subway station. Buildings and hardscape filled lines of sight. My body registered this landscape as urgency when all my body could muster from within was heaviness, slowness. If settling into my own metabolism, my own timetable, was part of healing, New York City felt as if it raced all around me, a syncopated attack on my fledgling stride.

Living in the city after all those years in the slow quiet of Maine felt like trying to remember a childhood tune while in a crowded nightclub, music blaring. This new life without Rob, the scene now refreshed, was better in many ways. I told myself that, trying to take stock and to be grateful even as I dragged my exhausted and eight-month pregnant body out of the apartment at night to wait tables. In some ways I had the life I most feared and had spent the past fifteen years mitigating against. I was a forty-year-old, pregnant waitress with no horizon in sight. I was still the person who, fifteen years before, had chosen a quiet and largely solitary life, in the middle of a rural place. I had spent no small amount of time and creative energy figuring out how to purchase and then renovate two beautiful old houses in Bangor, each with apartments to rent. Those houses were there to protect me from this very moment, but they were now lost, too. As much as the city was refreshing in its distinction from the place I now associated with pain and treachery, I was not there by choice. It was simply where I landed, the final point in the trajectory of sudden expulsion from my marriage and my life.

The city had its own metabolism, but so did motherhood. The bodily entanglement required by this new relationship changed my understanding of what was me and what was outside of me, certainly while I was pregnant when, for example, I began eating meat after 27 years. Especially steaks and hamburgers. This new sense of extension into space, of interconnection, continued even after Lulu was born, breastfeeding being the most obvious example of so many daily exchanges.

My reaction to the city was a tightness, a coiling, but in motherhood, I softened, if only slightly. I surrendered a bit to the new waters in which I found myself. My identity was fluid, moderated by so many sudden changes, not unlike all those years ago in junior high, it had no place to land. A friend remarked that it must be exhausting being a mother, constantly considering another's needs. My relationship to my son's needs was not one of active consideration any more than I considered what I'd like for dinner. I won't draw the comparison between the consideration of my own respiration, or my heartbeat, because his needs were not quite so automatic, but they were firmly in the territory of sustenance, of biological imperatives. There was a diffusion of identity, of ego, that came with sharing my body with someone else. Extending it into an autonomous space inhabited by another will, another ego.

I sat in a group Vipassana meditation at the Dhamma Center in midtown Manhattan and I marveled that someone else's sneeze, across the room, should send such waves of feeling through my body. A simple adrenaline rush at being startled. I was struck at how I'm *affected* by others, in my body. People and things who are ostensibly outside of myself, produce these deep stirrings within, waves of sensation.

I often continued this musing as I would walk Pony, Petey, Buster, and Flash on those New York mornings, Lulu strapped to my chest. However, there was a dark side. I became aware of a slow growing rage that accompanied those walks, the subtle sensory onslaught, the gauntlet of perils that besieged even springtime hope.

It would all begin when trying to leave the apartment, gathering the coats, definitely the baby's and sometimes all four dogs, depending on the season. A process no one was particularly keen on, making the challenge of lifting everyone's spirits while completing tasks they'd rather not, all the more daunting. Coats, baby carrier, leashes, poop bags, house keys, and cell phone. I would arrange this efficiently, minimizing the always looming risk of crankiness (canine and human). I would also try to minimize the number of squats I did holding a twenty-pound baby.

Next, I made my way down the five flights of stairs and two doors (heavy doors that opened towards me and threatened to close on dog tails and noses.) I watched my steps amidst a tangle of leashes. I couldn't see ahead of me as I stepped out the door, not onto a landing, but down another short flight of steps. Here neighbors would sit, trying to enjoy their morning. There I was, pack in hand, bursting towards the sidewalk propelled by four urgent bladders. The wild card: would a passing dog incite this already precarious circus act into complete chaotic lunging, barking, and frantic snapping? I told myself that deep breaths would keep everything just tethered. I attempted to keep my balance and some charade of equanimity. If all went as smoothly as possible, it was nonetheless accompanied with the kind of hypervigilance that knew, bodily, how tenuous any calm.

The rest of the two-mile journey continued in much the same way. A woman passes by, "You've got a lot going on," she cleverly observes me bumbling along. I laughed to myself: "Man, I'm making it look easy." (Although, thank you to the young woman who remarked to her friends, "that lady is the MVP – she's got four dogs *and* a baby!")

Our walks (in all manner of weather conditions) were punctuated by squatting to pick up dog feces in what I've since learned is called a hell strip. Some people call this patch of terrain the road verge. However, as I would squat (remember that twenty-pound, squirming baby and picture my sweater now grazing the ground), the breeze-stoked gyre of dog feces, cigarette butts, chicken bones, grease-stained paper, and fluttering plastic felt more like a hell strip to be honest. I'll give you one more image; congestion, both human and canine, approaching from all directions as I maintain this delicate balancing act. I take refuge in oncoming traffic, letting others pass on the sidewalk as I wait to resume our morning perambulation.

I try to metabolize the energetic shrapnel. The phrase "emotional contagion" running through my mind, lest my displeasure ruin my child's chances for emotional self-regulation and become a textbook "don't" for Cesar the Dog Whisperer.

Here I am. Fully dispersed by 9 AM.

My experience at the time was not unlike all those years ago in my childhood and teenage years, feeling beset in gym class by mandates and rules bent on denying the truth of my metabolism. Now those mandates sounded like: Be thin, but not too thin. Cook, clean, nurture, be more aggressive, but not too aggressive. Accept unequal compensation while accomplishing more of the household maintenance. Do not expect maternity care or family leave. The work of the so-called stay-at-home-mother, invisible to the GDP. This I already knew. However, it's the response, the counter-demands, that felt simultaneously oppressive and less achievable. I felt called to love my body as it was, to care about my health, but not appearance, to embrace imperfection, and to generally act in consciousness of the double standards, the oppression. I felt tasked to reveal my too-fat and my too-thin, to show my scars, my acne, share my #metoos, and declare #timesup. Any lack of self-acceptance, self-care, self-esteem, wellness practice, or self-advocacy was just another way I could fail. I read an article that proved the practice of gratitude is how *mentally strong people* lead healthier lives. If I were to fall from this high wire, it would surely be through ingratitude and mental weakness.

As a palliative, I encountered endless musings about how to find, or more accurately, how to *achieve* (if character is invoked, our success or failure measures our very integrity) the ever-elusive 'balance.' It occurred to me, beset as I felt, that this kind of balance was not desirable. Balance, packaged in this way, promised a state of perpetual tension. It was the illusion of stability created by so many opposing forces. I had that kind of balance. I hated it.

As part of the routine of efforts I made to find out who I was and how to function in this new life I'd been dropped into, I attended a women's panel discussion on wellness. Three quite elegant and successful women adeptly discussed the mental and physical benefits of self-care. They punctuated this discussion with the selling point: "When you take time for self-care, you will actually become more productive." During the question-and-answer period, I inquired about where they felt the spiritual belonged in this discussion. One woman responded, albeit awkwardly and all but admitting she was grasping, that she was raised Jewish and sometimes prayed.

The balance being sold on that panel, for one, was being sold. Everyone was offering an app or otherwise monetizing some practice. It seemed like palliative care for suffering people in a dying culture. What I believe we actually want is closer to the idea of integration. We don't want to be further fractured, further pulled in multiple directions that simply pull equally in all the directions, like some sort of new age drawing and quartering. We want all the parts to work together instead of at opposite ends of the horse-drawn rope. Even our zen is preposterous: Be here, now. Live in the present. Don't forget to make the maximum contribution to your 401K, because *your work will never be enough*. You will always be dependent on capital, on excess.

There is one final, perhaps ultimate demand: Forge an identity. If you happen to find yourself unemployed, hone that identity into a brand. If my identity is actually moderated by this fundamental dispersion, this inexorable confluence of mutually exclusive imperatives (sex, career, and motherhood, just to name a few) it is truly a Sisyphean joke.

I sat in a group Vipassana meditation. Afterwards, there was a speaker, he said, "the path is not 'be here now,'" but instead "the path is suffering, this, Vipassana, is a way out." Finally, the resonance of truth.

I was suffering in New York City. I was suffering in my fifth-floor walk-up with four dogs and a baby. I suppose all this thinking could be expressed more simply: my nerves were shot, a compass needle spinning. And I was so very sad. I was grieving my own death. I had worked so hard to build a lifestyle that would heal and honor a sensitivity and metabolism that I had ignored and neglected for so many years growing up. That's what Maine and my marriage to Rob had done for me. What was worse, I was beating myself up for suffering. Suffering itself was a mark of ingratitude, of failure.

Here in this articulation of the suffering, in the darkness between my experience and what I was being sold, I saw the way out. I had to embrace my bodily reality for its implicit wisdom. Something magical and transformative happened between the bodily experience of transplanting to New York and of motherhood with the complete dispersion of my identity. I was no longer who I was in my former marriage, my former art career, and my life in Maine. My ego left and my body awakened. My sense of inextricability came alive. It was as if my lifelong intimacy with material things, in art and life, emerged in these new circumstances, remastered in Technicolor, an undeniable and living awareness of the one and the many. I cast a theory: Surely there is power in the invisible extension into space, the ceaseless dialogue between myself and the world around me. Yes, sometimes, the onslaught is real and those details press in, but I, in turn, in my element, press out. Or join in, like double Dutch.

It became increasingly important to inhabit that dark space of dissonance rather than retreat into a singular, if visible, entity. To retreat into the light. Letting the sense of all my parts well up to meet the world in all its disparate beauty, feeling my way, through the mirror things and the lens things throughout the day, I slowly began to apprehend my own integrity through the grace of my connections.

8. Leaving the Path

"I would like to spend more time painting." I sat in a small blue-gray office on a sprawling green corporate campus just outside of Boston and honestly answered the final question in a third-round interview for a PR position. I had been in my first post-college job for just over a year and I offered the truth. I've never quite been able to lie. Which perhaps has been a small, if not double-edged gift. It edges me toward the right path even if it takes a while to get there and goes against my apparent self-interest in moments that in hindsight, seem bordering on ridiculous. In retrospect, I felt the moment I didn't get the job. The expression of my desire to paint was a rheostat dimming the once eager women who interviewed me. Their faces flattened. They leaned back a bit in their chairs.

Rob and I had moved to Boston soon after college and this interview self-sabotage marked a turning point. There was nothing acute that happened to me there, nothing overtly bad. Instead it was a malaise that seeped into my emotional temperature, into my imagination. I started dressing in black pants and modest sweater sets. I played this little game with myself, perhaps it was more of an experiment. What would happen if I started dressing like the boss? A navy blazer and dark denim on casual Fridays. I was promoted eight times in two years.

The immersion in this life felt safe, regular. Rob and I lived with roommates, but our relationship plodded along, uneventful. Perhaps I should have felt more comforted by this life that promised a smooth ride from there, as if I could've turned on the autopilot and been good to go. I worked with a woman who had long black hair and bright blue eyes. She always wore her enormous, sparkling engagement ring to the office. She became pregnant and as I watched her grow, slowly, my imagination of my own life took shape slowly around the image. She was beautiful and yet as if behind glass. Whatever her beauty was, this image of success and happiness, it did not call to me. I tried to imagine it would: Rob and I married, our love shining through a giant diamond and our enfranchisement sealed in the ancient rite of progeneration. In some ways, I'm surprised that I even noticed myself slowly becoming numb. Sitting at a desk and staring at the layers of gray and blue from morning until evening, every day the same. This was it, the life I'd been trained for all these years. I was twenty-three years old and I'd arrived safely at my destination.

I believed I really wanted that promotion. The woman who would be my boss was quite a bit more glamorous than the bosses I'd had before. I noted her red designer handbag and I desired, not the handbag itself, but the life refracted in its image. Sitting there on the floor next to her desk, it gently offered hope to the oppressive blues and grays, its leather suggested life and death in the face of the ghastly immortality of plastics and polyesters laminating the corporate landscape. The shape, color, and texture of that simple bag felt like inspiration, even like hope. It whispered to me in that interview, "You want to paint more, go ahead, say it."

I knew I had to leave Boston. In 2001, Rob and I headed to a little cabin on a lake in the middle of Maine near his parents.

When I gave my notice at work, they tried to get me to stay. They suggested this move to Maine could be like a sabbatical, (there was no precedent for such a thing), but I knew my time there was over.

I started work in the costume shop of the local professional theater for the summer Shakespeare Festival. Rob's mother was the resident designer. It would just be for the summer and then we'd move on, plot our next steps. Maybe Louisville, Kentucky. After college we took a little over a month and drove around the country. I wanted my gut to tell me where to live. I fell in love with Louisville at the time, but I didn't listen. I was offered the job in Boston and I had no template for living another kind of life. No compass for choosing anything other than the safe, middle-class path I was raised to follow.

When I began working at the theater I became part of a new, different kind of work culture than I'd been used to in Boston. The costume shop was on the second floor of the theater, up a gently curving stairway from the main lobby. Huge windows lit the high ceilinged room, which glowed through the lens of dust and multi-colored cloth. The metabolism was different here. The way my body lived in time began to change. There were no regular hours. Projects erupting in urgency, waiting for later, and everything in between now replaced a sentence of sprawling regularity.

When I wasn't in the costume shop, I would draw and make quilts in the dark, rustic cabin we tried to make our own. Rob and I would sit on the dock in the evenings talking about the day's creative work. We'd make food together, often from the latest Martha Stewart magazine. Once we battered and fried herbs, whole leaves of mint, sprigs of parsley and thyme, to be served with a dry white wine. His parents would come for dinner and we'd have cocktails by the water. His mother drank bourbon. He introduced me to waterskiing off the back of a small motorboat his father kept. He'd begun working for the family plumbing and heating company, but only part time. He was a writer and now, this life opened more space. *I spent more time painting.*

Our lives had taken an irrevocable turn away from a life of certain expectations and into the uncharted territory of individuated truth. That truth only just glimmered, like a small glossy seed catching bits of sun. It was the first step down a different kind of path. We were blind to what lay ahead. Armed only with the tools, skills, expectations, and beliefs from our old lives, these ways of navigating had taken us where we'd been, but not where we wanted to go. That seed was new to us and it had no instructions for care.

One summer of Shakespeare Festival quickly turned into a year, and then more. I continued designing costumes and adjusting to the culture of the theater, some parts darker than others. "He prefers to ask forgiveness over asking permission," someone told me about a director. I found the observation both startling and chilling. The theater struggled with various volunteer efforts to make things the best they could with limited resources, always counting on benevolence, ingenuity, and passion to flesh out the margins. We scraped together volunteers to sew and to donate old clothing and fabric.

I began quilting more. Manipulating fabric all day in the costume shop kept my mind thinking in textiles, in the architecture of fabric. I started to feel myself disappearing in the costuming much as I had in Boston. I could design and execute whatever was necessary for the performances, collaborating with the director, the other designers, and working with the actors, but I was finding no space for art in that world of design. There were technical and aesthetic questions, but no existential ones, and I longed for those.

My favorite play that season was Harold Pinter's *Betrayal.* There was somehow more I could offer, a deeper place to go. It was a small play, mostly two men and one woman. Emma and Robert were married. Emma was having an affair with Robert's close friend, Jerry. An intense, psychologically driven story, each character has a unique potency. This was different from so many of the historical plays where the research was more about class and era. Gestures of personality could be far less nuanced than in a contemporary production. I could now contemplate the ideology of pleated versus flat front pants. I could explore the difference between a man who wears gray and a man who wears brown. What is the attitude of a bowtie versus a necktie? Leather versus suede? What does a woman's collar reveal about her values? Is she driven by trends? Confident? Sexual? Even there however, design always had an end in sight, a master keeping close watch. The costumes always had to serve the play, the director, and the audience while simultaneously holding some part of the actors and other designers close. I ultimately felt as though I were coloring within so many lines, there was nothing worth fighting for. While this was endlessly fun, it partook very little of my voice. I could not connect to purpose in this work, just to a certain set of skills.

The set department functioned much like the costume department. They'd scramble for resources with each production. One day, someone realized there was a lightbulb out in an enormous prop room housed in a building offsite. For the couple of dollars it cost to purchase a new bulb, they'd received a room full of furniture, lamps, books, swords, telephones, tambourines, pogo sticks. I realized that things we'd spent so much time, so much energy searching for and duplicating were right under our noses all along.

I left the theater. I packed the quilts I'd been making into my minivan, partnered with Rob's mother, and for the next decade, I headed out to art and craft fairs across the country.

9. In Between

I didn't grow up with quilts. We always had comforters, duvets, blankets, but no quilts. Rob's mother introduced me to quilting. She and her friends in Maine would make quilts together and she lent me a book of Amish quilts on one of the many visits Rob and I took to Maine when we were living in Boston. I think, to this day, I love few designs as much as an Amish Log Cabin, especially in the Fields and Furrows variation with no border, just the pattern running to the edges, bound with a simple ¼" edge, as little as possible obstructing the infinity of the pattern. It was the design for the first quilt I ever made.

I took the book back to Boston with me and followed the directions to compile the list of fabrics I'd need to begin my first project. I visited a little fabric shop in a fancy area of the city several subway stops from where I lived. It was filled with expensive cotton yardage and women who tended a bit older than I who made it clear they were also a bit wiser when it came to quilts. It quickly felt like a kind of club where there were right and wrong ways of doing things. A door had opened into a world I hadn't known existed.

I selected my blues and my yellow-golds, my fields and my furrows. Light, medium, and dark tones. I eagerly brought them back to the apartment Rob and I shared with three other roommates. I had an old, plastic, Singer sewing machine and I set it up on the desk in my bedroom. As soon as I began, the ideas came in a steady stream. Creating a pattern and then diving in, not knowing if it would come together until so many steps later. First piecing the individual blocks, then piecing the blocks together, layering the top, batting, and bottom layer, quilting them together, and finally, binding the edges. My curiosity to see the finished work remained strong until the very end. I'd arrived in a kind of work that inspired me, kept me desiring, kept me living. Not unlike all the loves of my life, there was a wholeness to the work. It was analytical and planful, while at the same time being intuitive. It needed the body and the mind. When it was finished, it was both useful and beautiful, intimate in everyday life. More than the sum of its parts.

It wasn't terribly long after that first experience with quilting that I moved to Maine and began making and selling quilts at craft shows around the country. Working with my hands, the deep knowing of color and pattern. The metamorphosis of meaning that effervesces from combinations of simple material things. The wellspring of life that springs forth from the infinite microcosms of material variation, repeated over and over in space. However, something was missing.

I loved quilts not only in themselves, but in the way all of this wondrous manufacture became part of my everyday world. I saw the infinity all around me now, the incremental changes operating in the most intimate spaces, our behaviors and feelings. I moved my mind toward those small fluctuations, those moments of possibility captured not just in cuts of patterned fabric but in an unexpected heartbeat or wayward glance. Quilts became how I lived.

What I slept with, what I curled up on the couch under, hung on my walls, and gave as gifts of love. This integration of living into material and back into living was pure magic. When I showed up at craft shows and even at artist residencies and exhibitions of craft, the focus was on the materials and the techniques. It all felt like that initiation in the small Boston fabric shop: there's a right way and a wrong way to do this. The focus on the mundane, albeit skill, technique, and craftsmanship, felt myopic. It either dismissed or foreclosed upon the expanse of my imaginings, on the intimacy of my relationship with objects.

In my time quilting professionally, I was often asked to teach classes. Being known as a quilter, people wanted me to teach them *how*. They wanted answers: "Do I press my seams to the right or the left? How can I applique curved pieces? What is the best kind of batting to use? Hand quilting or machine quilting?" This pressure forced me to think about what I truly valued about this kind of work. The truth is, I couldn't care less about the rules. I barely held them in my head. If I saw something in my imagination, I would figure out how to make it. Sometimes that meant trial and error and sometimes a video on the internet.

In the same way, I never remember recipes because I never make the same thing twice. I consider them guides, suggestions, frameworks within which improvisation takes hold. Granted, I once tried to make chocolate cupcakes out of a parsnip puree leftover from Thanksgiving dinner that tasted not-so-faintly of garlic, something my sister will never let me forget. Nor will she eat anything I bake anymore. "How hard is it to make something taste good when the ingredients are just sugar and butter?" My mind proffers rhetoric, an implied challenge I always fail to resist.

I wasn't afraid to make those mistakes. I was uncomfortable surrounded by people who wanted those rules to be hard and fast. Like an outsider and an imposter. I never aspired to be the voice of the bottom line they seemed to be after.

Instead, I'd figure out how to teach classes my way: *Freedom Through Limits*. I taught the three-day workshop back at Haystack for the Maine Craft Association's member artists. The class was all about how ideas come from the constraints and infinity of the material. It was so cold that weekend that I filled an empty wine bottle with hot water from the coffee and tea machine and slept hugging it each night. We made dozens of weird quilt blocks in that workshop, each successive one born from a seed in the previous one. A metamorphosis of forms. I received a flood of thank you notes after I'd returned home. One of the students, a teacher, invited me to teach at her school for a weeklong residency the following school year. I would accept the invitation only in an unsettling, personal revelation during my time there, it would be me who would learn.

After several years of creating functional quilts, sized for use as "king," "queen," "twin," and made from machine washable cottons and batting, I was called to let go of those constraints. I was freed to consider the philosophical implications of the work, the meaning of pattern itself. In a piece titled, *In Consideration of Counting: In Memory of Necessary Omissions*, I created a hash mark pattern with two-inch blocks of cotton that consisted in a diagonal white line on an ivory background. The creation of each block created some waste, trimmed cotton and thread. I collected all of this waste and once I'd pieced together the "counting" blocks, I stitched together blocks made from waste. Each of this next collection of blocks created yet another batch of waste, this time smaller, threads and threadlike slivers of cotton. I continued in this way, by the end, the 90" x 90" textile was composed of just little piles of thread, barely enough to hold on to. I stitched until there was nothing left.

Quilts had become a powerful meditation on repetitive action, on the way structure creates meaning, on what we leave out when we want to make sense of things or create a coherent image.

I had been working with Rob's mother, but I told her I could no longer do that. The work had become too personal. Over time, the quilts I made now hung on the wall, objects for contemplation instead of use.

In 2008, I wrote about my quilted work, a piece called *Black Finery*, for a book it was featured in: <u>Quilt National 2009, The Best of Contemporary Quilts</u>. The 60" x 60" work was made from one-inch strips of black cotton sateen, pieced together in overlapping rows and at various angles. I embroidered and hand quilted the entire work.

> Quilts embody ideas. They also have function and purpose in the home. Through manipulations of fabric and stitching, I explore the intimacy between manufactured objects and daily living. The idea of finery emphasizes both the created nature and elevated status of this quilt. Its homogenous, incremental piecing refers to elemental concerns, both material and philosophical. These concerns, namely relationships, boundaries, and scale, are all framed in the context of home.

This work was preparing me for the task of rebuilding my life from the ground up after its peremptory and unforeseen end. I was learning the voice and the ethics of the material world. I was learning how change is possible and how to locate that possibility in the most elemental objects of everyday life. I was learning that you can return home safely, but only if you figure out how to re-arrange the furniture.

In high school, I also had braces on my teeth, despite that they were fairly perfect except for a gap in between the front two. Think, Lauren Hutton, sans glamor. The orthodontist spun a cat-astrophic tale of the gap slowly growing, pushing my molars, caus-ing them to rotate, to turn in my mouth, a chain of events bound for disaster. Three years later, after removing them, the gap started emerging again. He said he needed to put some bonding on the back of the front teeth. I begged him not to. The adults in the room insisted and prevailed. "Don't drink hot fluids and don't eat anything too crunchy for 48 hours. No apples," he warned. When we got home I ran my tongue over this small piece of cement be-hind my front teeth. If I weren't so practiced at overriding my own discomfort at this point, I would've cried, rolling and thrashing on the floor, just as I had that rainy morning so many years ago. Instead, I sat in the sunshine on the front porch steps and ate an apple as violently as I could muster. The small piece of cement fell onto my tongue; I spit it into my hand. My shoulders relaxed and a steady breath returned to my body.

By the time I left high-school, I was fully formed in the light and darkness of my material experiences, like a plant moving and growing under the sovereign sun. I had learned to use my clothes and my surroundings for peace and protection, as mantras and as calling cards. I had also learned when and how to deny my experience—to dishonor my boundaries—for the sake of others and for self-preservation in a culture I found increasingly inhospitable. I wanted connection, to fit in, and the lesson of this period was clear: the quality of my life depended on how I would deny or uphold my truth. This was all at the level of instinct. It would be years before my art practice and the destruction of my life would force me to reconcile spirit and body.

10. The Bell School

People fall in love with Maine. The rocky coastline. The lobster. An austerity and imperviousness that feels vast and liberating, especially to those fleeing the heat and hardscape of the city in the summertime. Flat bucolic vistas punctuated by peeling farmhouses read as authentic Americana, inspiring a slowness, a return.

I never loved it. The coniferous trees felt rigid and harsh compared to the soft deciduous leaves of the mid-Atlantic forests I was used to. The icy waters and rocky beaches forbidding, nothing like the open, endless sands of Long Beach Island where I spent summers growing up. Maine's cool summer air was populated with black flies making one almost nostalgic for those mosquitoes of my youth. I missed being hot.

Rob took me once, on a beautiful warm day, to a one-room camp on a lake in Beddington. It had no running water, not much of an interior to speak of, no sheathing on the walls and no furniture. It sat in the woods just on the edge of the lake. After getting undressed we could barely make it to the frigid water before the onslaught of biting insects covered my skin. I tried to escape into the water, but the cold, its own kind of attack, was not a relief. We spent the rest of the afternoon on the towels we laid out on the rough plywood floor of the cabin.

Yet Maine seduced me with its possibility. No one ever asked, "What do you do?" This struck me for years. Growing up outside of New York City, people identified with their jobs. They identified others through their jobs. In Maine, I rarely met someone who did only one thing. Everyone seemed to be composing a life of disparate talents, projects, and pursuits. One particular vocation was not usually a meaningful shorthand for identity. In Maine, any sustained conversation would have to do better than that. Seeing no path laid before me, just another way of saying many paths, this way of being held great appeal. It seemed to embrace complexity and discovery.

The cost of living in Maine was much less than in New York. I could start to admit dreams of gardens and an art practice. I could imagine supporting myself by making quilts, something I actually loved to do. More so, I could imagine liberation from the mandates and ambitions of capitalism. Indeed, when we made the fateful move from Boston to Maine, these pressures palpably lifted. The narratives and expectations of performance that weighed heavily since childhood, they too lifted as I settled into Maine. The space created energy and hope for desires I'd never before let surface.

This was a shared dream, one hard wrought in books and dreams and endless conversations with my husband. We carved it loose from our histories, our educations, and most of all from our desires for another way forward. We protected one another from the exigencies of a world that was harsh on our time and space, those incubators of our humanity. With a loan from my parents, we bought the Bell School in 2004 for $60K.

I still have the fading piece of paper Rob's mother printed out from the online listing, the white schoolhouse sitting back on a grassy lawn cut by a circular gravel driveway. It was shaded by the just-turning-red-and-orange autumn leaves of huge old maples under a crisp blue sky. The view was as if looking up from below, a vantage the building tended always to inspire. It was a tall building, crowning in a now empty bell tower. I slipped the printed paper inside the plastic cover of a looseleaf binder where I collected my ideas and designs for turning this magical place into our home.

"I don't know why it's still standing," remarked the engineer we hired to tour the property. The 1879 building had been used as a school as recently as the 1980s and despite this, it had no plumbing, no heating, no insulation, and no working electrical system. Walking through the heavy double front doors into a small entryway, I was greeted by the smell of mildew, dampness on old wood, and various rodent habitats. The little room was lined with wainscoting with hooks still at the ready for coats. Below my feet, a door cut through two layers of old pine floorboards giving access to a crawl space below. To the right was another small room, empty except for a wooden ladder rising through the ceiling to the attic above. The heart of the structure opened up beyond these small entry rooms. The huge, 25-foot-by-30-foot, open classroom with ten-foot ceilings, despite decades of neglect, still inspired awe. A small, black wood stove sat in the middle of the back wall, like an altar, drawing my eyes across the expanse. The walls, like the entry, were lined with wainscotting. A series of blackboards were punctuated by evenly spaced windows. The original balloon framing had been subverted by some recent attempt, I can only assume, to retain heat. This was done by dropping the ceiling about five feet from its original height. Each rafter had been cut from where they originally met at the intersection of roof and walls and were hastily scabbed in below using various scraps of wood to cobble it all together. A ceiling was then tacked to the boards in this new location. Upon exploration of the crawl space, we discovered the house was sitting half on bedrock. The rest of the foundation consisted of stacked rocks topped with thick slabs of granite. Posts were sculptural piles of stone or old tree stumps. The floor, dirt. Woods surrounded the house and were beginning to take it over. Acres of poison ivy encroached from all directions. After the engineer's assessment, I no longer sought that kind of authority. If I did, we would not move forward.

Instead I took to tradespeople, books, and my graph paper.

Serving as architects, general contractors, and crew, Rob and I got to work. We moved out of our apartment and into his parents' house, heading to the schoolhouse every night after work, every weekend, and any other time that presented the chance. What we thought would be months stretched into more than a year. In the winter we'd pack thermoses of stew and sit in the dusty construction zone. His parents helped us. My parents helped us.

Gutting a house seems so simple, and yet tearing down plaster and lathe, stacking and salvaging hundreds of old wainscot boards, dismantling a crumbling chimney, and eradicating archeological layers of debris was just my visceral induction into the metabolic clash between the imagination and the hands. We hired out certain tasks such as putting in the septic system, hanging the drywall, rebuilding the dilapidated front doors, jacking up the house to install a bilco entrance to the crawl space, rebuilding the chimney, and shingling the roof. The rest, we did ourselves: the plumbing, heating, electrical, framing, water purification system for the well, kitchen cabinetry, bathroom fixtures, tiling, all of the trim, the painting, much of the insulation. I remember laying an entire new second story subfloor: rough sawn hemlock on the diagonal. Crawling on my back between the bedrock and the crawl space ceiling to staple insulation around the ends of PEX tubing Rob had run for the radiant heat.

I was carrying the weight of the project, the plans. Although Rob supported it, he did not drive it. Having borrowed money from my parents created an onus of debt, a silent promise to create a kind of spiritual dividend on their investment in me, in my desires. I needed this house to be *special*. Often upon running into an obstacle, I would call my parents under the guise of needing advice. Truly I was seeking a bit of faith and assurance that the house wouldn't fall down around me. Of course, they were more risk averse than I and their tastes did not run to these kinds of projects. They lived their lives in highly-regulated urban and suburban New Jersey and my father was a lawyer, always mapping contingencies, if not disasters.

After our conversations I would run to the town's administrative office, a long white trailer on the side of the two-lane highway that passed only on its way to and from other places. I pulled into the dirt parking lot, newly charged with lists of terms and variables I'd never considered. Each one with the potential for sabotaging the whole endeavor. "Do whatever you want," was always the bewildered response from Lois, the gray-haired woman who worked there. We encountered surprises all along the way, each one quite scary at the time. I had never done anything like this and could barely figure out what I didn't know. I was beginning to learn that the rest of the world did not operate quite to the standards I'd thought were universal. This dissonance felt like anxiety, like a space fraught with the potential for disappointing someone. Either I was too uptight, or I'd failed some elementary due diligence. I was straddling two worlds.

"The roof could collapse with a heavy snow load," warned the experts once they discovered how the rafters had been cut and dropped. We ran cables through the ceiling of the first floor in an attempt to stabilize the structural integrity, to try to pull the walls together and prevent them from bowing under the weight of a flattening roof. The position of these cables unfortunately meant reconfiguring the stairs. Each bit of the unanticipated reverberated elsewhere in the house.

The Bell School never had a second floor, only some attic space never meant for bearing weight. We needed to run a series of posts and beams starting from the foundation, to ensure support for this new level of living space. I'd budgeted for fiberglass insulation, but when we'd stripped the walls, we discovered not one regular board! In 1879, there was no dimensional lumber. Each crooked piece measured about four inches deep, just short of what we needed to get the appropriate R-value for the frigid climate. We decided to use spray foam, relatively new for residential buildings at the time. In addition to costing over three times as much as fiberglass, it changed the environment of the house. Venting a house with spray foam is different than a house with fiberglass. We no longer needed a ridge or gable vents, but we did install an air exchange system. We were also tightening a house on bedrock that had never been sealed in this way. Our original radon testing would be meaningless. I decided to preventively install venting during the construction process rather than discovering a problem afterwards. When the power company came to hook the house to the lines at the street, they told me the meter would have to sit on the front of the house to avoid the wires hitting certain trees. This also meant that power lines would run across the newly framed view outside of the second story windows. We paid a couple of thousand extra to run the lines underground.

Each dollar spent encountering these surprises took away from some more glamorous part of the vision, (a bathroom sat for years, just a dusty repository for old cardboard boxes I used to ship artwork to clients) and created a pit of scarcity in my gut. These numbers felt so real to me and yet so far outside of my metabolic scope. Wagering these chunks of money created the bodily feeling of overextension, of living beyond one's boundaries.

Once the house was built the design seemed so intuitive, as if it were always that way. I wanted to stay true to the building, to keep the openness, retain the symmetry. We wanted to create the space to be the people we wanted to be. That meant a room for Rob to write and a room for my art practice. It also meant space for guests. I wanted a place for my far-flung friends and family to not only visit, but to stay, to be not just tourists in our lives, but as much as possible to make a home within our home to nurture those relationships. To that end, I wanted not only an extra bedroom but a bathroom, too.

I wanted the space to be efficient and functional. We created a cocoon that felt both safe and nurturing. We replaced the old broken stove with a beautiful white enamel Jøtul stove that would end up sufficing to heat the entire house. Oil heat in a state that lives out seasons of protracted winter in old housing is not easy. For the ten years we lived there, we spent a negligible amount on heat. And that beautiful stove was one of the first things I ever purchased for the house. I found it at the chip and dent sale at the

Black Stove Shop in Bangor. At the time $2,000 was the most money I'd ever spent on one thing. It scared me to write the check.

I hunted down old claw foot tubs from this little classifieds periodical called Uncle Henry's, mixed floor stains to achieve just the right color, and collected paint swatches endlessly to alternately temper or enhance the quality of light as it moved through the seasons. Each tile, the height of a knee wall, the dimensions of the landing at the top of the stairs, the placement of the skylights, these all created a movement through the space, a peace of being, and a container for the kind of activity I envisioned there.

I spent countless hours in the garden. Each activity in the house was bookended by some activity outside the house. If I spent some time in my studio or cooking in the kitchen, I would then spend some time raking leaves or creating raised garden beds from the bricks of the original chimney. I collected plants from Rob's mother, my father, and so many others. Rob would laugh at how long it would take me to leave the house, even the tiniest plant would get my utmost attention, noticing every fluctuation in growth, in movement. I surrounded the house with pathways built from rocks I dug out of the ground, spending hours upon hours hauling them from one place to another and placing them just so. I plotted each garden so that it would move. The color, size, and texture would shift and change through the seasons. It would protect the foundation from water. Insulate from north winds, shade from southern sun, and screen from the closest neighbor. The view from each window became a careful plan, its own painting in four dimensions. I viewed the gardens in both time and space, days, seasons, and decades. I imagined what it would look like when I was old, imagined where I wanted to be and I planted the seeds.

We created the Bell School and it created us within it. We were able to get it just to the point of habitability: heat, power, plumbing, and a simple kitchen, no frills, before we moved in. We'd spend the next decade saving and working out the details. I wanted room for people: we rarely lived alone in that house. The first night we slept there, we camped out on the floor with our friends Putnam and Selena. Then Dan moved in, and Melissa. Putnam. Later, Cameron. It fulfilled my designs in ways I couldn't fully anticipate, nor appreciate until years after I'd lost it all.

We wanted to work and to create and that's what we did. Rob wrote several books, published short stories, and was nominated for a Pushcart prize. I finished my MFA and exhibited regularly, winning grants and awards internationally. Cameron finished college and then graduate school; he also exhibited internationally and won prestigious awards, even becoming one of the youngest people to be included in the Whitney Biennial. We read and critiqued. We hosted holidays and art events. We filmed an eight-course dinner, held in silence, from an elaborate menu of only white foods, fusing performative art practice with Vipassana meditation with domestic life.

Every Thanksgiving, the Bell School filled for a week of activity. Dancing, cooking, eating, drinking, and late-night conversation. One year, a group of friends sitting in bed, drinking wine, and performing a reading of Rob's latest play, an existential drama enacted through cat puppets entitled, "What's Eating Pussy?" We laughed endlessly. I remember it especially because we took a photo, and despite later burning all my photos in the wood stove, the image remains strong.

We could improvise and intend, but the building had its own rhythms and mandates. We lived with and through her. I woke up every morning in the tall, pine, four-poster bed my mother and grandmother had bought for me when I was a girl. It never quite fit anywhere until it arrived at the schoolhouse, and then sitting on the wide plank pine boards we'd carefully laid, its posts for the first time stretching freely under the high ceiling and broad sky-lights, it found its home. I would sit up in bed and turn to look out the window centered over the headboard. Rob would bring me coffee; he'd already been writing for hours. I would watch the gardens from this vantage, seeing all the seasons and years in the size and colors of the plants below, future and past, all before fully entering the space of the day.

Building the Bell School changed who I was as an artist. I was making and selling quilts throughout the prolonged construction period. As much as I loved them, they started to feel like my sketchbook. They were a source of joy, practice, and ideation, but the ideas they sparked were often other media entirely. Creating the space of home and garden allowed me to enter a spiritual space that transcended simple objectification. My home became a living collaborator. My work on the house opened the door to pursue more conceptual work, too. My embodied understanding of how the material choices in the house changed how we lived allowed me to tap directly into those choices, to consider ideas that trans-cended the bounds of functionality or a particular medium.

I created sculptures, often in diptych, setting up a system in which one part was used to consider the other, elaborate mirrors. In one, titled *Study*, two seemingly identical gold quilts hung side by side. Upon closer inspection, one was made of gold fabric, embroidery floss, and glass beads. The other, with bits of old postcards, nails, screws, and other debris.

In another piece, I created a structure consisting of two small rooms, in mirror image, separated by a central wall. A viewer could look at them from the front, like a life-sized diorama, but the rooms themselves were not connected. Each room had damask painted walls in tonal shades of gold. The back wall was lined with bookshelves on which stood identical books wrapped in gold paper. Each room had a desk, with a small, quilted cloth over the top - the pattern in mirror image. A chair sat at each desk.

Another work consisted of two four-by-four platforms, created with planks of wood laid in rows. Each platform was on four caster wheels, making them mobile. One was painted in tonal shades of off-white and the other in tonal shades of gray. Brass nails tacked the wood in regular patterned lines. On top of each platform sat a small bed with layers of quilted mattress, each quilt stitched from inch-wide strips of cotton sateen, and punctuated with rows of embroidered French knots, an echo of the planks of wood punctuated with nails. There was also a small hooked rug on each created from rows of knotted wool, an iced layer cake with a slice taken out, and a small row of chalk. Each unit of this work was almost identical, except the color was slightly different from one to the other.

Building the Bell School not only changed my direct relationship to making art, but it expanded my creative life outside of the studio. I found in the work of building this home, a kind of real art. An engagement that demanded every bit of creative attention, but that in the end, came off the page to enter the transformational plane of everyday life. It was this work that led to the purchase of two more nineteenth-century houses in Bangor. With additional loans from my parents, my friend Lisa, and banks, we were able to renovate these spaces and rent out five apartments in them. This became an integral part of how I would conceive of my art practice. These buildings created security, both long and short-term, which allowed complete creative freedom to flourish.

Creating the Bell School was a childhood dream which I never fully allowed because unlike in Maine, I never would have been able to have a relationship to a space like this where I grew up in New Jersey. Driving in the car as a kid I would stare longingly out the window at houses with land. I always felt the proportions of the suburbs were wrong, they chaffed, but driving into the more rural areas, things spread out a bit, making way for beauty to emerge. Soft green grass rolled gently over fluctuating elevations, but what really moved me were the trees. I imagined living intimately inside those forested hills, more like I imagined the Lenape people before me, "part of" instead of "apart." It seemed more natural to have more land than house, more house than garage. These proportions changed as a reflection of priorities and activities. The dimensions of the suburbs made me uncomfortable, nature relegated to the form of homogenous and submissive lawns. Houses seemed teetering beyond their means, like those images of the wicked stepsisters trying on the glass slipper in Cinderella. In New Jersey, however, those houses comfortably scaled to expanses of land were only for rich people. I didn't dare have that dream because I never desired money, only space. I thought that private land was an illusion of space for those who owned it. I believed that the irony of possession was the absence of true belonging, that money was in fact that antithesis of space. The nay-saying experts I encountered in Maine would, in New Jersey, be responsible for countless permits and decision making, relegating me to the sidelines of my material experience. We would not have been able to use our hands and our time to build the way we would live.

I certainly could not have followed this dream without the loan from my parents, who even if disinclined toward such projects themselves, trusted and supported me to the sum of a mortgage.

I also knew I could not have followed this dream without Rob or his family. They were entrepreneurs and in that, they were fearless, playful even. They knew how to do things with their hands and if they didn't, they wouldn't hesitate to just figure it out. They gave me permission and courage. They backed it up with their material support. On day one they showed up and tore down walls. They painted, ran wires and pipes, burned brush, and all along they housed and fed us while we worked. Their living room became a storage unit for our furniture and they never complained. Rob's mother would fill black thermoses with stew on cold nights before we headed out to our construction site after our other work that day. They believed in our home and in what I saw for it and in their support they invested in this dream with us. This was the first time my vision became manifest and they were my team. It forever changed me.

The first time I saw the Bell School, I was twenty-six years old. I'd never been to that town before. It was a nowhere place between nowhere places, for no one unless you happened to be born there or were seeking that space in between, that liminal view. Twilight. I headed east away from the interstate and towards the coast. I turned onto the road that would become mine in the next decade. The elevation changed, and became higher. Suddenly, I was surrounded by hills, horses, and Christmas tree farms. Sweeping vistas were covered in deciduous trees. Giant maples lined the road. "This looks like New Jersey," I marveled, surveying the softness of the land and believing I'd arrived home. I didn't know yet how this mimicry of the land, this illusory similitude had led me far from it.

11. The Wisdom of Connection

"I didn't really fall in love with you until you fell in love with someone else," Rob told me one day, out of the blue, a decade after Cameron and I first met.

I saw Cameron for the first time in 2005, as soon as I stepped from the gravel parking lot onto the wooden deck upon arriving at an artist residency on the coast of Maine called Haystack. He was tall and lanky with impossibly perfect curls and dark blue eyes. Yet, my palpable response to his presence had more to do with a sense of movement than with appearance. Something tangible, yet invisible. We grasp at forces like magnetism and electricity to explain the kind of tugging and sharpness. I was *moved*, although I didn't quite know how and certainly not why.

When I found that he and I were assigned to the same studio, I was deeply relieved. I felt inexplicably safe. His proximity allayed the familiar, but long latent, social anxiety that blindsided me, walking across a dining hall, food in hand, scanning the room for an empty seat at tables crowded with strangers.

I experienced my feelings more like the memory of feelings. I felt like a person I'd been long ago. This alienation was provoca-

tive, like consciousness itself. I possessed the inevitable estrange-
ment of a traveler and this revealed intimate things that never seem
to change, though sometimes they're forgotten. This reverie made
me miss Rob and I began, almost immediately, writing him letters.
I reflected on how we'd been ten years ago, when we'd met at a
tiny liberal arts college on the East Coast. Our connection was
forged by some shared version of what I was feeling again in that
present moment. An inquisitive and observational drive meandering back and forth over the line between excitement and anxiety.
I bummed a cigarette from another artist and smoked alone on the
deck, enacting another memory, a regression.

That first evening of the residency, all of the artists gathered
for a communal dinner of homemade pizza in the lodge. After eating with my new studio mates, I suddenly felt acute pain in my
abdomen. A doubled-over, face-flushed, leave-me-alone, but
someone-please-help-me kind of pain. Without missing a beat,
Cameron, confirming my most immediate intuitions, took
charge. He made contact with the staff after hours, procured medicine, tea, and sat next to me until I was well.

The two of us spent the next weeks working side by side in
the studio. We learned how to make nets by tying different kinds
of strategic knots. We used crochet for sculpture. We tied silk and
cotton yardage around small and various objects and dipped it into
steaming, noxious vats of dye. He made me a silk scarf with his
newly acquired skills, but added a well-placed iron burn, a contra-
distinctive gesture in this place where everyone seemed to put the
world aside for a utopian immersion. For us, the shine seemed
suspicious, calling to question what it obscured.

In addition to these sanctioned pursuits, we made creatures from spent pistachio shells. The exquisite corpses emerged from bits of string, bobby pins, and ink throughout the days.

We paused in pleasant surprise to discover our mutual Wu Tang love, further demarking us an incongruous demographic.

We laughed at the messages left in the guest book and added our own under each other's names. We marveled at the behaviors of people away from their daily lives: I interrupted my roommate getting an awkward massage from a man named Ed. Ed had written in the guest book, too: "Life is short. Haystack is long."

The day our studio group was tasked with presenting histories of our work to one another; I nervously fumbled with my slides. He loaded the projector for me.

Not only was vulnerability OK; Cameron *helped* me. The effect was so foreign I could not then name the experience. Even as a child my well-intended parents would push me, hoping that through immersion or coercion, I would unlearn my pronounced and innate reticence. I learned instead that even the smallest bits of life were painful and no one was there to help. Independence should be forged at any cost, that's how one survives. It was my moral obligation to *overcome*, my fear itself a kind of failure. An identity forged in overcoming who I was, an autoimmune affliction of the truth. Through these new kinds of interactions it was as if something inside me dislodged, like a bit of ice melting in a glass of cubes, and soon everything falls just a bit, into a new place, and slowly becomes less rigid, more fluid.

I was flirting, but I indulged it, not because I didn't assess that risk, but I determined there was none. First, my new friend was surely gay. He even referred to his current partner with gender-neutral pronouns, not a habit for straight people. Second, he was twenty-two years old to my twenty-eight. The difference was a lot at the time, especially since those particular years marked different stages of life, he was in college. I was married. I had a house, a business. Finally, this residency was only two weeks and he would soon return to Chicago, 1,200 miles away.

For this moment, I needed the profound sense of safety and belonging that I felt in our small exchanges and quiet work. That sense of security on one front, allowed an opening for growth on another; I glimpsed a new horizon for my work. One day in a group discussion, he said, "I just want to live my quiet little life." The contrast between the humble content and his enthusiastic confidence was startling. It resonated with me so thoroughly, more pieces clicking perfectly into place.

The last day of the residency came. I walked alone on a wooded path toward my cabin, a lump forming in my throat. I sat on the ground to quell the vertiginous welling, instead, I began to cry, overcome with grief. Unnerved and mystified, I interrogated the feeling as it consumed me. *What was my problem?* I was in love and I would never see him again.

I returned to my daily routine, changed. My husband and I continued our work renovating the old schoolhouse, transforming it into our home. I tended to my tasks absently. I was listless, tearful. My stomach ached.

One day, weeks later, I received a letter in the mail. He missed me, too. The partner he'd so vaguely referred to? He was breaking up with *her*.

"These are the challenges marriage is made of," I told myself. "Events unfold over long arcs of time. The nature of feelings is transience, the nature of marriage, commitment," I tried reasoning with myself, inspiration to just wait this out.

"If you feel the same way in five years," I told myself, "then might be time for action." The problem was, I had already taken action, albeit involuntarily. This act of consciousness so many years ago was one of the first times I can recall practicing what I now think of as strategies I would articulate so many years later in the formation of the holistic styling practice that would become my mode of creative work. I observed things as they were, not as I wished they would be. I accepted the truth of my body, the complete metabolic change that had occurred and remained. I described my self-observation instead of judging it. Although I used the word and concept "love," surely an evaluation, I treated it as a daily fluctuation, an ever-changing movement of the body. What I witnessed was that I was not present in my chosen life anymore. I had to fix it. This meant being truthful about my experience to bring it back into alignment with the intentions I had for my life. I reached an impasse where I could no longer rationalize away my embodied experience.

One night, as Rob and I sat in the cab of his blue truck parked in our driveway, I worked up the courage, "I'm in love with someone else," I told him. The only way to protect my marriage was to bring this inside, believing the true work and hope of love is the creation of wholly personal answers to our most intimate questions.

"But, you can't love two people at once," he said softly, staring at the steering wheel. He rarely looked directly at me. He wore glasses and made it a point of taking them off in preparation for an intimate exchange. He liked the blur of vision, the obscurity of his companions. I think it's one of the reasons I have a hard time remembering his face and when I dream, his eyes are always darting, never focused, like someone intoxicated or enraptured. Or in the most disturbing case, darkened like after an explosion.

"I guess you can," I said, heartbroken. In some ways, I think I've been heartbroken ever since. I had to give up the formative expectations and vision I had for my life, for the person I thought I wanted to become, those shreds, however small, of desire to be that woman in Boston with the love-shining-ring and gravid enfranchisement. The quality of that giving up was grief. This queer space had opened up between the truth of my experience and everything I thought I knew and wanted, sounding dissonant alarms familiar from so much of my childhood. Just as all those years ago I felt the compulsion to protect my difference, here, too, I felt fierce, like life or death. This new space, the one that put me at odds with my husband, whom I loved deeply, with my family, and my community, was most precious because it contained the truth. Anger had helped me protect the truth of my experience for so many years, and I knew it would now, too.

If something saved me in this pivotal moment in my life it was this: the alignment of curiosity and desire with an intensity of metabolism, of bodily experience. Imbued in the secrets of my

DNA was surely a history of turning over tables. I've never witnessed either of my parents submitting, never seen them clamor for popularity. In fact, it is something they both seem to despise. They even delight in the truth of their perspectives, maybe especially in a fight. The truth, for me, was too loud to ignore.

Despite the encompassing physicality of the change this love wrought, I didn't understand what it meant to *listen* to my truth then. I frankly didn't know what sense to use, was it even listening? Was it looking? In so many ways, especially in the day-to-day, I was probably further from the truth than most. I was so practiced at dulling my *sense* altogether. Instead, I was trying to reason, to skip experience and land on something clear without all the messiness. I was in a near-constant state of rationalizing, narrativizing, and planning.

I was moved by overwhelming desire and curiosity. I wasn't moving from fear, from scarcity, or from necessity, after all, I already had everything I thought I wanted. If anything, I was moving despite those things. I was terrified of losing my marriage, of losing my identity as part of this "successful" couple. Perhaps most of all, Rob and I had created a universe between us, one that extended into the space around us through our home and our work. It was a love, an ethics, a philosophy of living, a temple. This love allowed me my sovereignty. The thought of losing that meant certain death.

In the year that followed the residency at Haystack, Cameron and I continued to write letters and talk on the telephone. "I love you," I told him, "but nothing about our day-to-day lives is going to change. You should find someone else."

My sister and I drove to visit him with me almost five months after we first met; she didn't want me to be alone. She and I drove over thirteen hours and checked into a hotel in the middle of Chicago for two days. The next time I saw him would be another eight months after that. Our relationship slowly became a part of reality for me and Rob.

At Haystack all those years ago, I'd remembered an older version of myself, or maybe a smaller one that I'd kept hidden. I needed to go back to the place where I'd lost the thread of a certain identity, the place where my curiosity and desire were overtaken by the pressures of the world around me. Like a little girl learning double Dutch, rocking back and forth until she spots the moment where she understands the rhythm, where she knows it in her body. It's a version of belonging that calls her to jump in.

12. What We Talk About When We Talk About Love

Rob, Cameron, and I didn't know how to be on this path, together, and so we reached for books. We made art. And we talked to one another, endlessly, daily, in the mornings and into the night.

"That's just penis envy," Rob explained to me. The three of us sat around the island in the kitchen at the Bell School, late one night. So late and so many drinks that we'd decided to smoke our cigarettes in the house, something reserved for a special kind of abandon.

"I understand what you're saying, well, what Freud's saying, actually, but that just doesn't resonate with me. You can say it all day," I replied. Rob would get really into particular authors or theories and hold on to them for years on end, practicing the application of the ideas in and through all the scenarios of our lives for that time. Writing in the style of his latest inspiration, sometimes spending years at a time in the universe of one particular man: Faulkner, Carver, Barthelme, Borges, Freud. He would become so adept, that the ideas were as if his own, rarely allowing daylight between them and his truth. I, however, rarely read. Even the smallest bits of information, a line of poetry or a painting in a museum, would feel like anxiety in my body. My metabolism needed more time to make than to consume or I would experience great disturbance, something like urgency. A feeling like I needed to warn someone and I didn't have the words, like I didn't have the complete information and so no one would heed the warning, but nevertheless the danger was real. And so it was that Rob would talk from books and I would respond from someplace else.

The light glowed yellow through the amber glass of the pendant hanging above the sink, illuminating the cloud of smoke forming in the room. I opened a window to let the smoke out, the cold air in. The conversation meandered in those days, each of us bringing the refrain of our current interests, our projects, to the table. Testing new language, new manners of expression, new discoveries brought forth from our individual laboratories. Smoking made me feel alive because in those moments, and maybe only in those moments, I wasn't afraid of death. The breathing kept me present. The drinking allowed me to rest, it also allowed me a respite from the head. Although our conversations were always cerebral and many of the words now lost, what we would create, night after night, was a space of connection. Our inhibitions lowered, our speech more about immersion in this thing we valued together and less about any specific content. We would plan our dotage: three rocking chairs on the porch.

I wish I had an anchor for my memories of my earliest life with Rob. Perhaps a memory of a beautiful place or a beautiful memory of any place. A place where Rob and I were together, alone, before meeting Cameron, a setting for the beginning of our story. I remember certain streets in Annapolis, where he and I met. Those streets disappear at the edge of the water. My image of them is dark, nighttime, and they aren't attached to the rest of the town. I could never find my way back there, even though I believe I'm remembering real places. Countless images of sitting together by the water in tiny parks or grassy alcoves that just end there, leading nowhere but still and glossy water, opaque. We talk late into the night. We were two kids, forging something in the dark although we could only hazard poor guesses as to what.

"You are my mirror," I argued one of those late nights. We were always tenuous, always breaking apart. It probably wasn't arguing so much as begging in a style I thought could masquerade as dignified. At the time, Rob read Raymond Carver, obsessively. He would write story and after story in his style, in his mood. This gnawed at me; his stories gave a kind of image and flesh that fed my anxiety, my neediness. I saw Rob's attraction to the cynicism, the alienation, the curt detachment in Carver's bleak relationship portraiture and I felt that aesthetic universe penetrate our interactions. Raymond Carver nurtured a despondent vodka-in-the-freezer kind of love and I campaigned hard for something different, more like a bottle-of-wine-in-a-backpack and leaving everything else behind, on foot. I wanted a partner with whom I could plunge into the unknown. I saw myself as the only one fighting for our togetherness, but I suspect now that wasn't the whole story. It was the push and pull that kept everything in motion. Together we created the energy, the gravity, that held us together. As if holding hands and spinning as fast as we could until one day we could no longer hold on, we lost focus.

It was the impasses though, the deadlock, even the adversity that compelled me. The places it hurt not being able to move through or past. If he could see me, maybe I could see me, too. I wanted him to know that I, too, knew we were both alone. "I don't need you," I would insist, explicitly, lest he feel too trapped. It pained me to say, after all, it seemed wounding and destructive to make this the mantra of a relationship. I used Rilke as a mutually agreeable palliative and made the case for being alone together in the most beautiful and acceptably erudite paraphrase. I didn't yet know how this relational space can transform and evolve past this point of hyper self-awareness. This head-knowledge of spiritual truths wreaked havoc. This fun-house effect of consciousness. Words became elaborate puppet theater mistaken for the puppeteers, the playwrights and the ancestors before even them.

I didn't understand the fuel we were living on. What we knew of love was fear. For a long time I think I believed that we create meaning, that rich terrain of intuitive wisdom and connection, from sense, the plausible stories we tell that uphold our identity and our relationships. Now I think the reverse is true, we create sense from meaning. Love was the sense. It was the story we told about what we knew, the meaning, in our bodies: fear. We make it all up afterwards. There's no real or not real when it comes to love. Did I truly love Rob? Yes. Mortally.

My memories of that time are now dead ends themselves. They stop and go nowhere, surrounded by darkness. There's no trace to or from anything else and no way to get back.

Even now, when heartbreak rings some quotient of truth, it is maybe mostly because of the broken part. Grief is a tough fit at first. The mind balks after all, there is evidence to suggest Rob isn't actually dead even though the person I was married to certainly is. Some form persists, looking and sounding and moving very much like the person I used to know. I'm sure he goes grocery shopping, in the very same store we used to go grocery shopping together. And drives around in the very same car. I knew it wasn't him anymore. I know it's hard to believe, but I'll tell you how I knew: his eyes changed color. We were standing in the entryway of the Bell School and in a rare moment he looked right at me, into my eyes, and what I saw weren't his eyes. They'd changed color, ever so slightly, but for certain.

"I don't know why artwork should be beautiful." Cameron described his motives as the three of us sat around the table. "Hasn't anyone seen a sunset? Who thinks, 'I can do that?'" I'd rather think about the relationships between things." Rob mixed another round of cocktails.

We tried on the lenses of books, artworks, and images, each of us immersed in our own creative and imaginative worlds, but we tried them on for one another. We were at home in a love of ideas and trust came from a mutual reverence for this space. There was intimacy in the provisionality of this testing ground, exposing our vulnerable explorations, but more than that, we trusted each other's minds and sensibilities. We trusted each other's *style*. This was not a trust any of us found very easily. This was an incubator for our creative works, our thoughts, without each other's nurture and protection, we were imperiled. Together, we found mutual guardianship.

Rob wrote a short story, "The Neighbor War" just before meeting Cameron for the first time. He cast us and the others living at the Bell School as engaged in a war, explicitly queer against convention. The sides were characterized by their sexuality and their relationship to the material world. He expressed a great sadness at my relationship with Cameron, whom he named Julian, but described an ethical trajectory, a queer mandate, for their relationship.

Rob's stories emerged as all of our work did during those years, as deep and mutualistic explorations of who we were, in love, in family, in society. We recognized in our dispositions and in the work itself this "common foe," this anti-material, conventionality and patriarchy that bubbled up as the voice of oppression and repression within each of us. It was scarcity that rarified love, making it dangerously precious, stealing it from its proper home in abundance where it could thrive in all manner of relationships. Our mutual sovereignty depended on our mutual support, our creative license in work and life.

Our creative works drew on the intimacy of the lives that we lived together. A radical self-honesty had to face the boundaries of our own internalized narratives, no matter how safe they seemed. We tore everything apart so we could rebuild it together. "The Neighbor War," perhaps above many other attributes, pushed a deeply political agenda for the kind of luxurious life rooted in true abundance, rooted in the idea that "there is enough." Certainly, enough love. Scene after scene was set with creative acts of sustenance, honoring the mundane and the material: "Pauline made Morel, Asparagus, and Fresh Pea Risotto in celebration of the beautiful autumn day. . . Sam and Tom went to the farmers' market and got ingredients for Pappardelle with Caramelized Onions, Pancetta, and Arugula." Even the uniforms of *our* army adhered to these standards of abundance through luxury: "The lieutenant wore a silk arm-band and a coat with attractive brocade on it." This all, starkly contrasted a worldly neglect and inherent violence of the neighbors who at varying points are described as looking crazed, letting their children lead them into battle, not raking their leaves (contrasted with our neatly raked piles), and profound scarcity, ultimately trying "to eradicate Tom (Rob) and Jane (me) . . . because of oil."

We waged this war within ourselves for years, our scarcity and our abundance. Our desire to live beautifully and creatively versus acceptance in our own families, security in the cocoon of career and financial stability. Exploring our relationship to one another was a way of fighting for ourselves. They were acts of faith, practiced daily, and affirmed night after night in these discussions. In artwork after artwork. In the beautiful feasts we cooked, often marveling in gratitude, "Who eats like this!" In the beautiful home and garden we created, each of us contributing in our own way, Rob built a beautiful fence, creating each gate into the garden. He tended the life blood, the infrastructure: the plumbing, the heating. Cameron and I designed. We cleaned and painted, procured furniture, and worked in the garden. This was the vision, the temple, we tended it together, materially and in our dreams.

Rob manifested emotional involvement and tender perspicacity in "The Neighbor War" character Sam, who not only was better than Rob "when it came to certain matters dealing with emotions and subtlety and the human heart," but, "Also, Sam knew more about wines." The connection Rob made between emotional presence and the sommelier's intimacy with wine stood in contrast to the emotional distance, the frigid counterpoint: icy vodka, in Carver's universe from so many years before. That was a change, an evolution, all these years later. It was wrought in terms of the quality and intimacy of our relationships to material experience. In its own cerebral and literary way it was searching for a path back into the body, a savant-like prophecy of the way not yet fully forged.

The material world we created around us showed us to ourselves. We came from the world and our world came from us.

13. Divorce

I've been concerned my whole life with what it means to know the things we know. I realize as I sit here that this almost-obsessive drive was probably rooted in qualities that manifested young, but for years sat nameless and unfocused. There was the time I became inconsolable watching *The Fox and The Hound* while others seemed to enjoy the pathos in the way I suspect it was intended: more like entertainment and less like existential horror. Sometimes, when trying to fall asleep, a stuffed animal slightly askew would need to appear more comfortable before I could relax. In larger gatherings of people I was aware that a change in temperature, in lighting, or in sound could shift the energy and emotions in the room. This kind of discernment created a baseline sensory experience for my life, a kind of hypervigilance. An awareness of our invisible extension into space, into things. The admixture creeping in from the edges, moving through us.

I was always drawn to animals, but most especially dogs. My childhood I spent begging and pleading to no avail. Around the age of thirteen, I campaigned. Hard. I would leave daily signs and drawings, relentlessly, throughout the house: "I Want A Dog." Each one colored, adorned with illustrations of Labrador Retrievers, Beagles, Collies. It didn't so much matter what kind of dog. Sometimes the 8" x 10" pages would be folded into my parents' drawers, or under a toilet seat. Taped end-to-end they'd accordion out of a cupboard. Until one day, my mother, having had *enough*, took me to a psychologist. She insisted there must be something wrong with me, an emotional problem of some sort, to want a dog that badly. While there was undoubtedly an element of truth, some sessions later the professional verdict came: "Why don't you just get her a dog?" I don't think my mother ever forgave the psychologist, nor trusted one ever again.

When my parents finally relented, we got a small terror of a puppy, a Dalmatian and named her Bailey. She was intelligent and sensitive and unique in certain proclivities from the outset. My mother was the one first drawn to her. She singled her out from her litter mates because she noted her tendency to be *independent*, even at 6 weeks old, wandering off from the others. In her puppy "kindergarten" training, the sweet-faced runt stood on the sidelines growling at the fluffy Labrador Retrievers unfortunate enough to flop and bounce in her direction. She was more still than the others, more vigilant, aloof. I think high-strung is a way of describing something that is vibrating in a perpetual attempt to escape its own body. Aggression was a feature of her personality for her entire life, showing her tiny needle teeth to those bubbly puppies at the very beginning.

We took her to training after training, the kind that recommended putting a dog onto her back to create a proper pack structure. I remember my father doing this, with rage, when Bailey snapped at him one night. What she learned in that moment, and all of the similar ones, was quite simply, more fear, more rage, more aggression.

I studied Cesar Milan on episode after episode of *The Dog Whisperer*, long after Bailey died at the impossibly old age of fifteen, after she'd gone with me to college, to Boston, and then even to Maine. I watched him teach clients how to walk their dogs and even if they were successful in mimicking his gestures and movements, what they never quite mastered was his energy: calmness and intentionality. I watched him embody what he tried to teach: leadership is service. If you do not serve the needs of the dog and control your own energy, regulate your emotions, you will never lead or have peaceful relationships.

What service requires first is understanding the needs and desires of others. This is a practice of listening. To lead oneself, one must discover one's own needs and desires. This wisdom does not come from the head, it resides in the body, and we have become skilled liars, mostly to ourselves. We like to evade the itchy discomfort of our truth. It is easier to experience it as an urge to act or to numb and avoid, instead of as a call to be still. We are immune to the steady leak of energy we expend vibrating out of our bodies, our presence. We call it nervous, stressed, and anxious.

Sometimes the evasion of bodily truth gives way to periodic eruptions. Physical violence was a regular feature of my childhood experience, as was it for my parents and their parents, too. It was a culture. I didn't understand at the time, but I don't think we can truly have self control, control over our violence, unless we heal the body. Bailey was learning it as I was, as my father and mother learned it at the hands of their parents. Each successive generation trying their best to absorb the shock, to filter it through their own bodies in some inarticulate but pressing drive to spare their children. Bailey, as any sensitive creature would, absorbed the energy of the household and manifested all manner of dysfunctional, aggressive, and anxious behavior. Not only did she become another symptom of the dynamics, but that made her yet another cause. She was a casualty of the unconscious cycles we all fulfilled in that house. From the moment my mother's initial attraction was sparked by the independence of this creature, her disconnection, she became a part of us, capable of fulfilling her role. My mother to this day remarks with fondness on Bailey's intelligence. Independence and intelligence were always worthy, even despite other horrors.

My mother would often describe my father as ugly, she'd make a joke of it, as if it were a playful assessment. I'm sure on some level she felt powerless in what was a near-constant contest with my father, perhaps like she had raised at my grandmother's brutal and often violent hand. "What was that for?" my mother, just a small child, cried out in astonishment. My grandmother had hit her in the face, suddenly and from nowhere. "Nothing," my grandmother warned. "Imagine what will happen if you do something." Back then, my mother would sit on the floor of her mother's closet and pull at the clothes until she heard them rip, just a bit, at the seams. An act of subversion slight enough to go unnoticed and real enough to become relief. "You look just like him," she'd say to me about my resemblance to my father, "his clone." Never connecting the parts of this proposition she'd set up. Maybe not uttering the clauses in a single breath spared her coming to terms with the cruelty of it, but did not spare me a certain understanding of my own image. I only heard, "you're ugly."

My mother was, and remains, quite beautiful, although I never noticed it growing up. Perhaps it's the birthright of beautiful people to take appearance for granted, like a form of health. She always wore stylish clothes and makeup, but that didn't register for me either. She kept her makeup downstairs, in the half bathroom off the kitchen papered with brown, concentric and interlocking diamonds (they always seemed to me like the faces of wolves peering from the forest). I would watch her apply eyeshadow, eye liner, mascara, and red lipstick. Always red. Her nails, while kept short, were also often polished, those red, too. She dressed to go out, but she seemed under no compulsion to keep up appearances. She was much more fluent in a fuck-you energy than a please-you energy. She was glamorous but I didn't know it, because she was brash and bawdy to match the elegance. She almost always left the door open when using the bathroom.

My mother would make dinners of roasted Cornish game hens with dried fruits and wild rice, followed by a dessert of custard filled pastries topped with whipped heavy cream flavored with vanilla and powdered sugar. She never pandered to a June Cleaver image of motherhood. There were never granola bars or party favors. I went to a friend's house after school and suspected disingenuousness in her mother's cool inquiry, "Honey, would you and your friend like it if I made you some popcorn or cookies for a snack?" I wondered if she had interests outside of her child. My mother, not a regular smoker herself, was known to choose the smoking section in restaurants because it was the "child free" section and "who wants to listen to other people's whining children when you're trying to enjoy a meal." She was always willing to own her opinions, her will, even, maybe especially, if she knew it was unpopular or confrontational, the very tone of her voice conveying a simple, but seductive subtext: "If you don't like what I'm saying, then fuck you." My mother's style did not serve status or obfuscation, something that even then I saw in other kids' mothers, some of whom had plastic surgery or who gravitated towards statusy brands, instead she was bold. Unapologetic.

My mother always has a song at the ready sparked by the smallest turns of phrase that arise in mundane conversation. She speaks five languages with varying degrees of fluency. She delivers all of this with a great deal of humor and frequent laughter.

When I was young, my mother did not allow me to grow my hair long, or wear it in certain styles, or to paint my nails, shave my legs, or wear certain clothing. This control over my embodiment was attended by rigorous and ethical critique of those perpetrating the styles I wished I could possess. An aspirational perm and pink fingernails meant for me a hope of fitting in, that my voice might be heard. I think she hated the notion of my belonging if it meant sacrificing elements of my childhood to the compulsory costuming of womanhood, most especially in a sexualized way. Although herself adept at these expressive forms, she balked at the premature cultivation of affect. I believe she saw, in these aesthetic pursuits, a foreclosure of a more essential focus and, with it, the hobbling of a certain moral sensibility. Perhaps she is notable in her absence from the sea of mothers concerning themselves with the various shapes and sizes of their daughters. She didn't seem to give a shit what anyone thought about my appearance, that terrain seemed, unlike my behavior, marked by a healthy dose of differentiation. Perhaps that's the privilege of someone beautiful, someone more comfortable in the world and with people. Someone who found herself less at odds.

I, however, saw these physical modifications as the pathways for connection. The strict limits imposed by my parents let flourish sartorial and ethical walls between me and my peers, my alienation became conflated with being good, with being smart. Although painful, these distancing limits were also gifts of awareness. They created consciousness and conscientiousness around sartorial activities, especially gendered ones. My inability to participate gave me the distance to observe and what I saw was that the stakes were high.

The rules I wrapped myself in grew tighter, like a rope around a tree, slowly cutting its flesh, altering its growth, its shape. I look through old photographs and see a tense and crooked smile. It follows me through the years. I wonder if it's been deformed by that invisible rope, twisted by the hand of shame. Sometimes I see that smile in others and wonder what pain is binding them. I've spent my life working in ways that would lessen the intensity, unless of course I was compelled to seek it out, never successfully finding the balance. I was always practicing this precarious dance between advance and retreat, the need to become whole sometimes only producing more fragmentation. One day's active fight would turn the next to withdrawal, completely worn out by any engagement, any attempts to communicate. These shifts would happen inside as well as out. One moment feeling as though I would be consumed by my emotions, at their mercy, and the next, incapable of feeling them at all.

I painted my high-school bedroom all white. I cleared the walls of any decoration. I cleared the surfaces of the dressers and nightstand. I asked for white sheets and blankets. My mother found an old comforter with small yellow flowers and green leaves punctuating a white background. "You can use this," she said,

"I'm not buying you something new." Those bits of color tormented me. I turned it over for the comfort of the empty space, only it had some blood stains on it, tarnishing that experience, too. To this day I'm drawn to empty space, white and spare. Sanctuary.

For years I worked towards dampening the senses. There are various ways to do this and I tried many, but escape to the mind became a primary coping mechanism and a way of earning love that not only distracted from the senses, like a matador waving a red flag, but was also sanctioned, more like workaholism and less like rage or alcoholism. (Although I've spent my share of time in all of those places.) At the end of the day, it was still an escape, avoidant, and perhaps a more dangerous escape because of its cultural standing as a positive quality. It's actually the stuff of champions and CEO's, its reward is power over others at the expense of power over oneself. That made it harder to recognize as a problem.

The further I divorced from my embodied senses, from the animation of intuition and spirit and its one and only vestment, the more any innate faith I may have possessed slipped away. I lost joy. I lost wholeness, an integrity that occurs when the mind and body are not fractured, when each apparent part is functioning according to its truth and purpose instead of vivisected for our cognitive consumption. I became confused and indecisive because my internal alignment was off, my parts were not in sync with one another. Emphasis on the mind was a way of looking for something stable, but at the time, and for most of my life, I didn't know I was using the wrong tool.

Years later, as I watched episodes of The Dog Whisperer with Cesar Milan, his narrative made sense of poor Bailey, of all of us really. Her needs weren't met, and yet, she didn't have the tools to meet them herself. I realized that my so-called retreat to the mind, my use of logic and reason as a defense, was just an anxious dog lashing out. Logic was never meant to lead, but to follow and serve. It cannot set goals and desires, cannot be inspired or moved. It has no compass, and when called to that task it becomes like an animal, chasing its tail, spinning aimlessly, productive for productivity's sake, *ambitious*. The mind has no joy.

When it was time to go to college I weighed my options and by the very end there were really only two: the Great Books Program at a tiny liberal arts college on the east coast or art school. I pushed further into the abyss and chose the books. Rational thought is a building block of our Western heritage, starting with Plato's chariot mastered by rationality right through to the birth of specialization, Kantian imperatives and Enlightenment ethics. The rise of the West meant that the same kind of hierarchical parsing we cultivated in our thinking, we would create in our reality manifesting in species, races, and classes. We would mirror this kind of meaning-making with linear, time-based, patriarchal, racist, and capitalist structures. Inevitably, groups became marginalized through this kind of meaning and to further rationalize that effect, we stripped credibility from those groups. We did and continue to do this by impugning non-consensus reality as lies, unprovable, subjective, and irrational. We strip the natural world of resources, poison it, no longer knowing our connection.

I was so divorced from my body that I had to learn these things through the head and as I learned them, I had to create things: clothing, houses, relationships, art practices, that would move this knowing to a place of being, to a place of wisdom. I had to move the knowing into things and into the body.

It wouldn't be until many years later that I recognized non-linear and spatial practices as alternative and creative paths to meaning-making. By making things, hours and hours in the studio cutting and stitching fabric, making marks on paper, cutting, gluing, coloring, and painting, I slowly learned to connect to my body and spirit. Faith and the unspeakable kind of wisdom happened in connection, not information. For the first time I began to feel my own power, and not because I was in control or exercising my will, making decisions, but from surrender. In art-making, I found something to surrender to: the place where my ideas met the world. I surrendered to style.

True stories quite literally don't make sense in the way we like to think of it, unless we omit the nagging suspicions and fleeting glances that would never hold up in court. Making these omissions too shameful to report. They destroy our coherence, and women, most especially, are rendered powerless through an image of incoherence. We are relegated to the irrational, hysterical, and the emotional, all ways of demeaning the part of reality not subject to consensus, the part that is our own personal stories, our dreams, and experiences. This strategy is one that positions rational thought as not just a means, but as an end, as an ethic and practice valuable for its own sake. It steals multiplicity from truth, leaving it singular and scarce, accessed only by an elite which the strategy itself has created. Through this strategy truth becomes the story shared by the elite. Truth then becomes the consensus narrative of those in power. We compete for it. We see this flood our institutions and cultural practices.

Style meant living my true stories. These stories, however, are like the body, like the heart, they demonstrate that same indifference to compulsions of analysis, instead favoring something that requires our full metabolism for digestion. Style is something re-cycled, like waves rolling over and then back under themselves, refolding and layering, mixing bits of detritus with fractions of sunlight, recurring over and over, but never quite the same. Style is equally at home in the easy fluctuation of a summer breeze and the downward plunging of waterfall over rocks.

Style is presence at the union of body and spirit.

14. Making Nets

"You never look at me when we talk," I noticed aloud to Rob, not infrequently. "Do you think you're autistic?" I half-joked with a small knot of concern taking shape in my gut.

He tried to look at me, but seemed to truly not be able, "I can't concentrate on what I'm saying," we lived versions of this conversation over and over. Once years later we sat in the four-poster pine bed, his back against the headboard and my body turned toward his and had the conversation again. This time, so well worn, the knot of concern became a stand in for the intimacy. At least it was a knot reserved for us. We had a routine of gestures and observations, conversations spanning decades. These were so many knots and they became the net that held our story. I felt the presence of the gardens beyond the window in the yard below. The exposed dirt of the raised beds seemed soft and inviting.

In college, we sat up late at night, sometimes in small parks tucked out of the way, near the water. Sometimes sitting on a twin bed in a small, spare dormitory. Late at night after seminar sitting on the stone steps leading from the quad to back campus. He would take off his glasses. "Why do you take off your glasses when we talk?"

"I like the way everything becomes a bit blurry."

I saw him once sitting with a beautiful girl at a party, in that time at the beginning of college, before we were a *we*. He took his glasses off and slid them into the chest pocket of his black and red plaid shirt jacket.

*

"I don't want you to talk to Cameron anymore," Rob declared just after I'd told him my feelings. It came out clear but artificial sounding, like trying on a costume, using a voice somehow necessary but foreign and somewhat unappealing. The stiffness belied both the terror and the shame of expressing his fear, or perhaps the desire within the fear. We sat in the four poster bed, the raised beds below, just over the headboard and beyond the window.

"I can't do that," I choked back tears and searched for words. My mind scanned expanses of darkness to find them and there they were, insufficient, the only offering from the abyss. I grabbed at them. "I can't. I love you. I love Cameron." We sat in silence, me imploring and Rob, his arms crossed, protecting himself from me, from himself. Our bodies, sitting on the bed, angled against one another. Only more darkness through the skylight. "If you have to make a choice I understand," I lied, I wouldn't really understand, but I would've accepted the inexorability even if it killed me. I saw nothing else.

Sitting there on the bed, I ran my hand back and forth over the familiar pattern of the cotton quilt I'd made for us. My chest was as if crushed, incapable of drawing in full breaths. I pulled at loose threads, laying them flat and smoothing them along the surface of the quilt, pressing them into the seams, hiding them. I'd spent so long wanting Rob to want and now I faced my inability to give him what he asked.

If he'd left me then, I don't know if I would have survived, maybe he wouldn't have either. I always believed he was impervious to me, ready to abandon, or perhaps never really quite there at all. It was the effect of so many years of telling me how little he needed me, in fact, how he didn't need me at all, ever solicitous of his independence and his unencumbered time. It is hard to say if ultimately I gave life to my fears, or if my intuition held the muffled truth all along.

I pictured myself laying on the soft brown dirt of the raised bed outside, the one closest to the house, closest to that window. I felt myself resting my head in the dirt, my eyes closed and face turned toward the sky. I would press a gun against my forehead, centered, just as I was centered in the garden bed below the window centered over the headboard which was centered in the bedroom we'd built. Gently I would pull the trigger. The sound perhaps softened by the bullet thudding in the dirt after passing through my skull. My blood would flow neatly from the wound into the ground below. I merged with the earth and released the pressure in my body. Not the volatile pressure of a volcano, but instead the voluminous weight of an ocean pulled by the moon, attached to the lump in my throat and the throbbing in my skin. An unbearable sadness I would never speak aloud. I swallowed these traces of my selfishness.

I lay awake next to Rob in the night. His back to me, always his back to me, I put my arm around him. Sometimes, asleep, he'd make whimpering sounds, sad and vulnerable, like a small child. Other times his breathing seemed to stop altogether, I would become fearful only for him to gasp, once again taking in air. In these moments I saw him as tender, as human. I realized I was scared of someone who was also scared. He was not impervious at all, and yet, that was not something available to me. I knew that he would never understand those soft sounds and gasps I heard in the night, would never allow space for them in our waking life together.

I didn't deserve my grief and so these feelings, too, just more knots.

15. Pains and Perils

"You have to make a philosophical decision," a friend warned when I first met Cameron. The intimation was that I hadn't thought things through. Perhaps she wanted to say "ethical" instead of "philosophical," but was too erudite for pedestrian moralizing.

"But, we already have," I thought to myself. We chose the only path that was not arbitrary, the path that however hard to bear, adhered most closely to the truth.

I felt guilt, but not in a way I could have expected. I felt guilty for being with my husband. Was my internal compass broken, or did my instincts reveal a truth I couldn't understand? This was another moment, when leaning into the truth of my body gave me an answer that defied my expectations, and quite frankly terrified me, but I listened. I was in uncharted territory and once I committed to that terrain, there was really no choice but a vigilant attendance to the experience. There was nowhere else to rest. This is the gift of the dark. It hands us our presence.

I wanted marriage to be the end of personal drama, of doubt, and the beginning of pure existential and creative work. I believed it could be this way, not from my home, but from television. From movies and literature, where love is an end. It's the life raft we're handed to get to where we're going with an assurance of safety. Marriage promises in its various ways to usher us to our romantic destination. However, what I'd failed to fully imagine, in part perhaps because I've never seen it detailed in literary or cinematic visions, and certainly not in my home, is what happens once you arrive. There's plenty to depict the peril, the soulless disintegration of the married abounds in tales of adultery, violence, or just some low level foggy ennui. Sometimes a couple of kids will buy you eighteen years (give or take) of distraction, although their fates, too, foment in that ether.

I thought if I were safe in marriage, I could untether from the treacherous constraints of so many conventions that had failed me growing up. While I somehow got the message that marriage was an end, I had an unfounded and creative optimism for the new life that would spring up after the death of going-it-alone. I saw the uncharted home that I believed marriage could be, but only the right marriage, with someone courageous, creative, smart, and independent.

Rob was my perfect husband. He was willing to leave the trodden path and forge another way. He was intellectually and creatively brilliant, truly, enough to entrust the co-creation of a new world, forged under its own laws. Finally, as much as his independence pained me when I interpreted it as indifference, the life I was after required it. My only hope was to find a man who loved me just enough to mutually protect our shared space and not enough to own me. To find a man whose love was the inspiration to build our freedom from the substance of mystery.

And so I brought everything to my marriage first. My marriage was the largest circle in a set of Venn diagrams, everything that happened was within that circle. At our wedding we read aloud from Wendell Berry: "Marriage is a perilous and fearful effort... It creates pain that it is the only cure for." My universe functioned only under the rules of that marriage, but not blind to the reality of its experience. Marriage was my shelter, a wellspring of courage. It made meaning by virtue of its very structure, calling me to face and solve the problems it created, by revealing my reflection in another. Rob and I had created the shape of this union to embrace our own inexorable curiosities and to support our elaborate, mutual sovereignty. Surprises are not always accidents.

Our so-called pains and perils were hard to parse. Our marriage now included this third person. More so than conventional marriages, it was political as well as personal. This felt especially true in the rural town where we lived. My husband worked for his parents, conservative Christians who stayed in the small town where their family had lived and run businesses for generations. Despite his daily lunch with his mother, he didn't share much about his personal life. The decision to reveal our relationship to his family was left to his discretion. I didn't want to violate his privacy.

The treacheries of convention rose up to vanquish difference and the unknown. I received a letter from my first college roommate and longtime friend, detailing my innumerable shortcomings through the lens of this most grievous culmination. She was on the cusp of getting married herself and seemed incapable of holding onto the idea that if I, in my transgressions, weren't sealed in an overall character of moral failing and dictatorial callousness, then she wouldn't be able to rely on her "goodness" to save her from similar peril. "You pet me like a dog," she wrote, maligning a history of my genuine affections. Next, it would take the form of medical authority. "When any one of you becomes healthy, this relationship will end," Rob's therapist diagnosed. We'd entered into a symptom of sickness.

My sister, not unlike almost everyone close to us with whom we'd shared our secret, struggled, too. Upon sharing with her therapist, the verdict came harsh and clear: "Your sister is not living her authentic life." These judgments didn't make me question myself. The nerve we touched, the universal resistance, made clear a collective wound. I was so used to thinking differently from others that this, although painful, was not different in kind from so many other moments in my life. The absurdity of convention was rarely lost on me.

Our experiences only exacerbated our varying degrees of ever-present alienation. As artists, people happy to observe, we had become accustomed to sitting on the periphery. After all, we are taught that seeing is from the outside, *objective*. Despite this, the targeted cultural gaslighting stung. It drove wedges between us and our other relationships. It centered authority outside of ourselves, deemed us foolish, cruel, sick, and inauthentic. Often the highest benevolence was simply the condescending anticipation of failure. The self-fulfilling nature of these kinds of projections was never lost on me. Staying away from people became a way of staying alive. I had renewed empathy for other unconventional relationships in hostile times and in hostile places. "You don't want people burning crosses in your yard," my father understood the stakes and my desire for privacy.

My mother-in-law and I were close. We worked together. We talked everyday. It pained me to feel as though I were keeping something from her. "You'll find someone someday," she told Cameron at dinner one night as the three of us stared at our plates, finding it suddenly difficult to swallow any food. The secrecy produced feelings of guilt. It weighed heavily for over a decade, finding destructive expression in anxiety, obsessive work habits, and excessive drinking.

We were effectively in the closet for over twelve years. We were fractured and fragmented.

"Can he even get it up for you if you don't bend over?" a friend speculated on Cameron's sexuality as a way of insinuating a generally lurid and corrupting vein of suspicion into what she considered a reckless and degraded situation.

This secrecy was counterbalanced with unwelcome scrutiny. The three of us were increasingly committed to our relationship, even moving in together. Cameron and Rob became close; they were as family, planning a future. Eventually, Cameron and I told our geographically-scattered families. Cameron's were concerned but supportive. Mine, I suspect, were ashamed, and mostly expressed anger and disapproval. (We spent some time not speaking. I told them, in some manner, that my life was hard enough and I would not admit their active resistance.) Slowly, as they spent more time with the three of us, they accepted the relationship, albeit begrudgingly. We enjoyed holidays together. We traveled. We behaved much as any other family. Despite some level of acceptance, I felt uncomfortably overexposed – a private aspect of my life, one which 'normal' heterosexual couples could expect to be left private, was now open to the salacious, speculative, and critical fantasies of others. Walking through life vulnerable in this way extracted a kind of energy from me that was not elsewhere replenished. It drained me. I was running out.

On the other side, there were great joys and illuminations for having given over to this relationship. The joy that resides in truth admits more suffering than conventional wisdom lets on. There was pride in attempting to face something so inexorable and yet culturally repressed with thoughtfulness and compassion. The three of us, at times, took great pleasure in considering and discussing it over the years, how it highlighted dimensions of relationships generally ("in order not to be alone, you need to be two, but in order to be a couple, you need to be three"). Nothing could be taken for granted, imparting a beauty and generosity often lacking once love's urgency wanes and gives way, even if slightly, to the mundane. Radical honesty reigned among values for twelve years, a new prerequisite for engagement. Without it, nothing would survive, and I learned this once it was too late.

Now, and here, in New York City, I hear a lot about polyamory. In 2005, in Maine, that was not the case. The kind of truth I wanted to live put me at deep odds with the world. It was yet another kind of separation and alienation from the pervasive values and entanglements I saw around me. I'd lived in this dissonant space for so long that I absorbed its pains as a matter of course.

Just after graduation, Rob and I headed to St. Louis for the wedding of some college friends. We joked about the sermon long afterward. The pastor compared marriage to a triangle whose sides A and B represented the husband and wife. (An awkward nod to our collegiate study of Euclid.) Alone, their union was unstable.

The addition of the third side, C, for Christ, stabilized the marriage, a triangle being the most stable shape. Our trio did, in fact, last longer than many romantic relationships of any kind. I don't think it was three people that allowed for the relationship to persist, but the honesty. Where it failed was in the places honesty hadn't been realized, and those places were still deep within ourselves, separated from our consciousness, from our daily practice.

In my marriage I reenacted the conditions and patterns of my childhood. I was looking to return home, not unlike my attraction to the land around the Bell School. I built an identity motivated often by a fear of being unloved and a sense of scarcity. I didn't know how to navigate between independence and intimacy. As a woman, I didn't feel entitled to both and for me, love meant the former. I was lucky in so many ways to have the opportunity to grow in the safety of this little world we'd built at The Bell School. I often wonder at the name, both its strength and weakness. Why should a home be a school and not a place of deep rest and belonging? It was a place to nurture the mind, not unlike my first home. On the other hand, it was the place where I followed my truth as it appeared. The simultaneity of these two romantic relationships provided a dialectical proposition for growth, instead of a cyclical refrain. Perhaps therein lies the strength of the triangle. It is the strength of perspective, of complexity.

I considered my life with my husband one of building: our home, our relationship, but most importantly a very hard-earned story of love, identity, and purpose. We were both bound by creative purpose. I was playing out the familiar advance and retreat of my childhood against the chronic retreat of his. Sometimes, I filled up all the space he left in his wake, becoming intolerably needy. Or, I tried to keep some level of dignity by retreating, feeling nothing at all.

When I met Cameron, I was able, mostly, to keep an equanimous distance from Rob. Cameron had responded humanely to my experiences of pain and vulnerability, however small, in our fateful first encounters. It was enough of a glimpse of something different that I couldn't go back. Truly, I believed I was engaging my husband in a way he could respect and in a way he desired: I did not task him with emotional content. I didn't express need of any kind, instead, we connected through the head. A place that gave us both great pleasure and meaning.

What I didn't quite realize at the time was that Rob was both disgusted by and attracted to the advance. His isolation could not properly be performed without an audience and I became increasingly disinterested. I'd left him more isolated than he'd actually wanted. An expanse of desires I'd never admitted were met in my relationship with Cameron. I had the space to recalibrate, I had no urge to push my husband beyond the safe distance he liked to keep from me, the place he was most comfortable. I no longer begged for his presence. This brought a great deal of what seemed like peace to our marriage, until he wanted to trade peace for the urgency of renewed desire.

16. Double Jeopardy

"Well, you know, you did have Cameron. It seems only right that Rob has someone else, too." I was pacing the sprawling lawn of the City College campus just north of my apartment in the late summer heat when one of my closest friends uttered the sentiment I would come to hear too many times in the aftermath of it all. I was hit in the gut. I was relieved we were talking on the phone instead of in person; I don't think I could have handled the full weight of her presence accompanying this second betrayal.

Similar comments trickled out of the mouths of people I was close to, tentatively at first, through slightly squinted eyes and down turned corners of mouths, as if easing the blow of their opinion. The lilting tones of their voices rocked back and forth in another failed attempt to slow the crushing impact of the "I-told-you-this-would-never-work" subtext. It felt like the people around me were sighing relief: the heteronormative couple bond had been restored. The world made sense again.

Homosexuality was classified as a mental illness in the DSM until 1973. It was then replaced with the diagnosis of "sexual orientation disturbance." I could not fathom my inner circle not being able to learn the lessons of a fickle history, a lens besmirched with patriarchy. The apparent redaction of extrapolation from otherwise functioning cognition. But of course, these things are never a matter for the mind, which was my golden revelation in the decade I spent with Rob and Cameron; fear not only buries the truth, it spins a special narrative, both seductive and threatening, meant to conceal the grave forever. These look like arguments from authority, arguments to preserve the status quo. The ones that need a movement of "me too's" to just crack the surface. They are arguments adept at denying the invisible, the multiplicity of truth, and the entire terrain of reality that exists outside of consensus.

Rob surely endured a unique pain in our relationship, not insofar as there was pain, but that it was his own. My friends seemed to suggest that I should have never believed his consent, to say nothing of his active participation and explicit defense of our relationship, because our so-called arrangement was too corrupt for credibility. Their remarks betrayed them as never having understood or accepted our relationship in the first place. We'd gone back to the beginning, the place where we'd endured the remarks from family, friends, and therapists alike: this will all fall apart. I felt them grasping for the moral of our story because the mess and the pain of it all needed some cautionary rule. The favored way of avoiding pain is being normal. In the eyes of the world, things had returned to normal. In retrospect, I don't believe there was anything Cameron, Rob, and I could've said or done to convince people we were capable of consent. Believing we were in some way compromised was always the easier sell. Even if we'd lasted forever, it became clear we'd always be subject to some narrative about what emotional disturbance or relationship problem had produced such an anomaly.

I'd long questioned the so-called "test of time." This instance was no different. The relationship that Rob, Cameron, and I had together does not need to be reflected through the lens of the end. It stood the test of presence more than any other relationship I'd been in. We were re-writing the rules and that required more from us than following the well-trodden path. My marriage had ended, but I would still protect the sanctity of my story because in the heart of that story was love. In the heart of that story was my map, charted by spirit and anchored in values that I still hold dear. Even despite its end, my marriage, in all its specific glory, would remain part of my truth.

Rob used to protect us, to protect our relationship, from this kind of subtle attack. His wit was as sharp as his disdain for the status quo and he'd comfort me as friends and family leveled these kinds of blows, most especially at the outset of our relationship with Cameron. Sometimes he'd remind me of something philo-sophical, like the Rilke we'd chosen to read at our wedding, years before we could've imagined Cameron:

". . . where people act out of a prematurely fused, turbid com-munion, every move is convention: every relation to which such entanglement leads has its convention, be it ever so unusual . . . why, even separation would here be a conventional step, an im-personal chance decision with strength and without fruit. . . . But if we nevertheless hold out and take this love upon us as burden and apprenticeship, instead of losing ourselves in all the light and frivolous play, behind which people have hidden from the most earnest earnestness of their existence-- then a little progress and an alleviation will perhaps be perceptible to those who come long af-ter us; that would be much."

Rilke goes on to offer patriarchy as the great corrupter of love. Rob and I knew this Rilke so well. Even from our earliest days, we'd built our relationship on it, so mostly it didn't need to be said and he'd offer instead a simple, ad hoc, "That person is an idiot." While not philosophical, he understood that the truth we'd honed together, our story, was a salve.

But, now, he'd pulled the rug out from under our universe and left me out there, to say nothing of Cameron who was left to tend his own pain in the shadow of mine. When it came to marriage, if Rob recanted his story, I was no longer defensible. Rob betrayed our honesty, our ethics, and our trust. He tore apart our story by upholding an ethic we'd disavowed in the practice of our lives so many times, from leaving Boston, to choosing art, to building the Bell School, not having children, and spending over a decade actively engaging in the complexities and realities of our relationship to one another and to Cameron. The fissure that Rob opened up between us let everything ugly we'd fought against seep up through and trickle over the edges: a second betrayal for me to face alone.

I felt I had little recourse to human compassion, or even if there were some quotient of compassion, it was tainted, even if slightly, with judgment. I often turned to shamanic journeying for guidance and to cope with my pain and the alienation. On one such shamanic journey, I saw the Bell School as a temple. I opened the heavy wooden doors to see dishes smashed and furniture broken and overturned. It was a desecrated temple. I ran screaming from the house, tearing my hair and my clothes and running into the hills. The message came clear, "unsanctioned grief is madness." The healing, too, came in the vision. In the journey, women came to grieve with me, to witness my grief. This was the antidote to the pain and to the madness; this being seen. Empathy. Before the journey ended I was given an assignment. I was told to write Rob a eulogy, to reclaim the intimacy, the good memories. I sat in bed and wrote page after page, black ink on unlined sheets of thin printer paper stacked on top of a green notebook. Periodically, I'd look out at the New York skyline, allowing tears to fall, and then returning to the page. Sometimes I wish I still had the eulogy, a reminder of anything good, but I don't because I burned it. I carried the stack of ink covered sheets to the stainless-steel sink in the kitchen. I lit a match and watched them turn black and then silvery. And whatever I put on those pages is now gone.

That second betrayal, the invisibility of the treachery, is the stuff that breaks women in divorce. Grief was a natural pain, like childbirth, but grief unsanctioned turned towards madness. I couldn't grieve when the people closest to me seemed bent on denying my experience of my marriage.

Rob's mother found her father's dead body, shot in the head, a suicide, when she was just a girl. At the funeral, an aunt slapped her across the face: "Your father's dead and you're not even crying," she reprimanded. I knew this story in my bones before it was told to me. Not the specifics of course, but I knew what it was to be unseen and for that to exacerbate the darkest moments with cruelty. Each demand to see my feelings and each misunderstanding of the signs of my pain was just another proof that vulnerability was not safe at all. These unsubtle people surely can't be trusted with what is most dear to me. "Well, Gabriella had Cameron, so it's not such a big deal," I heard of the rumors. A denial of sadness. A denial of my story thanks to the slight of hand wrought by the juxtaposition of events out of time and careful omissions and fragile details. "We had an affair, but did you know Cameron and Gabriella have been together for years?" The equation was entirely recast in that simple, yet profoundly deceptive sentence. A slap in the face.

It's hard to be sad in the face of injustice because inevitably that sadness carries acceptance of the very premise inside. How was I supposed to metabolize my own pain, while still being capable of fiercely protecting my truth? I am sad because little girls who don't perform as they should are slapped in the face in the depths of their despair. Crying metabolizes sadness and turns it into other things that can be released. Often responsibility is released once we mourn. I want to be responsible, however, to my own story. Anger keeps me responsible. Instead of mourning my own queer edge, letting it go, it keeps me out there, fighting for it.

When I first met Cameron I told him that no one ever believed that I was sad. He began sending me sympathy cards. He saw the tenderness I guarded so fiercely. I asked him recently why he believed me. "Because you told me," he answered simply.

Sadness, like all emotions, is a story. Stories are not the truth, they are just maps. They are projections from the past. Maps are based on culture, they are based on geography, and they are based on conventions of design. All of these things change, none of them are capital letter Truth. Truth is where the body meets spirit and when we can inhabit this space we find ourselves needing to tear up a lot of old maps. Including our own emotions. I let my sadness run through me. I will be sad about Rob and everything his name suggests to me for the rest of my life. What I won't do is learn too much from that sadness. I won't use it to make a map. That's simply not where I'm going; it's not my truth.

17. Prophecy and Incantation

"I hired you, Eddie, because you look like Thomas. I gave her you." Jeff Bridges' character in the movie *Door In The Floor* explains this to the young intern he'd hired for the summer, ostensibly to be a writer's assistant. In fact, he ended up being a companion and lover to Bridges' grieving and despondent wife, played by Kim Basinger. A couple years prior, they'd lost their teen sons, Thomas and Timothy, when the car they were all riding in was split in two by a giant snowplow. Kim Basinger wasn't to be rescued from her grief. She leaves both Jeff Bridges and their young daughter, never to be heard from again. The flash of realization in these lines, this explanation handed to the young intern, was a kind of horror at the fatefulness of this seeming act of will, the ultimate fulfillment of the semi-conscious desire. Why couldn't he have just stood in for the son? Allowed for a mother's final goodbye perhaps? Jeff Bridges' character could never have fully known that to begin again, the world that they knew would have to end.

I think I started building bridges and tunnels out of my marriage way before it ended. These bridges and tunnels looked like women; they had names, first Melissa, then Nora. I had no idea that was what I was doing. I followed my intuition in art and in life until I was exactly where I needed to be, despite not looking anything like I'd imagined.

"Maybe the whole reason Rob and I were ever together is so we could be friends," I joked lovingly with Melissa over a glass of wine at the Bell School one night. We sat talking by the fire, bright in the wood stove, as we did in that time.

Melissa would not be the last woman Rob loved that I, too, would love. That I would take into extreme confidence. That I would invite to live in our home and become part of our lives. I met her just before I met Cameron in the summer of 2005. Our friendship began just as I fully realized my love for Cameron and accepted havoc into our lives.

"You know those race horses, the thoroughbreds? They're so high strung that they always go to the gate with a friend," Melissa continued. We often sat there together, after dinner, by the fire, in the time we lived together.

"Yes!" I felt the same: "We're buddy horses!" We could be anxious, maybe fragile, but we were driven. We had undeniable instincts. I once read an article about the filmmaker David Cronenberg that described him as "compulsively himself." The language gave me a sort of permission to pursue an idiosyncratic path in the world. I repeated the phrase silently in my mind, a mantra, to stay faithful to my own vision. Melissa was the same, although perhaps she felt less sanctioned than I, more beset. She was often harder on herself, susceptible to doubt. She wasn't as angry, instead tending to feel somehow responsible for the injustices she experienced. There was something about this adherence to a certain way of life that we shared, a potentially deadly curiosity. (She once barely survived washing down a bottle of pills with a cup of bleach.) This disposition was costly to relationships and careers, certainly to stability. Often to mental health. The world was not an easy place for us. This Rob knew and I suspect was part of the attraction. "You're the most beautiful when you're sad," he'd say.

"'That woman is so beautiful. Of course that's the person Rob left me for.' I wanted to hate you the first time I saw you," Melissa reminisced.

We'd met one night at a party at a mutual friend's house. This meeting was almost ten years after I knew that she existed. Rob had told me about her when we'd first started dating all those years ago. It was crowded and Rob and I were already sitting on the couch, involved in some conversation, when I heard her entrance in the other room. I had butterflies in my stomach. The party just became a lot more interesting. I had always wanted to know this woman, the one with whom my husband stayed up late reading poetry and smoking cigarettes. At the time, they both lived in apartments above Frank's, a bakery where Melissa worked in Bangor. I imagined their romantic Bohemian universe, scented with fresh baked bread and hot black coffee, and I wanted to know more. It was as if her image brought me closer to Rob and to an image of his desire, which of course brought me a glimpse of myself in a new way. Seeing her would change how I saw. It was a flight of fancy that I found intriguing, all of us mirroring something back to one another through the nature of our desire. The party was crowded and when she entered, people flocked to her, the volume rose a bit in the room, everything brightened. She has a kind of magnetism that inspires and draws others to her. People feel more alive in her presence. She lives in the truth just past expectation, a place of delightful surprise. Sometimes she's downright shocking, and at her best, she's a revelation. She had just arrived back in Maine after several years in San Francisco on the heels of a particularly nasty divorce. She eventually made it through the crowded kitchen and into the living room where we sat. She found her spot on the couch next to Rob and looked into my eyes, "Hi," she smiled knowingly, settling in as if that moment were always going to happen. I got her phone number and called later in the week for a date, some Bangor young professionals event. She suggested we meet for drinks first. Only a short time later she would move into the Bell School.

"Why would you invite your husband's ex-girlfriend to live with you?" The decision was met with skepticism, at best.

Years later, after she'd been living in New York City for a few years, she sent me a dress: a short sleeve, knee length print she found at a little shop. Little white horses, bits of orange and blue, floating on a black background. She'd gotten one for herself, too. Buddy horses, a friendship mantra, a calming whisper of solidarity at the gate. After my divorce, we remembered back to what was once a joke: "Rob was only there to bring us together."

In 2015, I began a series of art works entitled "You Be Me." Two women sit in a bathtub or drive together in a car. They always play the same game, "You Be Me." They take turns speaking in the voice of the other, a dialectic of imitation, in content and manner. These moving cars, this bath water, blurring the boundaries further, building a connective tissue. I wrote scripts, made videos, and created collages. I practiced replacing girls with other girls.

With moving them into the background, making them indistinguishable from a landscape, from a swath of hair, the hills that surrounded my house, and the back of an animal. I created a kind of puppet theater in these works, women telling one another's story. Becoming one another like jumping rope double Dutch style, entering a unifying space of rhythm and movement, the transfer and contagion of energy. Just the body sitting in for another body, learning to speak its language.

Around the same time, a new girl began working at the restaurant where I worked, she was young, still a college student. I saw her carrying produce in from the farm truck. I felt a bit of repulsion at the sight of her. Years ago, while we were both in high school, my friend Monica told me about an experience she had waiting in line at the check out in a drug store. "I turned around and saw this woman. I thought she was so ugly, like, my stomach turned. And when I looked back towards the cashier at the front of the line, kind of taken aback, I realized: the woman looked like me." I too, felt that special kind of repulsion reserved for our own shadow.

We became fast friends, Nora and I, connected in that uncanny way reserved for people who see something of themselves in one another, maybe especially the dark things. Soon she was going through a break-up with her on-again, off-again boyfriend. A red-haired kid, sensitive and quiet, also pathologically avoidant, not unlike a young Rob. She asked if I would cut her hair, an intuition about the powers of the material world that many of us enact in times of heartbreak, crisis, and transition. I invited her to come sit in my garden at the Bell School. It was a humid summer day when she came over for that first time. I don't remember being in the house, just sitting in the backyard. I felt uncomfortable at having to touch her, as if I were transgressing my own boundaries, but I wasn't so good at boundaries then. I marveled at how the thick, greasy chunks of her blonde hair were so unlike my fine, dark strands that I was used to cutting. It fell heavily through the damp air and into the grass. The scissors would saw through unless I used care in separating out very small sections. She cried. She was lonely, but also had failed at this relationship, again. My hair was short then and I cut hers to appear like mine, at her request or my suggestion, I have no memory. This was to let her begin again.

Soon, I would invite her to move into my home, although she had also invited herself because a movement was beginning. I invited her into my home, the one that I built to make space for others, so she could learn how to be me, perhaps so I could begin again, too. There was something slow, languid, and unspoken about our togetherness, just barely masked by a lot of chatter and laughter. Late night whispering and hugging.

"Maybe Cameron and I will fall in love," she fantasized aloud. I pulled her aside and explained the relationship. She became one of the only people in Maine who knew the truth and that gave her the privilege of intimacy within my world. I let her see the pieces, the fragments. I let down the pretense of being whole and it was a great relief. She was someone outside of the three of us, with whom I could be myself. That space did not otherwise exist for me. I let great energy and love pool in that space. I explained there was nothing open about our relationship. She knew the stakes, but I never asked people to keep secrets for me because I know that is not possible. Our stories are always collective.

She sometimes played as if I were her mother, part of an on-going banter. I obliged in my way, despite not relishing the idea. Afterall, mother was not an image I had of myself, nor one I nurtured. Despite that, I could help her from the vantage of fifteen years hindsight. I encouraged her desire to become a midwife. I helped her get on her feet and to save money by giving her a home. I taught her about finances, urging her to open an IRA, which she did. I always entertained her relationship woes, even on occasions that were inconvenient, like the time I was traveling out of the country only to field calls about yet another impending break-up.

We danced. We went to meetings at a hilltop, oceanside spiritualist camp. We laid in bed cuddling with the dogs. We put on makeup. Just like years before with Melissa, Nora and I became both mirror and lens for one another. We cut and dyed our hair. We dressed in the same clothes, we experimented with and shared makeup. We costumed ourselves for one another in revelation and play. We held ourselves up as images of the other, innovating in the space of our own images. In the morning, I made coffee and cleaned up any stray cups or dishes that hadn't been tended the night before. Nora would retrieve the little plastic bag of granola from the bulk section in the local food coop that she kept in the cupboard by the refrigerator. We sat at the butcher block island. She ate her granola. I wrapped my hands around a fresh cup of coffee.

Near the end, when it all was just on the cusp of breaking apart, I started packing. I had entered a contest, in desperation, for what and from what I didn't know. It was pure instinct, like an animal heading into the woods to die. In the contest, I would win a bed and breakfast in southwestern Maine, just on the border of New Hampshire. I focused all my energy on this vision. I drove through the mountains and lakes and drove back and forth past the front of the white building. I waited there, out front, to see if it would be my home and it did not answer, not with a sudden flock of black birds, not with anything, but I was already packed. I just didn't know where I was going. Rob never came with me to look at that inn; Cameron did.

I packed for this inn over a period of months, in my own way, in works of art. I collected all the memories I could find and arranged them neatly and beautifully into small wooden boxes. I made sure these memories were the elaborately specific ones, trinkets from my childhood that sent shocks of remembrance through my body whenever they emerged. The memories were so small and idiosyncratic, so unmapped, untethered to the narratives that otherwise held my story together, they could never be replaced or recreated. I left the more obvious things out, books and clothes, art supplies and house plants. Even artworks. These things were the generalities. No one would really notice that the small, unusual things had disappeared, the ones that told a story no one else knew: bits of string and toy cars, a dull beige, plastic virgin Mary only a couple of inches tall, they were harder to see anyway. It wasn't difficult to make them disappear. Their absence would never raise suspicion. I packaged these things, these memories in their boxes and then wrapped the small boxes in strips of white paper and glue so that they could not be opened again. Looking at the small, mummified tombs was a reminder of necessary omissions, the kind of things we leave out to make sense of the world and to maintain our cogency, our credibility. They were not, however, reminders of those things themselves, those would be lost forever. I found old books and boxes of childhood photographs and each one that sparked even a trace of pain, I placed into the roaring flames of the white enamel stove. The pain was always the same: it was someone else's image of me. Yes, I saw ugliness, but mostly because they were perpetrating a truth that wasn't mine. They were lies that everyone else seemed happy to believe.

In response, Nora decided to hide things, too, also with craft. She knit a small pillow to conceal spent casings from bullets that had been used to shoot an old set of law books, which, a few weeks prior were lined up for execution in the backwoods behind the Bell School, some part performance, some part recreation. (I did not shoot. Instead, I would, over weeks, clean up the remains, composting the books.) She presented these pillows to me, a gift, albeit a facile and darkened mimicry portending the violent end to order, packaged in this small, blue, woolen Trojan pillow.

I wrote a book then. I'd been collecting my dreams for many years, trying to know the world beyond my head, to connect with something outside of myself. I wanted to know about knowing and dreams were a way in for me, having always had a strong attachment to them. In the first days that Rob and I met, we'd sit on the steps of the quad for hours after our nighttime seminars. We talked about many things then, but our talk of dreams rings clear still. He wasn't so into them. In fact, he was dismissive, but in a flirtatious way. Back then, I'd not been totally broken of a mysticism that was at once latent and burgeoning. Perhaps his dismissal was part of the beginning, part of the movement away from intuitions, dreams being such a strong part of that.

These years later when I wrote my book, it wasn't a record of dreams as much as an account of female wisdom gleaned from the dreams themselves as well as from the way of dreams. Their manner. I let them inform the logic of my waking life, seeing all the non-sequiturs, all of the beauty in strange juxtapositions. A wayward pig running down the street in a snowstorm. An unexpected, late-night knock at the door while I cooked Japanese pumpkins in the dim kitchen light. Dreams allowed me to attune to the small, the seemingly inconsequential, to the possibility inherent in idiosyncratic moments.

Rob loved the book. In fact, he wrote quite an effusive, albeit intellectual, afterword for it. He also claimed that he understood its value and truth even beyond what I understood.

Nora collected her dreams now. She packaged them in a large envelope and mailed them to Rob at the Bell School some time after she'd moved in with her ex again. The two of them began pouring over them together. Titillated by the sexual content. Rob took great pleasure playing the analyst.

Later, I wore glasses I did not need, pretending not to see, and then I dyed my hair, blond like hers. My costume made us indistinguishable to the untrained eye perhaps so that when I was ready to leave, no one would notice my absence, not even Rob.

"It's you," Nora pointed at a Blue Heron as it alighted on the opposite shore. She and I sat on the gray rocks at the edge of a small inlet on a warm summer day. We absently gazed out over the water. I picked up several small rocks around me, turning them over, replacing them to their homes. I noticed one smooth, oval shaped stone, brown and the size of my thumb. It had a perfect tunnel as if drilled into one side. "What made this hole?" I couldn't imagine. I slipped it into my pocket, a reminder of this small mystery.

She texted, "Covering a small shift at work today . . . Freddy asks me if my hairstyle is an homage to you. Lolz. I just said 'Well, we are the same person.'"

You be me: game over.

PART 2 : The Heron

The Great Blue Heron is a liminal being. She's not blue, but inhabits the space of both black and white allowing others to read her as gray. Perhaps this misnomer is a misunderstanding, or maybe an unnecessary and insulting attempt at euphemism. She hunts alone at the edge, in the damp, ambiguous spaces between water and earth and sky. She does so mostly at dusk and dawn, these thresholds between darkness and light.

18. Wounds

"We had a sleepover," Nora told my suspicious co-workers to raised eyebrows during a breakfast date she was having with Rob at the restaurant where I worked. I was away in New York with Cameron for the weekend. I only heard this later, when co-workers admitted they'd witnessed Nora and Rob together with a kind of flagrance disconcerting even to them.

A few weeks prior, on an otherwise-pleasant June night, my grandmother, now ninety-five years old, sat scared in a rehabilitation facility hundreds of miles away. In her last years and months she encountered a string of minor and major incidents that became hard to disentangle from one another. A stubbed toe led to a foot infection, which for a diabetic like herself was devastating. A series of impotent antibiotic therapies turned into chronic gastrointestinal turmoil. Increasingly, symptomatic congestive heart failure was gaining; it would turn out to be the quickest route to the end.

She refused to leave her two-story home, despite desperate arguing, pleading, and criticism from her children. She insisted on crawling up the white-carpeted stairs when she was no longer able to climb them on foot. Blood stains now mapped the route from the kitchen to the bedroom. In this ever-mounting series of slights, she found herself, not for the first time, recovering in an institution.

"I know what to do," was her familiar battle cry and defense. So that summer evening on the telephone, her plaintive, "tell me what to do," unnerved me.

Nora came over to the Bell School, to comfort me. Early in the evening, exhausted and using alcohol to anesthetize, I headed to bed. Upon waking in the morning, I was startled to find Nora still there, in my kitchen, having slept in Rob's study. She sheepishly ducked out before coffee. The sudden sense of her expression struck me in a wave of light-headed nausea only weeks later as it flashed through my imagination, once I learned of their affair.

After twenty-two years of life together, twelve years of marriage, and eleven years in what I believed to be a radically honest family that included Cameron, Rob confessed that he and Nora slept together in the four poster pine bed my mother and grandmother had given me as a child, under the skylight in the bedroom I'd envisioned and built.

That weekend, I'd returned home from New York City with my cousin Alexandra who was visiting from Los Angeles. We drove from the city to Maine for an event I'd planned called *Chatter*. I called Rob from the road, letting him know we were en route. It was his habit to cook some sort of feast upon my return from such trips, especially if I had someone with me, like Cameron, or in this case my cousin. He hadn't done so this time which registered as strange, but somehow too intangible for my full concern.

I had conceived *Chatter* over many months as a series of salon-style events or parties hosted at the Bell School, among friends. It was based on the idea that female speech is unique, as is speech located in the home - outside of institutions like universities, museums, and art galleries. I wanted it to be part discussion, part *Moth*-style storytelling, part lecture, reading, screening, interviews, performance, truly open to any form. In the course of each event, four or five women would present anything they wanted: a recipe, a dance, a childhood memory, gossip.

In signals intelligence, "chatter" refers to the quantity of intercepted communications. "Intelligence officials, not having better metrics, monitor the volume of communication, to or from suspected parties such as terrorists or spies, to determine whether there is cause for alarm. Even if they cannot decrypt what suspects are saying to one another, a change in the volume of traffic may raise alarm, since a large increase may indicate increased preparation for action, while a sudden decrease may indicate the end of planning and the imminence of action."

Chatter is also ascribed to a kind of feminine speech. It's a relational activity, but the content of the speech isn't where the meaning is located, it's somehow in the activity itself, not unlike in signals intelligence. To chatter is to utter a succession of quick, inarticulate, speech-like sounds, as monkeys or certain birds. In the case of women, it is deemed rapid jabber, foolish and purposeless.

This first incarnation of *Chatter* was planned on a hot July night just after I returned from New York. Alexandra and Lisa were to read stories. My friend Kate shared her explorations in Bodysex workshops under the tutelage of the now-late artist Betty Dodson. I gave a tour of my gardens, the provenance and *raison d'etre* of each plant and its placement.

The night, however, veered off the rails, more bacchanal than performance. Nora performed a yoga routine to "Back that Azz Up" by Juvenile on the back deck of the Bell School. In a horrifying turn of events, ameliorated only by extreme intoxication, it appeared more like a lap dance for Rob.

Nora texted me the morning afterwards, "I love you and your cousin so much."

Rob came onto me. I told him no, made the excuse that my cousin was visiting. It was mostly alcohol that kept me from experiencing the pain of his escalating relationship with another woman. I drove Alexandra to the airport and looked forward to returning home after so much travel and social interaction. I was exhausted.

I walked in the door and Rob told me that he and Nora had spent the night in our bed.

The blood from my body rushed to my stomach, which sank. My arms and legs lost all feeling. I wanted to cry but couldn't move. I became small and tight, imprisoned inside myself. In this state I could only access anger and shock.

Chatter had happened in the aftermath of their affair. Rob hadn't prepared a dinner that night we'd returned home. He came onto me in our bed. We'd had so many conversations with Alex. Nora showed up in my house; she'd performed *that dance*. Every memory flickered in horror. He'd not told me for days, letting me live in that sludge, in that dark. He knew I was about to fall off a cliff but didn't bother to warn me.

I don't remember what I said. Only that I begged, desperate for him to realize the reeling and the pain I was experiencing. Each increasing sign of incredulity, of shock and desperation was met with increasing coldness, moving firmly into contempt. Until finally, he laughed at me. A grin appeared on his face and his eyes darkened, and out of his mouth escaped a chuckle, like an exhale that suggested I could be blown away. I was insignificant.

I punched him, closed fist, in the mouth. As my fist made contact with his face, I didn't believe the contact was any more real than all the words that disintegrated under his audience. It felt like a last spasm of hopeless impotence. And there I was, back in my ancestral line. Out of my body and out of my mind. I had made the violence my own, made it my story. It rose up through my untethered body and into my clenched hand as if my life depended on it.

I punched him not because of the affair, but because, in the climax of his smug confession, he laughed at me. His practiced absence intensified at any sign of emotion, making me feel as though I might disappear. The laughter felt aggressive, retaliatory even. I punched him because he wasn't even there. His lip bled over his teeth and it was only then that he returned to his body; the smugness dissipated.

"I'm so ashamed," Rob began to sob. He held his head in both hands and leaned against the cold, white tiles, the water that ran over us, futile. It could not warm, it could not cleanse. It was too late. He slouched on the tiles of the shower floor, the ones that replaced the bare sheetrock and dusty piles of cardboard boxes we lived with for years while we saved and planned. This floor was the manifestation of a luxurious life we'd held out before us for so many years. This was not the kind of presence I'd anticipated. This was not what I sought to call in using the space of this home, but it was presence none-the-less, because here, he wept.

"I'm so ashamed," Rob repeated over and over again, explicitly disavowing guilt in a way, part compulsive and part intentional, that refused to take responsibility for what he'd done. It was a day-time glimpse of those soft whimpers in the night, the gasps for breath that I never thought could bear the light. They'd somehow gotten free and they looked like sobs that wracked his entire body.

When I recall this encounter, my body recoils to think of how much pain I was in. I recoil to think of what I became, my capacity for violence and my complete loss of will or agency. I became perhaps my most disempowered in that moment and I find that image of myself so ugly and so unconscious that it hurts to remember. Yet despite that, a resignation has also emerged.

A fundamental absence and presence, an advance and retreat, pervaded our relationship for so long. To say that being in our heads was a disease of our marriage, while also a feature of the attraction, would be a gross understatement. So while I could not have prescribed the violence, it feels now like throwing a sort of life-raft to the body, imploring, like a slap to wake up, cold water splashed. As if one body implored another body, albeit way too late and beyond the metabolic scope, to let this sink in. These words, *sink in*, an invocation of the physicality of consciousness, of wisdom.

This violence was my body's desperate gasp, a death rattle, after all I was the one that truly betrayed it. My slow dissociation from my own material experience, from my body, my internal fragmentation that I'd long nurtured by giving my mind the reins, the full seat of government over my existence had now reached a climax. The divide between my material experience and my spiritual experience became so great, that violence was a symptom of a kind of death. I'd spent decades asking, in all the ways and turns of phrase, all the postures and approaches I could learn, for Rob to listen to me. The response was always the same: I was interrupting him. It was not the right time. He would shrewdly defend against intimacy with tactics that ranged from insults and criticisms to silence or even just scheduling concerns.

All those years, I didn't realize it wasn't to him that I needed to listen, it was to me. Shame kept me from listening to myself. He was as if the externalized version of my own mind, never flesh and blood. I'd misplaced my faith, my focus. I wanted to trust him instead of my own material experience. As painful as it is to admit culpability, to apologize, and to admit being in the wrong, it is a place of agency where atonement is possible and ships can be righted. Guilt is a dense fog, but shame is a black hole. Guilt allows for resurrection, shame does not.

After this initial confrontation, there were painful death throes of our relationship under the guise of trying to work things out. I think this lasted a month, maybe two dissonant summer months. The sunny days were now haunting, as if illuminating a world where I was no longer alive. The brightness just highlighted all I had now lost. He told me he didn't think about Nora much, that he wasn't seeing her, despite showing me her plaintive text messages claiming she knew better than to write, but was 'weak'. Manipulated and urged by these disclosures, I unwittingly spearheaded the farcical efforts to repair the damage. Every exchange under the aegis of these false intentions I recall in lightning flashes of renewed pain: He carried my grandmother's coffin at her funeral. We rearranged our furniture, visited a Shaman, wrote poems, contemplated moving. He suggested we have a baby. We both sensed our grave mistake: we'd forgotten the body.

Even in my frenetic state, one where I had all but completely dissociated, I knew that the only hope for survival was through the world, through the stuff of our home and our bodies. There was no amount of talking that could heal these wounds.

After years of keeping his hair cut short, he left it longer on top. I gave him a small, carved comb made of bone. Perhaps I wanted to nurture change. Perhaps I wanted a gesture that broached the topic of his body without subjecting my own to that work. A promissory note of sorts: I would wade slowly back into intimacy.

19. Rules of Engagement

The world that Rob and I built began to crumble before the blow that finally gutted our marriage. "How would you ever protect me?" was a playful refrain I'd offer Rob over the years. A bizarre college conversation between myself and several male classmates, including Rob, culminated in one of them shouting, "We all want to protect Ms. D'Italia!" (It was a rule of our college seminars that we'd address one another by Mr. and Ms. and this turned out to be a habit hard to break outside of class.)

Rob and I riffed on the experience over the years, finding much humor in the absurdity we saw in this unveiled patriarchal sentiment. "I'll protect you by telling stories," he would say. Ostensibly stories to our enemies, to those who would threaten us. The refrain is chilling in hindsight, as the story he ultimately decided to tell would be waged in attack, not defense. Perhaps the secrecy from Rob's family and the conservative rural place in which we lived would have always been too much to bear. However, it was when we invited that conventional worldview into our home, we poisoned the well.

Nora was engaged to the on-again-off-again guy, living with him, at the time she was having the affair with Rob. She was going from barista job to bartender job, working as a clerk at the local food co-op. She still harbored dreams of becoming a midwife, but she focused her practical and libidinal attention on romantic intrigue. She would break up, get back together, muse on the boredom once things had settled into a routine, shake things back up again with suggestions of moving in together, or moving out, or drunkenly kissing other men at bars. In one such incitement, she convinced her boyfriend to marry her. He mostly seemed to avoid things, but was complacent insofar as it aided the avoidance. He nodded a lot and generally had the appearance of someone who is surprised, interactions always seeming to interrupt a private reverie. He agreed to marriage. Perhaps it seemed the path of least disruption at a certain point, but he maintained one condition. They would not be married "for real." They theorized: "It's only a piece of paper."

One night at the Bell School, this engagement announcement was met by a small group of friends with some measure of surprise and skepticism. As the conversation tended towards diffusing the awkward reaction, Nora managed to back peddle away from anything that looked like an engagement or subsequent marriage. As it turned out the promise would culminate in what appeared to be a potluck dance party, affording the opportunity to dress up, another shot of adrenaline to a system headed into plateau.

I suggested she take a closer look at what she meant by marriage, that perhaps there was more at stake in the so-called piece of paper than she thought. What did it mean to invoke the sanction and support of a community? After all, I told her, "Gay people are fighting too hard to get married so you can have a sham wedding." Perhaps it all hit a little too close to home having spent the decade immersed in my own marital considerations and wrestling with the tangible effects of the spiritual enterprise. "Frankly,

I'm more in a ban-marriage-for-everyone camp, than a subscriber to the *marriage equality* oxymoron," I explained. "But if you're going to bother, to go through with it, words are meaningful, alchemical. The boundaries between individual cases and the larger community are deeply porous." If anyone felt the reality of the social and political enactment, the reality of familial implication, it was me. I already knew that the line between real things and imaginary things was not so distinct. I believed in connectivity, the transference of meaning. As an artist, I also knew there is no such thing as just a piece of paper.

The nature of Bell School conversations those days tended to be personal, but always through an intellectual lens, often making use of books or various theories to consider the topic at hand. Our conversations were explicit, probing, critical, contemplative, speculative, abstract, analytical. They weren't mincing or coy. After all, we lived communally and in a school. My lens was often to use these personal stories to contemplate my own integrity, my own consciousness, my own ability to consent. Hearing this engagement story, my stomach immediately turned at the implications. I saw myself as the figure standing in for all of those implicated by the cultural exigencies created in these private mythologies.

When I expressed my reservations that night, I also knew that Nora was settling for something less than what she wanted. I recognized the dynamic between her and her fiance as much the same as between Rob and I so many years ago when we were their age. I felt in her the sadness of my own youthful assurances to Rob that I didn't *need* him. I was afraid of my boundaries, afraid of the loneliness they threatened. The always-grasping felt like passion, desire unfulfilled or only partially fulfilled just left more desire and that had its own special allure. It was the kind of energy I could see her feeding on through the arcs of lull and provocation, to the exclusion of any compass outside of this relational one.

I knew that night that something threatening was happening between Rob and Nora. I wanted to believe it was a harmless flirtation, but I knew it was more dangerous than that. Their behavior felt like contempt toward me, which was something beyond flirtation and a much more serious bond. His behavior became solicitous, always refilling her drinks, directing his jokes her way. Once, he even pulled her onto his lap while we all sat on the deck drinking. I was humiliated and sad, but more than either of those things I was afraid. Fear made me push aside the part of my ego that could be humiliated or saddened. I was in survival mode. We understand death so little that it is always a metaphor, and what I knew in my body was that the dissolution of my marriage would kill me in a very real way, as it eventually did. At the level of consensus, we all erased the incident, it, too, as if *just a piece of paper*, alternately laughing or explaining it away, albeit privately.

What I feared most in her engagement proposition was the infectiousness of the nihilism. At the time, even my husband had coined a phrase for the ethos that hung over this couple, a trailing puff of smoke: "Fuck-it time." We had spent twenty years on a path of meaning making. An allegiance to the serious craft of living intentionally and truthfully, in service of our individual and collective creative vision. I believed in the strength of something that turned out to be quite fragile.

When I voiced my objections, Nora cried and went outside. She sat on a metal chair on the deck and insisted, indignantly and self-righteously, that her perspective was well-considered. My defense of the conventions of marriage was wagered to consider the value and content of our public commitments. Truly, I defended the paper, and its capacity for alchemy. Its capacity to create new realities. I defended ritual itself. In defending the real status of our communal enactments, I circumscribed the privilege of heteronormative belonging. I worried about the upholding of gender binaries, implicit in the dichotomous marriage structure. To ignore those things would be wading into a territory where we can not see the consequences of our own actions as they contribute to a series of events rippling with dire consequence for others down the line. Injustice is the darkness between our ideals and our most mundane and seemingly personal actions, the darkness between spirit and body. Nora continued to sob, maligned.

Rob defended her, "She's right!" He, too, took things at the level of idea, but his tactic that night was to pivot philosophically, as if in revelation. He argued a kind of Machiavellian and de facto logic. "This is just what people do," he became excited by the freedoms he glimpsed through these doors of extrapolation. This became a new m.o. "Whatever happens must be righteous." That first breath of fuck-it time, it turns out, can feel quite exhilarating. He appeared to feel great relief in relinquishing diligence.

This narrative revision crystallized in this moment had been tended over some time, its origin hard to locate. From this point however, it would continue gaining strength like a snowball attracting mass, clear to the naked eye. Rob admitted his affair to his parents, but in the same breath, eclipsed the past decade by telling them about our relationship with Cameron, which now was cast as my relationship with Cameron. When I'd first met Cameron, I rebuked the suggestion that a deficit in my relationship with Rob gave rise to my love for Cameron. Rob traded that logic for the conventional story, I had a boyfriend so now, he too, was justified, an undeniably compelling sleight of hand.

"It's over," Rob and I stood in front of the stove in the Bell School kitchen in the discordantly pleasant light of that August morning. "I know you did everything - the houses, the planning, I know it was all you," he softened toward me. For years I'd managed the finances. I planned, created budgets, and invested. I begged him to participate but was always met with resistance and even hostility. A copy of our household budget hung on the side of the refrigerator each month and I asked Rob to tack any receipts to the budget. I wanted to make sure there was enough money in the correct accounts. I wanted to make sure that we kept in the ballpark of the goal or that I could learn where we needed to modify the plan. He refused, but in a passive way. He agreed that this was all a good idea, but just wouldn't do it. If I asked him about it, he'd erupt in anger and name calling, accusing me of being that special sort of nagging woman, a characterization I found particularly cruel and unflattering. It also kept me on eggshells around him when it came to trying to plan in practical ways. This was so much of an issue that he talked to his therapist about it. "Why don't you just give her the receipts?" the therapist asked. Rob had no answer. These conversations between us weren't even private the way they might be in an ordinary household, after all we were living in a communal household, the budget was on view.

Rob's freshman year of college, his aunt opened an IRA for him with $2000.00 and now, at forty years old, he still had that mail delivered to his parents house. I pleaded with him to change the address, to tend that account. However, it was met with the same passive resistance as the budget. I all but begged him to let me make annual deposits for him, as the account still had, after twenty years, close to the original $2000.00. He said he would, but never did, and if I dared remind him, I would be met with insults about my nagging.

When it came time for divorce, although I would have legally been entitled to alimony after our twelve years of marriage, Rob decided to revise his thoughts on this part of our history. In fact, it wasn't even his thoughts. "Let's let the professionals handle it," he sent me a terse email directing me to his lawyers. I was informed that I wouldn't receive alimony unless I wanted to give Rob half of my IRA. (The sad truth is, I didn't even request full alimony, only a fraction of the amount and a fraction of the time span to which I was legally eligible. I was still, despite everything, living under the aegis of our old story, where there was still respect for one another and an accounting of the particularity of our circumstances.)

I was now forty years old, without my home, stripped of the rental properties I'd purchased as both income and investment. (Rob offered me those, but his lawyer stipulated that I had to take over the mortgages within six months and I had no income or job prospects. In effect, I was offered a few hundred thousand dollars in debt that I couldn't repay, tethered to properties that would now be hundreds of miles away.) My resume read: Artist. Waitress.

This divorce wasn't about money. It had become about erasing the story of my life in a public way with real effects. The revisions Rob made, or relinquished control over, transformed the stories by dramatically shifting the values on which they were hinged. Trading what was elaborate and specific, for the abstractions of convention. I was reeling from the shock of these reversals on a personal level, emotionally and practically, but what ran deeper, was the way that Rob's family, the culture, and the law, corroborated Rob's version. I guess it was no joke after all: Story was a weapon, in this case a knife wielded to the back.

That night at the Bell School, when the turn first became apparent, I apologized to Nora profusely. I felt ashamed for hurting her feelings, for taking the forest view when a friend was simply asking for some tree-level enthusiasm. I could foresee how it would all turn out, where this path would lead, and I couldn't embrace the rise of an ethos that would destroy me. I felt Rob turn further toward the door.

The engagement fell apart. Nora spent months compiling and discussing her sex dreams, more papers, with Rob. She stayed up with him late at night and decided to put his penis in her mouth.

20. At Sea

August 2017

Past Life Energetic Therapy with Joan Francis, Temple Heights, Maine

The curtains are drawn and the plank walls are lined with mismatched chairs, some hard, some low and soft. The cabin is uninsulated. A small table, sometimes used in tipping ceremonies, rests in the corner. A hundred years of saturation gifts the smell of wood and ocean breeze.

I will use my energy as a surrogate for your energy.

I will seek and find the energy holding me back; I'm not just sightseeing.

You're pregnant now.

You can stop the session at any point.

I'll rewind through the life.

Retrieving a life or lives that are holding me back.

Take a couple of breaths.

I'm in.

I am male, about 14. I am on the sea. I'm on a ship, the Amiga, I take it it's the ship's name. An old ship. Old wooden ship. A beautiful ship. A working ship. Transporting goods. A hold. There's a hold. I feel you're young.

Gosh you work hard. I'm scrubbing the decks. I'm on my hands and my knees. As I'm doing that, they're chaffed, my knees are getting dents in them. So hard working. You're so young. You don't know a great deal about land.

I spin back, I feel very young. Oh wow. There's a part here of where, as I go back to when you're 4 or 5 years of age on a passage ship with hundreds of people on this ship. You were there with your parents. While this passage ship was on journey on route there was a great deal of sickness I feel as though . . . the heat, the sweats, the vomiting. There was some kind of food poisoning or plague. But you survived. As the ship reached its destination there were a handful of travelers left. The captain of the ship kept you. You had such a young wee spirited energy. He recognized if you were deposited from this ship you would never survive. So he kept you as a cabin hand. So this has been your life. This is why you know a great deal about ships and not about land.

The captain became a surrogate father. You have fondly attached to him. He is an absolute tyrant but with you he is so gentle. He has bonded. It's as though there's times it's been so cold. Instead of you sleeping on the floor on a haybed, he's allowed you to come to his bed, not in any untoward way, just to take care of you, warm you. That's the tender part of him. Blythe. I hear the name Blythe. This is his name. He taught you everything he understands which is a great deal. So you're very wise to the sea, the stars, maps. These are things that require skill.

But you missed your parents. You missed the mother energy. He's been the father, but you missed the mothering energy, the softness, the cuddling. I feel in the dream state you remember this sadness. It becomes a nightmare energy. Watching so many deaths, so many people died in the sea. This is part of your sensitivity. So young to watch so much death but these memories slide into the background.

Each trip so many different people. So many different walks of life. Different nationalities. Some scary. Which you love. So many different people. There are times you have to be very careful because you've come up against the different personalities. You've learned to dodge, when to get out of the way. Know when to pull back. But you've held such a beautiful energy. You've got this . . . I use the word loving and caring. But there's this inquisitive . . . this like, you want to know everything. It's like the minute there's someone new you want to know where they're from, where they've been, what's happened to them, what they know . . . you want to know everything. Such a variety of people which has satisfied this curiosity. You didn't need to run off and have adventures, all these people came to you. You have this great knowledge of the world, yet you've been on this boat. Sailing. Fascinating to have such a vast amount of information for such a young person. You have a thirst to know everything that's out there. You love gazing at the stars. When it's warm and the air is warm, you lie on your straw bed and just look up. And you love that. There's a sense of connection, but you're aware of the vastness and you wonder what's beyond the stars. There's a philosophy in you. There's a great philosophy in you.

But, as this journey began it was fraught with danger. And for the first time, the captain, the cargo, it was volatile. It was a gunpowder. It wasn't stable. You didn't know that. It was to be kept dry. That was the main concern. Was how dry it could be. You were put to task. But sometimes the ship would take water. Your task was to bail it out. You had a pulley system of these buckets and you would fill the buckets and pull the rope and someone would take the bucket off at the top and the bucket would come back down. It didn't take a lot of water on, but it kept you busy. That was your task.

There was a point where you were down there for a long time. There was more water coming on board and you told the captain. You didn't know where from. You would pack it, but you didn't know where it was coming from. You were there more than you'd ever been before.

There was something about this crew. You didn't really like this crew. There were about 3 or 4. You didn't like their personalities. Their mannerism. You were wise enough to stay away. As you were down there, this had to happen day and night. The captain came down, because it was starting to get wet. It wouldn't have arrived to port the way it was supposed to be.

Something happened. You didn't hear it. You don't have a memory of it. There was a fight. The crew were fighting. The captain had been placed into the cabin for safety. The first officers were dealing with it but you were in this hole. And you're unsure, it all happened quickly. I'm taking longer to tell you than it really happened. Very quickly you were pulled, you were told to come up and you said you couldn't because you had to keep doing this and one of the crew a really tall, umm, sallow to the skin, rugged to the face, really rugged as if he'd been in many fights, and he literally just grabbed you. By your clothing so your shirt was holding you, lifted you up and threw you down onto the deck. The other pulled you with your hair. You had the most amazing curls, you had this natural wave to your hair, and thick hair, but when he grabbed you he hoisted you up. You realized there was something very wrong. They were trying to get the captain to come out and they used you as that bait. That leverage. And as brave as you were you called out to him not to open the door.

(Deep breath)

Because you remembered. It's like these memories. You remembered back to when your mother and your father, as if it was yesterday, and you could see the people becoming angry because of this sickness and you remember how instead of hiding away as he was being told to do for his own health, the captain, he came out, and you remembered this at that moment. You remembered his bravery of trying to help the sick. So here you are as this young boy called to him because you recognize as young as you are that his life is going to be taken here.

And you called him to stay there and to shoot them. And this one, who you never liked right from the beginning, he smacks you and you fall to the ground, you burst the side of your lip with the force of his hand. At that moment, it was so fast, he then leaned on you, he put his knee into your chest, nearly crushing your ribcage. But he put his knee into your chest and pries open your mouth and cuts your tongue out.

But you never even screamed. You didn't scream. And all the time you were thinking of your captain of all the times he had taken care of you. And the captain opened the door. And you were trying to talk, but you couldn't speak. And then there was this few seconds of connection. And the whole time you were being pinned down you looked at him and you could see the father energy. And at that moment this really tall brute of a man crushed your chest.

And you felt as though you had failed him (cries) you felt as though you had failed him. It's what I call misplaced karma. It wasn't your karma to take on. But you couldn't save him. You were only a boy. You were a beautiful soul among all these really ugly people and I don't mean looks. And you were choking on your own blood. Your lung had been pierced by your ribcage. But that moment of connection was incredible.

So here you were at fourteen and had such an amazing life. (crying) The love that you had there. My god. You had such a willingness to work and care. Wow. Gabriella.

21. Turtlenecks

In 2007, a couple of years after first meeting Cameron, the three of us had found our own sort of rhythm. I took my one-time Haystack student up on her invitation to be part of a teaching residency at Mt. Desert Island High School as part of a Maine Arts Commission grant. I worked in her classroom where she taught home economics. Although I was located in her classroom, the grant funded several projects that were to serve the entire school and so my door was open to all students and faculty. I prepared lessons and projects that could serve all parts of the community. During the residency I stayed in a large apartment above Kathleen's garage in Southwest Harbor. Each night I would return to the apartment, the strong smell of gasoline wafting up from the boats below. One night, Kathleen thanked me, "In all the years I've worked at this school, I've never been able to have a connection, a dialogue with the art department. You bridged that gap."

While I may have been fostering connection on the one hand, what would happen next told a different story. As part of this extensive grant, the school offered many wellness services to its staff throughout the week I was to be there. Reiki was one of the offerings, which at the time, I'd never experienced and after what happened, I never would again. A slot opened up one afternoon. I walked into the small and brightly lit office this woman had set up as her office for the day. Her table sat, improvisationally, at the center of the space, in front of a tall set of windows still shining a warm light in the early days of Autumn. I lay down on the table.

"Have you ever had Reiki before?," she asked.

"No," I responded honestly and excited for our session.

She proceeded to tell me a bit about what she would do, a warning of sorts. I don't remember what she said. I don't remember if she laid her hands on me or not. I remember feeling her presence, certainly, even a kind of touch, but there was no telling between awareness of my own body and the energy of someone else's touch. It didn't so much matter except for that transformation of bodily boundary into something energetic, something extended. I have no sense of how long the session lasted, but what happened next would stay, clear and persistent, in memory.

"You are being torn in two," she seemed slightly rattled. "I don't want you to be afraid," the tentativeness of her demeanor undermined the message.

"How could she possibly know about Cameron and Rob?" I thought as I gathered myself and my things and left the room. I was working so hard to keep a secret and she read it in my body, she revealed to me that I was vulnerable. I became ashamed at the thought that if she could see my secrets, there were others that must surely be able to as well. I became afraid of my vulnerability. I became afraid of my body. It had betrayed me and it was probably killing me, too. If this secret lived there, in my body, it was not being stored safely - no climate control or special gloves for this volatile substance. It was leaking, poisonous.

To make matters worse, I was in the classroom the following day when a call came to the room. Kathleen answered. "It's for you," she reported to both of our surprise. I was instructed to head to the administrative offices to receive the call.

"Hello?" I picked up the receiver.

"Hi, it's me, the woman you had Reiki with yesterday?" Her rising intonation suggested I could've somehow forgotten the experience already. "I just wanted to apologize for yesterday. I didn't mean to say something so startling, to deliver bad news . . . I felt bad leaving you with that . . ." she stammered on for a while. I don't know if she was trying to ease her distress or mine, but the impression I was left with was only this: Whatever she experienced in that room with me disturbed her and her follow-up call was only further emphasis.

Almost a decade later, in 2017, I'd been in New York City just a short time when I sought out the healing of a shaman. (Reiki still bore traces of disturbing emotion. Mostly because it reminded me of the painful secrecy I lived with for so long, not because of Reiki itself. However, I was still very much interested in a mystical life. I sought out traditions of intuitive knowing and healing, having lost faith in traditional medicine and knowledge when it came to the most intractable afflictions.) He worked out of an office on the west side, not far from Broadway and just south of Central Park. I was still getting used to the city. It struck me as dissonant, seeking this kind of wisdom in such density. My only firsthand experience with shamanic practice had been in a small yurt in the middle of tall grass in rural Maine, nothing else around for miles. Sweating, I got off of the subway train and climbed the flights of stairs to street traffic and high rises. I got turned around a couple of times before finding the anonymous looking building and riding the grim elevator many flights to the equally anonymous hallway. I looked around at several gray metal doors and found the right number. A dark-haired man wearing a blue button down shirt opened the door and invited me in. It was an open space with tall ceilings and huge windows overlooking layers of more gray and shining buildings. Against one wall, a couch, towards which he gestured and I obliged by taking a seat. Putting my bag on the floor next to me, I collected myself a bit.

The session felt more like therapy than I was expecting. There was no intense drumming and circling, like there had been in the yurt. No blowing spirit guides into my chest. I simply sat and I told him my story, which was remarkably easy to do. There was no more secrecy, not just because I was no longer in a relationship with two men simultaneously, but because I was in New York City more than a decade after I'd first met Cameron. I was no longer fooling myself with the notion that as long as I could see myself through the veil of New England Protestantism, I would in fact be protecting myself from it. (Sometimes knowing the enemy treads awfully close to being the enemy.) Here, I was no longer around anyone who would bat an eye at an unconventional lifestyle. My depth of explanation, of backstory and justification, became unnecessary. The pain of more repressive environments, emerges self-evident. After all, how many New Yorkers arrive there just to honor their voices with true sovereignty, even if it costs them dearly? It is a refuge.

"That was you breaking free," the man described when I offered my explanation for all of the breaking glass at the time of Rob's affair. I had always thought it was a warning from outside.

"I'm sorry to not offer you more, but the truth is, you are on the right path. You were right to be open to Cameron when you were," he continued. "In Maine, you were offering gifts to those that could not receive them. When you offer a gift, you are to present it wrapped, beautiful. You will now be around people who can understand. Do not give your gift to those who are undeserving."

I moved to a table, like a massage table, across from the couch and he guided me through a visualization. I was in a garden, dense, with gates leading to more gates. Stunning and beautiful, but marked not with expanses, only paths begging to be explored. Glimpse of views just beyond, arched gates covered in vines, vignettes behind each. "You are here to teach people to live with mystery."

I closed my eyes and he began a ritual. "I see blue," I told him.

"Yes," that is because your throat chakra is blocked and I'm healing it. The throat chakra sits between the head and the body. It connects them. It is the voice, the bridge of our humanity. It is a locus of our truth and the capacity to connect that truth with the surrounding world.

I thought of the pained smile on my face, the one traced in a history of old photos. I thought of how I never sing. Even "Happy Birthday." I lip sync. The sound of my voice often sounds tight and constricted, or fast and breathless. I thought of how I lived in my head and felt alienated from the body. I now wondered about my lifelong love of turtlenecks. "You are being torn in two," echoed again all these years later. It was never Rob and Cameron. It was only me. The divorce: my mind, body and spirit. My voice had been the sacrifice.

Rob and I each had old paintings from around the time we were five years old. They looked as if they'd been done on paper from the same pad and with paints from the same jars. Perhaps all standard issue in American public schools from a certain era. I had both of these pictures framed and hung the two self-portraits. They flanked either side of the chimney and wood stove that anchored the Bell School at its center. I am pink and fill the page, my arms outstretched, long pink hair flowing wildly and wearing a blue and yellow dress. He is small and brown, standing on a round, equally brown earth. A small tree next to him and a small rainbow. He is a dark stick figure with red hair and eyes, across the lower half of the face a thick swath of black paint blots out what would be a mouth and nose.

It would still be another year after my visit with the New York shaman before I would visit Temple Heights on the rocky coast of Maine and learn about my father from another lifetime, the sea captain, who taught me philosophy, who loved me and protected me. For the love of whom I willingly sacrificed my tongue, my voice, my life.

22. Broken Pieces

Sometimes after breaking just a simple cup in the kitchen I'm shocked at how little pieces seem to emerge days later, in unexpected places, even after having vacuumed. Shards that could never be put back into an original shape. It's hard to even imagine how they once fit together at all. From a certain vantage, the dissolution of my marriage happened quickly. There was a span of a couple of summer months at the end of 2016 when my grandmother died and Rob was sneaking away at night under the guise of various activities. The time when Rob admitted to this only to double down on the lying in the weeks to follow. Compared with the twenty-two years of our life together, this was fast. I recall it, though, as a cup falling to the hard tile floor, a slow motion explosion, phrases and flashes of expression slowly flying through my memory, disconnected from any true timeline.

There were moments when Rob was there and when he wasn't. His eyes changed, even their color. Sometimes they seemed to lose all ability to focus or they would cloud over, like a victim of a bomb blast. When I think about what Rob did in that time, a story rises to mind and persists. There was this kid, when I was in high school, he snuck into a pool one night with some other kids. He didn't know how to swim, but he wanted to show off, or maybe he even thought he could swim, the way a lifetime of watching people do something with ease gives the false impression that it's easy, like dancing. And so this kid, he jumped off of the diving board that night at the pool. He died. I think my intuition reminded me of this story, as a way of showing me what happened. Showing me a way to understand without my ego getting in the way. It was showing me a path of compassion by giving me this analogy from a deeper place of understanding, one unencumbered by my own pain.

"I need to grow up and I can't do that with you," Rob told me as we stood outside on the street in front of the Bell School. "I learned this courage from you," he felt, with some collateral flattery, that he was following a truth as I had all those years ago when I met Cameron. There were so many things he said, fragments, floating, that as they come back to me ring true. I didn't want to accept it, because it made me angry, because it made me sad, because I feared for my life. "She's not as smart as you, not as beautiful, not as good in bed, and she has terrible taste, but she is my fantasy," he repeated. He would alternate between "she is my truth" and "she is my fantasy," (for him this was a very specific authoritative (and therefore dignified) reference to Freud.)

Maybe I resented him, not for loving her exactly, but, if this were his truth, for following it. As if it were a competition of knowing, and since I had not left him for Cameron, his willingness to leave me meant he would somehow win. Leaving me for her did not matter, except that what I thought was our decades-long creative and intellectual mutual striving, was not mutual at all. It was in fact a contest. In this act of leaving, he revealed he'd been a spy for another team all along and now he meant to win, especially through my defeat. It felt almost Oedipal, except with the genders and relationships tossed into a hat and slightly mixed up.

If ever that comparative bit he proffered, in that heated and desperate time, flashes through my mind, I immediately push it aside. It is unparalleled red herring material. Let's put it this way, its truth value was beside the point. It highlighted how little my confidence was at stake, and perhaps how little Rob understood what the stakes actually were. I loved Rob, and even Nora. My grandmother had rheumatic fever as a child and as a result, she had long term damage to her heart. What doesn't kill you doesn't actually make you stronger. It often has the opposite effect entirely. What Rob and I had built in our lives, in the Bell School, was a universe whose laws were overturned, as if the gravity were suddenly retracted from the earth. The narrative was no longer shared and what emerged in its place was weaponized.

Nora became for me the occasion for the deep levels of imbalance in my life and in my relationship with Rob to break loose, to proliferate, to metastasize. She rallied all of the demons that conspire to keep us from being whole. I wonder at her desire to be a midwife, to live vicariously on the birthing energy of other women, to be proximate to that power. A shaman reported her presence in a vision: "She's a vampire. She's using your vision, your image and your energy to stay alive."

I don't think Rob was really talking to me when he made those comparisons. I think it was somehow an inner dialogue that slipped out. He was trying to make sense of his truth, the one that didn't come from his head. The one that wasn't going according to plan. He was simply noting the dissonance between that moment when everything is ok and when it all goes awry; he knew he would die. He was feeling the limits of his mind and the rebirth of his gut, his heart, his compass. This was not a place he was comfortable. Perhaps it was all compulsion. Or maybe pure innocence before the deadly leap. Maybe it was brave.

What delivered the fatal blow was the existential horror caused by the trauma of such extreme treachery. It was like watching something you don't want to believe humans are capable of. It was a child with cancer. It was watching the inherent violence of nature. This, like a virus, leaves one's heart damaged.

*

There's this red bookcase in my son's room. Uncle Billy often built furniture for my mother and my grandmother according to their designs. He built this piece to my grandmother's specifications. It lived in her home for years until living in my mother's house. There, it housed a stack of old national geographic magazines. The ones with the golden yellow borders and spines. There is one image from that stack that has stayed with me for more than thirty years, although the magazines are long gone. A gazelle lays on the ground surrounded by cheetahs, they've caught her, but for some reason they haven't killed her. They are eating her alive from the hindquarters. Her face is screaming out, mouth open and tongue stretching, her neck reaching desperately upwards.

*

When I was fourteen years old, I was traveling in Italy with my family. My best friend, Tiffany, was having a sleepover at her house with another friend. Her mom was out of town and they decided to take the car out for a drive in the middle of the night. Tiffany had always been ashamed of the old car her mom used to drive, asking her to drop her off away from the main entrance of school, but now, they had a brand new Infinity.

Tiffany drove the car into a nearby tree, the one that sat out front of the post office, at about 35 miles per hour, seatbelt on. Apparently she argued with the paramedics when they brought her to the hospital, I don't know why. It was many hours of surgery later, but the doctors weren't able to save her. My parents got the call in the hotel room in Florence. "Tiffany Brittain is dead," they delivered the news.

All I could imagine was her happily skipping out to the car, the state of mind, the playfulness of youth and of life. What seemed most horrible is how that state could exist in such proximity to death. The not-knowing one moment, a laugh, frivolity, juxtaposed with the infinite oblivion of death. I see her now, skipping down the front stairs of her house on 18 Kennedy Road, car keys jingling in hand, in the dark of night, a smile on her face. I still drive by the house sometimes.

*

There was that movie about the guy who thought he could make friends with bears and then he was eaten by them. They found some audio recording, but people had to stop listening to it because no one could live with having heard it. The man screaming out in pain. Maybe he was heartbroken and shocked at the betrayal. I don't know.

*

When I was a kid, there was a little boy who decided he wanted to go swimming with the polar bears at the Bronx Zoo. "They're biting too hard," he cried out, too late.

*

Laika, a mongrel dog, was sentenced to a slow death, shot into space on a rocket by those who I can only imagine cared for her and showed her apparent kindness moments before the act of unimaginable cruelty. How did she feel floating alone, strapped down, hungry, overheating, gasping for breath?

Sometimes I truly don't know how to live with these memories except to try to forget them. I think I've spent a great deal of life mitigating against that moment between not-knowing and knowing something awful, something inevitable about pain and death, or even worse, cruelty. There are only two things that can fill that space: fear or faith. For most of my life I chose fear, as a strategy. If I could imagine the most horrible outcomes, at least I'd be spared the shock, the pain of the unknown. My mind filled up with images of car wrecks, plane crashes, cancer, and murder. A shield of horrors.

I couldn't grieve Rob when we were getting divorced. When Rob and Nora betrayed me, when Rob annihilated the temple we'd built together, it was as if I were that gazelle being eaten alive and despite my lifetime of imaginings, I wasn't prepared for the pain. He had a secret affair with a woman significantly younger than himself, who happened to be my friend, someone who looked up to me, who I took in when she needed a hand. He slept with her in our bed. Honestly, it was all so banal after so many years of claiming honesty and a kind of erudite perspicacity. To become such a cliche after such hard wrought intention, I mean, he might as well have slept with the proverbial nanny. But, don't mistake this for academic. It gutted my identity. It was as if I discovered the man I'd been with for twenty-two years was an entirely different person. "You've always had a flattering perspective of me," Rob told me eerily, in the death throes. I no longer had tender memories to grieve because what Rob showed himself capable of, the gutting of our story, the ghosting after twenty-two years, changed my understanding of who I'd been married to all along, of the marriage itself, and ultimately of myself.

Grief would have to come later.

When I make a quilt I start with a fabric I love and I look for others. Sometimes it takes over a decade to find all the right ones. As they form a pile on the shelf, I keep a watchful eye on their conversation. Is it worthy? Is it compelling? Is it beautiful? Each piece changes the others, irrevocably. My grief is just one fabric, flecked in pattern across a lifetime, appearing and disappearing according to its own mandates, changing in shape and in juxtaposition, but never truly going away. Grief is the body's memory of joy. It is the shade of green that Rob's eyes reserved for me alone.

23. The Unimagined

When I left Maine in August of 2016, my body was always shaking. I carried a knot of grief in my throat. "I can't make decisions from fear," I repeated over and over in my head as I wandered the streets of my new neighborhood, imagining how I might be a part of the countless vignettes I encountered along my way. Maybe one day I'd be buying flowers outside a neighborhood bodega or taking a certain route on my way to a new job. "I never want to wait tables again. I can't go backwards."

I applied for jobs as a live-in aid, an artist's assistant, an administrator in a small arts organization, an art teacher, a gardener, a museum docent. I wrote freelance articles on marriage, fashion, and other contemporary existential dilemmas. I exhibited and sold some paintings. I felt drained, fragmented, invisible, impotent.

When I left my corporate job in Boston almost two decades prior, I chose a certain path that ended when I left Maine. My impulse, after I left Maine, was to seek anything familiar, any lifeline. Sometimes that meant desperately trying to recreate what was lost, like trying to make snowballs with powdery snow that simply falls apart. Sometimes that meant trying to go back to the safety of that path I'd so long ago rejected, the place where I diverged from what seemed more reasonable, for what had been laid so neatly before me. I remembered how relatively easy it was to *advance* back then. Even that thought, *advancement, progress*, revealed itself as not vanquished within me, merely latent. I'd spent years forcing it into remission, trying to undo the deep cultural and familial conditioning. Back then, I'd worked for a company that offered so many opportunities to move and grow. I knew I was smart and competent and that in time, in the right environment, I could find some kind of stride. I could find a place to use my full strength, power, and complexity. Just as I had all those years ago.

In my art practice, I'd moved from functional quilts, craft, where the emphasis was on materials and techniques. In that space, I'd felt claustrophobic not being able to talk about the conceptual beauty and responsibility of living with things. So I'd moved into fine art. The pendulum swung too far, however. Materials became like passive vessels for ideas. Everything I did to point back to the material simply became about the pointing. Now, I'd choose a field, fashion and clothing, that aligned with all those intervening years of art making and domestic study. Perhaps here, I'd find middle ground, an elusive, simple integrity. Clothing seemed a medium that promised hope for the collaboration of body and spirit. Corporate life wouldn't be so bad, I rationalized. I'd do it better this time.

I was drawn to the retail store Anthropologie and applied for positions in several of their locations from Manhattan to Philadelphia. Each place held a slightly different promise cast in the shape and shadow of the particular city, the commute, the building, and the people. First, I was offered a job in their flagship store in Philadelphia. They were on the cusp of opening their bridal salon in that location and wanted me to be the bridal stylist. The irony was not lost on me. As much as they didn't know it and I tried to hide it, I was not the person to guide soon-to-be brides in their visions of white lace. I might have said yes anyway. I wanted so desperately to be the person to show up in that beautiful space, maybe wearing one of those key rings around my wrist that those women in retail wear, the ones with the power to lock and unlock things. My shoes would make some rhythmic sound on the ground, tapping on the terrazzo, echoing through the showroom. Rittenhouse Square seemed all the more beautiful that Autumn, for being a place that Gabriella-who-lived-in-Maine didn't live. I could see the new version of me sitting for a moment in the park on my way to work, finishing coffee in a small paper cup, excitedly meeting new bridal clients each day. Unfortunately, they didn't offer me enough pay to actually afford rent anywhere. The dogs were used to having two acres to run, a large house to nestle in the corners and peer out the windows. Most of all, they were used to people home with them. How could I suddenly keep them in a small apartment alone all day? If I couldn't afford rent, I certainly couldn't afford rent and dog care. My own misery was itself too much to bear. I didn't know then that they wouldn't, in fact, run free again for almost four years.

Next, Anthropologie had offered me a visual merchandising position in their Rockefeller Center store and then a stylist position in the Short Hills Mall. I wouldn't have to rent another place to live; I would commute from Cameron's apartment in Harlem to just a handful of miles from my parents' home, my childhood home. "I would *never* work here," the thought rang clear and echoing like the inimitable mall footfalls on the shiny white path winding past one exclusive and pristine brand after another: Max Mara, Christian Louboutin, Fendi, Tory Burch, Tumi, Louis Vuitton. I accepted the position. Actually, it calls itself "The Mall at Short Hills." It's a *destination*, home to the world's most prestigious department stores, like Neimann Marcus, along with specialty brands: Cartier, Chanel, Dior, Gucci, and Hermès. My interview there felt like a return to a microcosmic ethical universe, like a junior high girl clique in an affluent suburb.

I acted from my head and from my fear. I completely ignored the explicit message from my gut. I honestly don't think it could have given me any answer except: "Please, for the love of God, stop. Rest." I couldn't listen to that. How would I make a living?

The job barely paid for food, medical bills, dog care, gas, insurance. It certainly would not pay for rent, and so I continued to live on the generosity of my family and Cameron. The dependency did not make me feel safe. It had the opposite effect; it exaggerated and taunted me with my failure, my vulnerability; it made me feel imperiled.

"It'll soon be OK. I'll move up. Just as I did before, all those years ago . . ." I dragged myself through each day. I would meet with styling clients at the store, "I want to dress like you," one woman told me. I was wearing a robe from a small room at the back of the store reserved for so-called intimates and loungewear. The thin fabric was pale blue flecked with small pinkish red flowers. It wrapped around my body and snapped in two places at the waist. Two oversized pockets sat on either hip. I wore it over a pair of skinny black jeans, pointy, dark red leather loafers, and a brown, faux-fur collar that tied with a black ribbon that I'd had for years.

What I didn't realize is that I just wasn't the same person I'd been all those years before. Heading to that mall everyday, showing up under the aegis of style to sell people unethically sourced garments built on images of someone else's truth was adding insult to injury. I wasn't in my twenties anymore, believing I was eager to climb a corporate ladder. I couldn't find the energy or the space in my life for that path to emerge. My metabolism had permanently changed. Perhaps if this bottom had been a start, I could have held out hope, but it soon became clear that there was nowhere to go, no path towards something else. All of the beautiful things around me seemed shabby and flimsy up close. Years ago, when I was designing costumes, we used to talk about things needing to look good "six feet from a moving horse." Fast fashion is not so different. The fabrics were rougher or thinner than they first appeared, hanging in appealing clusters of color and shape. At the end of the day, especially during a sale, piles would end up dusty and trampled on the floor. What a great expenditure of life energy propping up these flimsy pieces of cloth, each adjustment on the hanger, each careful fold, each caress from human hands imbuing them with life. The window displays suffered from this proximity, too. Their disposability undermined the beauty. Errant drips of glue and wayward strokes of paint broke everything I'd once apprehended as whole into careless bits and parts.

Employees had to check out of the store when leaving. This meant stopping by the manager standing guard at the front door and letting them search your bag. No one was spared this ritual. The enforcement of security was the emphasis and priority of each position within the store. We were taught how to pat down and handle the clothing in the dressing rooms, how to patrol our zone of the store, and our walkie talkie communication system ensured we never left our respective posts. Of course this was called "good customer service," but the two were inextricably linked. Theft prevention actually seemed more important than sales. On the day I was tasked with this particular check-out detail, a group of managers from the region had gathered for an important meeting. An entourage of perfumed women peered down their noses at various things around the store, the soles of their shoes landing light and authoritative on the hard, gray cement. They noted things. They assessed. One woman approached to leave the store and I followed the protocol. She looked down at me and rolled her eyes, in a flash making clear the imposition. She was at once tasked with enforcing these protocols yet she felt above them and freely expressed her disdain. "Get on with it," she tapped impatiently, dropping her handbag on a stack of neatly piled sweaters and looking clear through me. My experience there further damaged my already mortally-wounded self-worth.

However, inside of this experience was a gift: working at Anthropologie gave me the opportunity to create a new wardrobe, one to pull me out of that place altogether. Their tagline was about creating an "unimagined experience." That is actually what I was there to do. I bought the clothing, piece by piece, that liberated me from my former life. It changed the trajectory from that of the person I was in Maine, to a new one for the person who now lived in New York City.

I think it's no accident we use the expression "walk a mile in her shoes" to talk about empathizing with another person's perspective. In these new pieces of clothing I could literally walk in different shoes, in different sweaters, different dresses, in a different perspective than I had in Maine. It wasn't rose-colored glasses, but it was something new, and at the time, that was enough. I couldn't imagine where I was going, but that job and each piece of clothing that came from it began to create a new path forward, albeit not there.

I still have the robe that the customer admired. I also have a long, dusty green, cotton Kimono with big pockets, although I've mostly convinced Cameron that it looks better on him. I have a white, cropped, boatneck sweater and a pair of 100% cotton Levi's Wedgie fit blue jeans. I have a beaded silk dress.

Finally, I have what I call my Komondor sweater. The large sweater, the color of newsprint, is covered with long knitted loops, like dreadlocks. It is thick, the sleeves are long, and it covers me from neck to mid-thigh.

The Komondor is a large dog, about 30" tall at the withers and up to 130 lbs. It is covered with a heavy, matted, corded coat. It, too, is the color of newsprint. The mature coat forms tassels or cords and will take about two years to develop. The coat of the Komondor takes about two and a half days to dry after a bath.

The Komondor is built for livestock guarding. Its temperament is like that of most livestock guarding dogs; it is calm and steady when things are normal, but, in case of trouble, the dog will fearlessly defend its charges. It was bred to think and act independently and make decisions on its own. The Komondor is affectionate with its family, and gentle with the children and friends of the family. Although wary of strangers, they can accept them when it is clear that no harm is imminent, being instinctively very protective of their family, home, and possessions.

The Komondor is a big, strong dog. The coat is her armor. As she protects her family, it protects her against predators such as coyotes, cougars, and bears. The teeth and claws of would-be attackers can't penetrate the thick coat.

Once, walking down 125th street near Frederick Douglass, a woman yelled to me as I passed by, "Girl, that is the *ugliest* sweater I've ever seen!" I laughed, deeply amused by the encounter, taking pleasure in her frankness. No teeth could touch me. I was that bitch.

24. Address

Cameron and I had been invited to curate a show in Belfast, Maine before everything came apart. The exhibit was set to open the summer of 2017, exactly one year after I'd left Maine. We'd always planned to curate a show of visual artworks that used text-based imagery and strategies, yet another iteration of mind meeting matter, the ineffable turned to image. The show statement read:

> The works in Address use writing, frequently emphasizing direct communication alongside graphic strategies. Such an emphasis mixes the social modes of signage and conversation with the personal and particular information found in gesture, material, and image.

> Short, declarative statements and the immediacy of imagery purport easy access to content and communicable information. The exhibited works complicate and enhance the simple content that text or image alone often seem to contain.

We worked on the exhibition throughout that first year I spent away from Maine, not knowing how I would face going back there.

We'd selected the artists we wanted to include in the show and as it neared, we talked with them about the works they wanted to include. Each one, unsolicited by title or specific content, came in more pointed and potent than the next, a magical poem:

This is Pompeii by Christine Negus

Looky Look by John Peck

Letting Go by Courtney Tramposh

The Past is a Wilderness of Horrors, Ditto for the Future by Christine Negus

Shame on You Monsters from Aram Han Sifuentes and The Protest Banner Lending Library

Dad's Balls Are Dad's Business by Steve Reinke

Since Evil Is A Substance Space Is A Problem by Steve Reinke

Tristes Topiques (Sad Topics) by Steve Reinke

We headed to Maine when I was eight months pregnant to hang these works in the place, in the community, where I'd been humiliated. It was the place I thought was my home, but like the people closest to me, the attachment proved insufficient, perhaps never really there at all. I felt in so many ways that Maine had betrayed me too. There was no person, no wilderness, no business, no family, no home to which I was rooted, the connections all appeared loose and weak. Maine let go of my hand and watched me fall.

25. Light and Peace

When I was seven months pregnant I headed to Delaware for ten days of silence at a Vipassana retreat. I arrived, handed over my wallet and cell phone, and filled out a clip board of stacked papers. I told them I was pregnant and that my son's name was Luciano Dove. I didn't know until I wrote it, but the moment it slid from the pen, it was the truth.

It wasn't that I had no inkling. Cameron and I, of course, discussed it endlessly and happily, but nothing seemed right. One night, we sat around the dining room table at my parents' house with my sister and her boyfriend, all laughing and throwing suggestions out, some more reasonable than others. I loved the name Luca, but all I could think was "Luca Brasi sleeps with the fishes" from *The Godfather*, so that was not an option. "Luciano!" The lights in the room flashed off and then on again. Apropos of nothing. It was a perfectly sunny, temperate afternoon. No strong winds or storms. Nothing like it preceding or following. "Granny," flashed through my mind. Mary had cast her vote from beyond, Luciano it was.

When I was in high school I used to hike these trails through the woods near my house. One day, I met this guy, he'd left the nearby Rabbinical College, somehow unauthorized was my impression although I don't really understand what the rules were.

He was questioning his faith, or perhaps not his faith, but his religion, and we sat and talked for quite awhile. His name was Dovid. "Dove," I thought. I held on to that.

When I wrote "Luciano Dove" on those intake forms, I knew it was his name and that I was not in control of his identity. I knew that my relationship with him would be wrought in action and deed. The bonds of family were perpetual acts of love, not static ownership. I committed there, in his name, to his sovereignty.

In the early days of my pregnancy, I went about my New York City routines, which mostly included simple acts of sustenance taken step by step and day by day. I shopped for as many groceries as I could carry home. Cooked. Walked the dogs. Moved the car from one side of the street to the other to accommodate street cleaning and avoid a ticket.

I worked nights waiting tables until a few days before I gave birth. I loved the restaurant and adored the people I worked with, brilliant creatives, passionate, and funny. Yet, I dreaded the advent of each and every shift. The work itself could be brutal, both physically taxing and often demeaning. It is often relegated to those so deeply committed to their vision, to a better life, that they have the fortitude to tolerate what can only pale in comparison to a greater dream. At forty years old and nine months pregnant, however, I interpreted my place there as a sign that my vision had finally and utterly failed. So I spent the days trying to suppress the dread and exhaustion I inevitably felt heading to work.

In addition to daily tasks, I tried to focus on the optimism of my future baby and as a way of making that concrete, I spent a lot of that time imagining how to dress my soon-to-be son. By the time he was born, I had carefully selected clothing for his first six months of life. I was pregnant in the heart of #Metoo and #Timesup. I couldn't help thinking, as someone growing a white, male human from my flesh, at my responsibility for the state of masculinity, patriarchy, and white supremacy. I began my evolving quest, man-repelling for baby boys, only, in this case, repelling his patriarchal-future-man in favor of *his* future (never forgetting how men suffer and deform under patriarchy as well, not the least of which in their intimate relationships).

As soon as I began shopping, the perils emerged: my son was headed for the major leagues or the military. He also had his choice of sanctioned interests: trucks, cars, dinosaurs, outer space, and superheros. Simply type "baby boy clothes" into google, or "baby girl clothes" to see the screen flush blue or pink.

Certain companies pay lip-service to egalitarian dressing. They mostly make 'boy-things' cool for girls, most especially things conferring economic advantage, STEM for babies. This strategy emphasizes the importance of creating an accessible iconography, defining a range of interests and assigning them to our children. This ideology, geared towards creating egalitarian economic producers (good capitalists), is often just undermined by the aesthetics of the garments. For example, frilly, pink dresses decorated with spaceships. Sure, it's important that girls can like science, but that is certainly a separate concern from considering the fundamental disparities between the sexes. Is it important that they are *still girls*? After all, what are girls and boys if these simple assignations, given at birth, disappear? I couldn't shake the memory of a passage from Salinger's <u>Franny and Zooey</u>: " . . . all legitimate religious study must lead to unlearning the differences, the illusory differences, between boys and girls, animals and stones, day and night, heat and cold." Imagine further, those that believe they've been born in the wrong body with regard to gender. What if there were another, Occam's Razor explanation: sometimes women have dicks and men don't. Perhaps we assign attitude, value, and narrative to the material world that is actually at odds with our truth, like forcing data to support a hypothesis that we're too afraid to relinquish. This kind of meaning making, our binary conventions, suit not much beyond current power. Accepting the truth of things, as they are, creates new worlds.

In the same way that we have strong associations with certain smells, I also have very strong associations with certain fabrics and patterns from my childhood. My wish for my son was that, if he remembered his early clothing at all, those memories would be a gorgeous underpinning, a depth of time, like a mossy undergrowth in an old forest or a well-loved storybook. His memories, carefully tended pictures, a kind of redolent imagery. Quite simply, I wanted him raised in beauty and intention. I wanted to protect him from the violence and artifice of binary systems, choosing queer over convention.

I wanted, even in the moments where I couldn't glimpse much of a horizon, to strive towards a future reality where there are no distinctions in dress between men and women, until then, I knew also that dressing my son in girl's clothes wasn't an answer. For one, it wouldn't avoid binary distinctions. More importantly, I had no interest in making my son an unwitting activist. We've instantiated gender differences, just as we've done with race. Denying these realities just inflicts further harm on those disempowered by the distinctions.

Making these decisions, even having these contemplations, certainly made me wary of the unconscious expressions of my hopes and fears. Although there's no way of relinquishing my ego completely, I observe my son, as well as my gut reactions. I find myself cringing a bit when someone refers to him as a "little man." It feels like fulfilling a prophecy we might reconsider wanting filled. I mostly don't want him to be the kind of man that I'm used to seeing. It is a nurture some of us have clearly come to regret, as pussy-grabbing, white supremacist rapists infiltrate the white house and the judiciary. As Simone de Beauvoir describes the being of women as "what they have become" instead of "what they are," so too with men. The way I understand adults and their effect on each other and on the world is not the telos I wish upon our children, not if I care about their peace. At some point my choices will contribute to identity and I would like to choose wisely. To this end, I created a provisional set of guidelines:

I avoid text and overt iconography. Perhaps, it's the explicitness that chafes. A foreclosing on the complexity that seems our birthright. Additionally, I have no interest in becoming a brand ambassador, a capitalist crusader.

I avoid sports and military themes. These seem like stand-ins for masculinity itself, just another form of "blue." It also prioritizes competition and violence, capitalist values best left out of the nursery.

I mix and match color and pattern. I combine traditionally gendered colors and themes, or I choose those with weaker gender associations. All-over patterns are better than single images. I avoid ready-made sets. I select items that work together for more flexibility.

I choose abstract designs and nature or animal themes.

Simplicity always works. Pattern, color and minimalism are not mutually exclusive.

I once read that Andy Warhol was "[making] the world safe for Andy." Through some mysterious alchemy, showing the world to itself, reflecting it, making oneself simultaneously part-of and apart-from, a mechanism for individuation. When we commit to serving difference from the moment our children are born, we should not be surprised when that difference appears later in the form of countless inequities such as pay disparity, voting rights, reproductive health, to name a few. When these gross injustices are examined under a microscope, you will see little pink bows and little blue booties, lest anyone mistake the caste to which they're born. Even our reluctance to relinquish those traditions we find so charming and cute could perhaps be our own resistance to letting go of the places within ourselves that map safety and love to these potent tropes.

I hope that as my son moves through life his individuality is complex and that he becomes aware of its fragility and contingency. I hope he is inspired and curious about its beauty. Small choices made towards this complexity increase safety and destroy illusory differences.

26. Harlem

By the winter of 2016, I ended up settling in New York City with Cameron after that bumpy few months of trying to navigate back and forth between his apartment and my parents' house. Cameron had been living in the apartment for five years when Rob pushed bottles of wine into my hands and walked out of the Bell School. I called Cameron in New York. I don't know what I said. Cameron, worried and helpless all those miles away, called my friend Lisa who drove an hour to come and stay the night with me. Cameron hopped on the bus from Chinatown in the middle of the night and made it to Maine by the morning. I awoke to find them both there. Later, Cameron drove me and the dogs back down to the city. I have no memory of the drive.

You can not build in New York City what you can build in Maine. The reverse is also true, but I had no map for possibility, only for known territory. The land is different, the people are different, the laws are different, the money is different, the climate is different, the buildings are different, the towns and cities are different. The desire that led to the existence of every material aspect, everything real, was completely gone. Was the creative life I'd chosen now responsible for all of this chaos and pain? Was this disaster in which I found myself a mirror for how ugly I had become? Although my self-doubt has never run deep when it comes to my compass, I feared the very worst, that all those ethical curses placed on our polyamorous relationship had come to fruition. This leveling of my life was my own doing and the only antidote was the restoration of the status quo, the heteronormative couple bond, the upholding of capitalist ideals. It appeared I'd lost the silent wager I'd made, maybe as far back as Boston, that I could do things differently.

I was so scared, the only intentions I could muster were base, subsistence level. Or, in moments of hopefulness when I'd push aside my resignation to conventional employment (which, frankly had I been qualified or able to find, I may have given in to), I'd simply regurgitate old ideas about being an artist and maybe one day owning some more rental properties to keep everything afloat. These visions that projected my past into the future were more like phantom limbs than embodied ones, ineffectual spasms only real enough to cause pain.

The way to live was only small. Cameron and I hung my five-foot by five-foot Pink Finery on the wall of the apartment. It was made of one-inch strips of pink cotton, pieced together in overlapping rows, sometimes revealing the layers underneath. I hand quilted and hand embroidered across the surface of the piece. This series began years ago as a material meditation, a translation of time into space. What if we never had the concept of time? I sewed the answer. Life became small, present, metabolic. Each movement unique and in each glimmer of that change lay a microcosm of possibility. A way out, albeit a slow one. The pattern could always change, if I remained attentive. This piece was a reminder, a mantra. Be present. Attend material fluctuations. See the potential in material things, not abstract ones.

Adjusting to life without my garden was heartbreaking and destabilizing. Especially when I was being strongly called into nature. On the other hand, the efficiency and intimacy of the smaller space felt elemental in its own way, unencumbered. A sanctuary. The walkability of the city, too, had a grounding effect, an antidote to the hours I would spend riding in a car in Maine. Through the lens of so much upheaval, all of my feelings about space and stuff began to reveal their underpinning in a complex and messy system of values and expectations. Transitioning was an ongoing, emotional dialogue that emerged between the depths of grief and loss and the heights of new gratitude and inspiration.

I carefully selected a few things to bring into the already furnished apartment, the rest would be relegated to storage for what would turn out to be the next few years. A footed brass bowl was my grandmother's. I kept it filled with fruit on our table. I can picture just where it sat in her kitchen. She kept papers in it and her reading glasses. It was kind of like her inbox. I think there were coupons in there, too. "Get me my glasses," she commanded from her seat at the kitchen table. The table and chairs were really the only significant furniture Cameron had before I moved in, but I'd helped him pick them out years ago. We'd picked the round, iron pedestal table because the tiny space would accommodate its shape and scale, while providing at least room for four, although we often pushed it to five. In a way the table anchored much of the apartment. It was simple, efficient, elegant, timeless, and durable. We'd never worry about dents or scratches. This is where we ate, worked, and lounged. The caning in the seat of one of the wooden bistro chairs broke. Cameron learned how to re-cane a chair from a video on youtube. He sat diligently weaving until it was new again.

Mostly the things I kept near were pieces of art, mine and others: quilts, illustrations, mobiles, paintings. These works would inspire me. They were ideas, and ideas were like clues building to an image of anything I might like to salvage. What was still good? What could I build on going forward? It was a way of living with mystery, instead of drowning in the fear of uncertainty. Inspiration in these things was a comfort, and invitation. I wanted to make the world safe for my family, for those who connect to my work.

I've known women capable of creating worlds inside of worlds – in their work and in their homes. My Aunt Jeannette. My friend Melissa. Each of these women create living theater in all dimensions. My mother's fresh meatballs frying in a pan, preparing for the simmering pot of tomatoes. My young eyes wide when Aunt Jeannette served steamed white asparagus wrapped in Prosciutto. The time while living at the Bell School that Melissa baked a perfect apple pie and delivered it to the man who'd towed my car out of the mud the day before. There are no fonder times than moments these women created in their homes when entertaining. It was as if they could fully ply their craft here, they could shine.

I was so proud of our house when I was young. It was colorful, full of artwork, beautiful furniture, ceramics, and textiles. My father's domain was the garden, but inside, it was mostly my mother. It was her studio: she cooked there, she cleaned there, she did laundry, she made space for her children to play, and she entertained. She rearranged the rooms to suit the flow of activity, not to fulfill the builder's imagination of our lives. The original dining room was a small room off the kitchen. It flowed into a giant living room with a large bay window overlooking the front yard. She turned the dining room into a parlor, layering green, floral print, chintz couches against walls papered above and below a chair rail: the top, a beige and pink floral chinoiserie, and below, a textured cloth. On the floor, a wool oriental rug with medallions in pink and green. Two salvaged side tables had layers of wood and glass, atop which sat stately, antique lamps covered in painted roses. My grandfather found an ornately carved coffee table with a removable glass tray on the side of the road and had it refinished. It sat in front of one of the couches, holding a small gold box decorated with the painting of a woman. Inside was a stack of wooden florentine coasters in gold, green, pink, red, blue, and white. In another corner of the room was a wingback chair covered in pink ikat. It sat under a painting, an abstract image of a woman rendered in yellows, blues and purples. My mother called her by the name of the painting, Cortinas Amarillas. When Lulu was just a baby, she'd take him to greet Cortinas and personify her voice, "Hola Cortinas! Como estas?" Their conversations were always in Spanish.

The would-be living room my mother turned into a grand dining room with ample seating for ten. On the longest wall hung painting after painting of women. My artwork, an oil pastel rendering after Les Demoiselles d'Avignon, hung next to reclining nudes, a woman in a boat, line-drawn women wandering a dreamscape, a woman leaning against a wall. It was a gallery of female images sitting above a marbleized buffet displaying crystal decanters on a glossy dark tray. A large ceramic pig's head, rosy pink and graced with flowers, hung cheekily on the opposite wall, a mix of high and low, of humor with tradition. At the head of the room stood an imposing china cabinet, displaying all manner of precious artifacts. Like an Austrian pepper mill that when cranked sprinkled fine particles of spice from the mouth of a pig while playing Edelweiss. This cabinet was flanked on either side by oval-shaped portraits of my mother's paternal grandparents, looking stern under their curved glass frames. My great grandfather's tie was penciled in, only a sketch.

My mother's interventions into space did not stop there. The would-be den or so-called family room was moved from its home on the first floor to a large bedroom over the garage. It was finished with a blue leather sectional, custom oak bookshelves and a window bench that Uncle Billy built. A red, white, and blue cushion and window valence finished that wall and entered dialogue with the red oriental rug and the painting of the New York Giants on the wall, seemingly at home next to a delicate tonal rendering of a forest. This rearrangement designated the once informal first floor space as a formal living room, as meticulously curated as each other space. A small cherubic bust, an elongated stone woman stretching on her own black plinth, an elaborately dressed Indonesian puppet on a pedestal staking claim to an entire corner, a couch covered in peach fabric with embroidered images of the Napoleon bee marking the surface.

On their honeymoon, my parents bought the memorable *Green and White Stockings*, a life-size, realistic oil painting of a woman from the waist down, clad only in dramatic green and white, thigh high stockings. Her legs were spread wide, her arm casually covering the shadowy place between them. They gifted me this painting when I moved into the Bell School and it now hangs in our Harlem apartment.

Although always intrigued by the juxtaposition of graphic allure with taboo mystery held in that painting, I mostly took these things for granted growing up. I felt and appreciated this quality of my life, but the rarity was lost on me. I was so close to women, most especially my mother, who were good at it, that only later did I realize this special gift was not a grace equally granted. Even in the ubiquitous light of daily life, my home enacted a coordination of color, space, sound, scents, and light that sealed memories with beauty. It created a form of hope called style that could resist a world pressing in.

I am sensitive to the fluctuations of feeling and content created by the environment, to the care and love present or absent. These environments always felt like wanting more, a kind of desire tugging at the senses, a curiosity for whatever shadow or wafting aroma may float from the kitchen around the next corner. A wanting to sink in, to be absorbed in the richness, or, alternatively to be made light, evaporating into the energetic efflorescence, swept up in the alchemy of material compositions. A darkened oil painting on patterned wallpaper tucked into a small bathroom at the end of the hall, scented with French-milled hand soap, a tiny bar sitting in a porcelain dish next to the embroidered towel. These places glimpsed by the soul are delivered to the minds and hands of those who know how to speak the language. The mother tongue of domestic forms. It is the language of luxury, a prayer honoring abundance. This is the very connective tissue that tethers us to the living earth.

While I was pregnant, I painted the entire apartment. I watched a bunch of Hitchcock movies and was inspired by the interiors. I noticed that the trim and the walls were all painted in one shade and I decided that in the tiny space, a similar strategy would create openness and simplicity. The doors were inexpensive hollow core doors that were stained a dark, high-gloss brown. One had an old Dora the Explorer sticker on it from a previous occupant. They were glaring and gloomy. We couldn't afford to replace the doors so I painted them with patterns, animals, and shapes. Years ago Cameron and I dreamed of something we called our "pattern house." We used to sit at a bar in Chicago after gallery openings and over gin and tonics we'd discuss our ideas for this living art project. Each surface would be richly ornamented, covered in pattern, but we would have the bare minimum of what we needed and nothing decorative that had no functional purpose. Two people, two forks. Wallpaper, no paintings. A quilt for the bed, no solid comforter. We'd map the details endlessly, wishing for a home in which to execute the vision. I love pattern and color and at the same time I love minimalism and simplicity. Textiles, walls, and doors are opportunities for layering pattern and color without adding clutter. I was motivated by so many things, but maybe most of all, I wanted to add images that would form my son's memory of his childhood, which would inspire his curiosity and create for him a sense of warmth, care, and playfulness.

There was a bathroom in my Aunt and Uncle's house with dark colored walls and a boldly printed shower curtain. I watched my older cousin apply eyeliner in the mirror. It was so glamorous. Sometimes colorful spaces are just around a corner, out of reach, but memory preserves the intrigue for years.

These introductions to joyful mystery remain strong.

Moving into Cameron's apartment, I held onto values I've always had and I tried to be intentional about the things I lived with. I generally stick to the rule that new things don't come in unless old things go out. I think I simultaneously care a lot about many of my things, but I also have a claustrophobia around too much sentimentality or attachment. These feelings cloy and have a way of chafing against the present. I lost so many possessions and artworks when I left Maine. There was just no room in the truck and no resolve left in my body. I piled them up in thick, black contractor bags and left them, an enormous pile, at the edge of the curved gravel driveway. I think this disposition saved me from a lot of heartbreak, but it has also been bolstered by the experience of loss.

I don't have photographs of people around, but what I do have are so many things of my grandmother's. I let go of my things, but saved hers, saved things that belonged to my parents: oriental rugs, china dishes, Florentine trays. I have a copper-colored sequin jacket that used to belong to my grandmother. She gave it to my sister before she died. No one could ever quite figure out how to style it, there's something about the shape more than the color or shine rendering is awkward on the body. I hung it on the wall in my son's room on an old hanger, heavy metal with a gold velvet bar across the bottom that once belonged to my grandmother's sister, Aunt Josie. My grandmother had a real penchant for flamboyance. She insisted on being buried in black satin pumps with rhinestone lightning bolts on the heels. The sequined jacket looks beautiful with the celadon walls and reflects light differently at all times of day. One last gesture, a length of purple satin ribbon tied to the hanger, just visible under the lapels. My son loves to look at it and I tell him about Mary.

Also in my son's room is a painting from my friend Monica, "Hello Again," washes of green over green. Monica channels her paintings; songs come to her in dreams and she paints them. When I was younger, when asked about my favorite color, I would reply emphatically, "It is red." It was my older cousin, Candice's favorite color and I thought she was so cool. I am also an Aries and always feeling an affinity for the fiery sign's characteristics, either in fact or aspirationally, I felt it a natural fit. One recent moment, seemingly out of nowhere and passing over me in a flash, I knew that was not true. "Hello Again," it had always been green. Chartreuse. Celadon. Moss. Hello green April-spring, animal birth. Hello beginnings at the end of ends. Hello old friends, always new, dearest Monica.

Cameron always had a studio in the city, his work is large and sculptural, and I've always worked at home. I can metabolize a day better when I work that way, intermittently cooking or walking the dogs. It feels more integrated. In this small space we were always ready and willing to rearrange the furniture for different projects. We sometimes moved our bed to the living room, and I used our bedroom to work.

Space is valuable as an artist. Space is also valuable as a parent. I remember a conversation with a glass blower I knew when I lived in Maine. At some point she moved from a tiny studio on the coast to a huge one, an old brick warehouse in Ellsworth, further inland and along the river. She described for me how her work was able to change and grow. The space around her changed her thoughts, her imagination. In the apartment, I started to focus on writing and creating videos because the constraints of space had changed. I loved the intimacy of our little family, how we shared the bookshelves and my son played with pots and pans. He always ate at the table with us, no separate highchair. because there was no room. No room to store a stroller or energy to lug one up and down five flights of stairs, four dogs and toddler in tow, means I always carried him close to my body and in time, he learned to be such a strong walker, able to go for miles with joy. His toys became our sculpture, our doors are his murals; we all love string lights.

We nurtured the intersections, because in a smaller area, they abound.

When I left Maine, I kept bemoaning the loss of my identity, but at some point I realized what true liberation I'd been granted, what a spiritual opportunity. Of course, I still mourn, grief is long and irregular, perhaps it is endless. It goes into remission only to resurface again, but I am wary of trying to replace my identity too quickly, perhaps even at all. Not that we can truly live without identity, but in that new apartment, the place where I was no longer what I once was, I could reflect and grow. I was becoming less terrified in the unknown, replacing it with mystery and her attendant: curiosity.

Our apartment was my quest for abundance. It was my new studio, a faithful manifestation practice. I was able to make our food and to play with my son. We were safe and warm at night. When I made the bed in the morning I knew, even that small act was a way of creating peace for my family. I could pause to think of my grandmother when I encountered her things. Walking to and from the grocery store several times a week with only what my hands could carry kept me in a rhythm of life that more closely matched my body's metabolism than ever before. This kept me fluid and listening. It kept me strong.

While not the final answer, Harlem taught me that home is more like a verb and less like a noun, that what I do and who I am are not so different.

27. Alchemy

When Lulu was not yet a year old, I got a call from Kathryn. We'd met almost a decade prior, in 2009 when we were both in graduate school, I in Maine, and she in D.C. We joined a group of seven other artists at a residency and experimental homestead called Mildred's Lane. We were both now living in New York City and Kathryn suggested we return to the place in rural Pennsylvania along the upper Delaware River, to celebrate the anniversary and final iteration of the project we'd worked on all those years ago. An Ordinal of Alchemy was a collaborative art and research project, organized by artists Mark Dion and Robert Williams. The best way for me to make sense of the project is to describe it as a multi-faceted, long-term engagement to contemplate magical transformation. Several groups of artists from all over the world moved in and out of the thematically shifting project, contributing catalogues, lectures, performances, installations, and the construction of a permanent structure, the Alchemist's Shack, on the Mildred's Lane grounds.

Both the project and its anniversary spoke to me now, as if a revelatory whisper, a reminder of the things that remained important and true even after so much loss: "You've been preparing for this moment." Mildred's Lane, as an experimental artists' space and the permanent residence of the artist J. Morgan Puett, hosted the Ordinal of Alchemy project. The 94-acre homestead is centered around the main house. In the humble way of an ancient tree, the house is both a dark and imposing structure. Although it is reminiscent of an old farmhouse, black and wood finishes and cold, gray, concrete floors make its elaboration as if organic. It unfolds, spontaneously and cohesively, as vignettes in a forest. Guests coming up the winding drive through the woods, approach from the back. Entering the house for the first time I observed stacks of books everywhere in the shaded darkness. There was a library on the left, more books floor to ceiling and piled high on tables. Further down the darkened hall, the large kitchen and dining area opened up to light flooding through windows and doors on three sides. The room spanned the back of the house where rows of doors lead to the large porch and majestic view: a large green lawn, the fenced kitchen garden, and majestic deciduous hills. Morgan's room, covered in layers of white linen, was down below. French doors opened to a stone patio under a pergola that wandered out to the same vista as above. Upstairs, a handful of other spaces were reserved for the revolving door of artists who came to live and work for varying periods of time. One such room was a modest loft lined with dolls and another, a sleeping porch running the width of the back of the house. It was sheathed with wooden planks and centered around an iron bed sitting under a rustic canopy of ropes and canvas in shades of ivory, honey, and flax. This place was the technicolor, fully realized version of the small bridge I'd begun building between the home economics department and the art department during my teaching residency only a handful of years before.

As soon as Kathryn suggested the trip, I said yes. We would drive four hours for a four-hour visit, but the potential in a return to Mildred's Lane was not lost on me. I knew that trying to see my way out of my darkness was not as simple as turning on a light.

I would have to become more like the darkness itself. I'd need empathy with this mysterious element to which I knew I belonged. I had to find some other sense. I'd been taught all my life to step outside, to look at, to analyze, to decide. I'd long suspected that was all wrong. A decade prior we'd literally laid foundation, stone by stone, for this moment. I had to reconnect with the site where alchemy made rebirth possible. A place where body and spirit connected in mystery.

At the time, I had been spending my time making some paintings in the living room of our Harlem apartment. By living room, I also mean dining room and hallway and office and soon, toddler playroom. Monica was able to sell a couple to some of her interior design clients on Long Island. I exhibited in a few small shows, but those were (and are) never about sales or material sustenance, only about ego. Don't get me wrong, I don't mean ego in an entirely bad way. I spent plenty of my life exhibiting work. It's just that exhibiting this way was more about being an artist in the company of other artists and other people who care about art, a kind of community. This was all proof and confirmation of my identity as an artist. The fragility of these propositions gave way after decades of this image, of myself, disappeared overnight. It dissolved in direct relation to the traces of my material existence that now no longer existed the way it once had, the way that I'd planned. My house and studio in Maine were gone, as was my network, my gallery.

I tried freelance writing but was never paid. I created and led a year-long project centered around the contemplation of the full moon, including monthly ceremonies, performance, drawing, writing, shamanic journeying, and divination all collected under the title Lunar Mythologies. I hoped Monica would call with more art-buying clients. While these things kept me busy, albeit in the scattered way that full-time motherhood often choreographs, the mounting feeling was one of failure. I wanted just one thing to pay me enough to continue, to make sense, to give back with even a fraction of the energy I was expending, and nothing did. The frenetic struggling to make these things stick in some way, to connect, to sell, ultimately created the feeling that I was failing. I was a forty-year-old unpaid intern trying to train and network in a new field and succeed as a full-time mother all at once. It was more than unsustainable. It was disastrous. The hole that precipitously and calamitously opened up and swallowed me was only deepening.

I was drifting further and further from my body. It was harder and harder to move through the space of the world around me. Electric waves of terror would seemingly fuse the fragmented parts of myself back together for just long enough to fill out an online job application, make some drawings in a sketchbook, or write an essay on fashion and identity. I didn't know who I was, but a lifetime of habits, ideas, feelings, and expectations surged in painful death throes of frenetic activity keeping me tethered to the old version of myself that no longer functioned in this new world.

What was at stake for me now was not entirely different from what it had been back in 2009 when I headed to Mildred's Lane for the first time. Even then, I was seeking clarity. I wanted to pinpoint a truth about my desire, about what I most valued in work and in life. At the time, I began pursuing something I called elaborate specificity. The elaborately specific was fertile soil for apprehending material experience, as it was, without the omissions and embellishments required by judgment, by feelings, by expectations, or by history. It was where the smallest fluctuations and mutations could be observed and embraced as hope for change. This awareness was wrought in countless quilts stitched one small piece at a time.

I made pieces where repeating patterns could change dramatically without warning or transition, perhaps a foreshadowing. I also made pieces that were relentlessly homogenous, allowing for the variation in hand stitching and the impossibility of exact repetition to emerge in the slight curve of a seam or the organic rhythm created by rows of embroidered French knots. I stopped binding the edges and I started layering not just left to right, but as if archaeologically, creating depth. These quilted works sat an inch or two off the wall, revealing at the edges strata composed of cotton fabric and batting, repeated over and over. I took comfort in the suggestion of infinity, of incremental change forever. Elaborate specificity had been a mantra of intentional design for the Bell School. It was in my love for two people at once. I wanted my spiritual life to exist not in spite of the body, aloof, but inseparable from it. I imagined my body constantly rising to the challenges of spirit, ever changing and ever open, in genetic communion with ancestry and the environment. Artwork had been a means, a material meditation, but I was always looking for a bridge to so-called real life. This desire needed a strategy, a practice.

Mildred's Lane was a place that validated my feeling trapped at either of two poles, the materiality of the craft world or the conceptuality of the art world. However, there was one crucial difference between my first visit and this return. What was once academic was now the life or death work of healing, of taking my profoundly fragmented self and making it whole.

In 2009, we spent the residency conversing in the early mornings, this after collecting dew from tarps, laid specifically for this purpose, in the back field the night before. This small attention to alchemy in the dawn even before gathering together for coffee on the long porch of the main house overlooking wooded hills fading into distant mist. We cleaned up after breakfast, carefully washing and arranging collections of mismatched dishes and glassware. These objects didn't have a place they belonged, instead each one was an invitation to reimagine the moment. An invitation to presence.

Kathryn, the other residents, and I spent a good part of our days and weeks digging rocks from a clearing on the hillside. This was a slow and methodical task in the heat and humidity of the August sun. We carried the rough, heavy slabs, one by one, from one area of the 94-acre site to another. We placed them carefully, laying the foundation for what would one day be the Alchemist's Shack. The shack, an outpost and guest space tucked at the edge of the woods about a hundred yards behind the main house, would become a space for magical transformations at the nexus of body and spirit.

Back in the kitchen, the refrigerator was home to still lives of fresh vegetables from the garden and eggs from a neighboring farm. These were reimagined with every touch. We were taking part in a communal dialogue, intervening into a site where artists from around the world convene to collaborate in this way. We considered social engagement in every aspect of domestic life and it was the most intimate work. We were engaged in our own bodily sustenance in Morgan's living home. One morning, after taking my turn in the concrete shower adjoining Morgan's bedroom, I dressed to join her for coffee. While I don't remember what we talked about, the invitation to her bed early that morning, the co-coon of textiles and fresh air filling the room through the open french doors, the steam from the fresh black coffee, was beyond information conveyed. It was about connection. The generosity of it all strikes me now. To relinquish the ego in one's personal space sets an example of vulnerability, of openness to mystery. Morgan invited people to rearrange her house, to shower in her room, to use her china cups, and to read her books. She ensured her home was filled with things that spoke and she taught us, by example, to understand their voices.

At Mildred's Lane, what to the world seemed common household chores, were treated as sacred alchemical engagements. Morgan had a vision of new modes of social engagement through specific innovations in fashion and domestic life. Her work aimed, like an arrow, at my intuitions about the true and intimate ground for transformative practice. She talked about there not being much left of material culture, clothing and textiles, from years prior be-cause these things were perpetually folded into the present, recy-cled and repurposed until they disappeared completely. A dress becoming a quilt becoming a rag. Always moving, a rhythm, a metabolism, like the turning of jump ropes. I knew I wanted to be in her presence.

As an artist, I'd focused my most vital energies into the details of my home, food, and relationships. In this way, my potency seemed relegated to the margins. After all, how can one focus on something meant to be blurry? Meant to be background? My art-work at the time, especially quilting, focused on locating critical social and political engagement in everyday life. The practices of everyday living which I lavished with my intellectual and creative attention, started to feel like a kind of background. I wanted more than anything to see all the things that have long been relegated to that space. Like a naturalist, taking earnest pains not to disrupt the natural habitat of this female and domestic space. In the language of Mildred's Lane: "Being is the practice." Viewing background as background is a tricky endeavor, once you look directly at it, it ceases to exist, it becomes foreground.

Morgan's work, and Mildred's Lane, are in part radical because they prioritize practices that traditionally have belonged to women. Having experienced the reverse, the affirmation was visceral. For example, living in New York in 2019, I gained an introduction to Brown Grotta, a gallery in Connecticut dedicated to, in their words "international art textiles, mixed media and dimensional art." "We like the work however, we just don't exhibit quilts," came their terse response. Even within the context of art textiles, the categorical exclusion of this feminist vernacular, this marginalization of the everyday, was loud and clear. They enforced the so-called high low divide by excluding quilts from a purportedly elite purview. For me, of course, it was personal. This was yet another avenue where I felt rejected in a space that, on paper, I should have fit in. I was desperate for access to potential clients, fearing for my livelihood. Even in this microcosm of textile arts for which I had already garnered national and international award and recognition, I was denied.

Kathryn and I drove out through the congested city traffic and onto the empty, two-lane highways of rural Pennsylvania. We spent the drive both reminiscing and talking excitedly about the future, in the way of people tipping inevitably and perhaps unwittingly into profound personal change. I parked at the foot of the long, winding, and eroded dirt drive, afraid of getting stuck in the mud somewhere in the woods between the main road and the house. We made our way on foot to the clearing where we saw the barn. This was the place where lectures, classes, screenings, and performances were held. Scattered to the east, north, west, and south were the handful of various outposts, just as I'd remembered them. Each one a question, a project, a creative engagement, and a living space, often housing visiting artists and residents. I was nervous about those intervening years, seeing Morgan and Robert Williams again after so long, but that feeling was quickly replaced with a continuity of history, a span of time bridging two distant moments. We were there to celebrate that final iteration of the Ordinal of Alchemy, to see the completed shack materialized.

I had always taken special note of the incredible warmth and generosity of spirit that Robert Williams, the artist behind the Ordinal of Alchemy brought to my experience at Mildred's Lane. He, his wife Gina, and their young son Jack were all there back in 2009. In a quiet moment, I told Gina about my desire to make work about my grandmother. She, in some all but imperceptible tone of voice or gesture now beyond my remembrance, and certainly with nothing so obvious as a perfect turn of phrase, sanctioned this desire in a way that remains with me. Robert, too, carried something of that encouraging air about him. He always wore a black t-shirt and black jeans, as if he belonged more to his own space than to the world, marking him as an observer. He tended towards the quiet, unless of course he was teaching or conversing about the ideas at hand, in which case he was a master buoyed by the contagious curiosity he brought to his work. "People that speak and think as you, often write books," Robert observed in one of our conversations. At the time, I was taken aback. I was at Mildred's Lane because I was trying, in some way, to cure myself of books. To leave the mind, and not just the conceptual world, but the physical practices that kept me untethered from my body. The sitting-still, running my eyes from left to right over little black letters that marched relentlessly to the beat of linear time. Shaping my mind to past-present-future constructions in both theory and practice. And yet, here I am now, typing one word after the next, hearing Robert's words again, a gentle suggestion.

Jack had accompanied his father for this return. Now, eighteen years old, I saw traces of the blond-haired kid in my memory, only now he was taller and broader than his father. He carried a camera, having found his own voice, and adeptly shadowed the grounds, observing through his lens. I'd been deeply moved, all those years ago, that Robert spent much of his working practice in collaboration with his son. It was a living example of integrity, that is, working at the intersection of cares, of love and values. It seemed so sincerely curious and relational in a sea of what, at the time, felt energetically egotistical and performative. I imagined something of myself in the image of this family. Something both present and aspirational. They seemed to be protecting something unbearably tender with some uncommon admixture of distance and passion.

I felt that Robert worked to see, not to be seen. I saw no trace of separating art from life and who better to lead us in alchemy than someone who practiced so authentically whole. As with so many aspects of this visit, what once was an appreciation became visceral. After all, I now had my own son and family, without whom work would be meaningless. I, too, had lost all will and ability to serve a treacherous ego.

Kathryn and I watched Robert's lecture in the barn that afternoon and toured the humble Alchemist's shack. Kathryn was careful to document our visit and I'm glad for the image of the two of us standing on either side of Robert in front of the shack.

I'm thankful for the image we took of the two of us sitting in the car when we arrived, sunlight illuminating our smiling faces. I took in the vignettes, an old, rusted merry-go-round, the careful architecture of a bonfire awaiting flame, the outdoor shower I'd used many times during my stay, and the farmhouse original to the site where I remembered my first encounter with a formidably sized Wolf Spider upon climbing into bed one night. That evening, Kathryn and I joined the current artists in residence for a typical Mildred's Lane feast, curated and prepared impeccably under the direction of artist Athena Kokoronis, who had been there during our stay. Her strategy was letting what was fresh and available meet planning somewhere in the middle. A skilled forager, she included freshly sauteed mushrooms in our meal. Long tables sat along the horizon on the hillside behind the main house. They were laid with white linens from Morgan's extensive vintage collection. As we ate, my memory wandered back to the night during our residency where I was tasked with collaborating on the evening meal. I'd recreated elements of the all-white-foods dinner I'd recently hosted at the Bell School. Back then, we all helped host the public for weekend lectures and events, just like the current cohort did that night. I remembered working alongside Athena at the kitchen sink, trimming asparagus and sipping from small glasses of Pernod balanced on a narrow shelf above the stove. That night, we finished our meal and rinsed our plates at an adhoc station near the spigot at the back of the house. We dropped our cloth napkins into a basket to be laundered for the next day. When it was fully dark, Kathryn and I hitched a ride down the long drive back to where we'd left the car. I felt full. I'd metabolized the present reality of this space and the characters that populated my memory of another time in my life. I absorbed it from my spiritually nomadic present. Now, I was ready to go home to Cameron and to my baby, ready to reconcile all of the pieces. It felt like being tired.

It was on the drive home that Kathryn made her simple but fateful request: "Will you help me go through my closet? Help me style my clothes?" She knew I'd designed costumes and worked as a stylist. She'd been with me one day in the city when I received unsolicited sartorial compliments from a stranger. It was, however, not in the ethos of those details that her request was cast. It was the long shadow of Mildred's Lane and the spirit of Alchemy that inspired her. The material world, clothing, was to meet spirit, in service of transformation, of becoming whole.

In the weeks that followed our trip, Kathryn and I set up a series of styling sessions. I intuitively reached for the many practices that I'd been using for years. I used the spiritual and embodied practices I was using to create visual art, namely: divination, meditation, psychometry, and shamanic practice. I created a magazine for her, a style guide. This magazine felt to me more like portraiture. It was collage that took the image of who she was, through this mix of intuited images, clothing images styled into renewed and empowered versions of who she was, material mantras and aspirations of where she was headed all materialized through the image of clothing.

All of the pieces I'd been juggling since leaving Maine--the tactics, impulses, and strategies for healing and rebuilding--began to take conscious shape. I could see the shadowy figure of what I would come to call holistic styling appear on the horizon, calling me to further work, to more practice. It was my work with Kathryn that brought light and cohesion to the practice struggling to emerge. It was an alchemy.

The space of everyday life is ubiquitous. It's the air we breathe and the waters we drink. Everyday life is invisible. It is the background. It is dark. The assumption then is that it is common, opaque, simple, and easy and that makes it deserving of disregard. That is a grave mistake. Everyday life is the deceptively humble alchemist's shack: the only place where magic is possible.

28. Identity Shopping

Living in Harlem in 2018 almost two years after leaving Maine, was a time of deep recollection. Sweeping up the bits of my life that remained discernible, that remained desirable. I didn't have directions, just some dismembered parts pulsating as if independently. I spent long days walking from park to park, starting at the northeastern tip of Morningside through to the northwestern tip of Central Park and that could be the day.

Who was I? I looked for myself in job descriptions. I looked for myself in other people, in motherhood. I looked for myself in my apartment. I looked in clothing.

It wasn't the first time I'd shopped for new shoes, but this time, the search was happening while I was searching for the way to unify all my languishing parts, to access some shred of agency. I needed the elusive pair that would end my desire for all other shoes. The pair to let me travel light, to maximize efficiency. I was rocking back and forth, looking for my chance to jump in. Each material experience was preparation.

I've always felt a pronounced allergy to any experience of excess. A visceral objection to material encumbrance. Part of this was undoubtedly my desire to leave the material world entirely, to become invisible, pure mind. On the other hand, I felt the nagging, consumerism-inspired anxiety created in the dissonance between the multiplicity of options and the dearth of satisfactions. I experienced things as a distraction. They pulled me in different directions and contributed to a kind of dissolution, leaving me fragmented and bereft of power.

I am aesthetically drawn to the ascetic. My fashion taste is in the ballpark of post-apocalyptic barbarian and Diane-Keaton-joined-a-cult. Black wool harem pants, a white linen t-shirt, and maybe some fingerless gloves. Denim work jeans and a thickly knit sweater. A shearling vest over a long animal print dress with motorcycle boots. Rob once described that ballpark as the "elegant retiree," this before the advent of so-called menocore (as in menopause, inspired by middle-aged icons ranging in style from Whoopi Goldberg to Miuccia Prada). "That's a wicked woman," a friend's child remarked upon seeing me in a long, black and ivory opera coat of my mother's with a two-dollar blue satin, Chinatown dragon hat.

This ideal shoe must serve a range of weather, support varied occasions, and function in different walking conditions. While all of these pose unique challenges, I'll wager that the topline to hem relationship presents the make-or-break situation, one with elaborately specific exigencies for each person. It's a moving target because these shoes must work with a variety of pants, skirts, and dresses. That relationship speaks to me like a metric of readiness, a metric of confidence, and of awareness. Like everything else, the proper ratio is never one size fits all, but I was looking for my sweet spot.

My memories of the incipient quest take me to grade school, where sneakers sufficed. Not to say that the type of sneaker was not a consideration, but once that part of the decision was made, it was truly the shoe for most of living. The narrow range of situational requirements in that time of life eases the task. I had a pair of pale blue, Converse high tops that lasted through quite a bit of fifth grade. At some point near the end of high school, I moved on to black low top Converse, which I revisited again fifteen years later in graduate school. A mistake I've now made too many times, alas, those shoes do not have arch support.

In graduate school, I committed to a pair of black, mid-calf, motorcycle boots from J.Crew. (At the time, I also wanted the sweater to end all sweaters, a tall order. I ended up with a gray, cocoon shaped cardigan, which Rob, with a special knack for sartorial nomenclature, coined my "Romulan" (an extraterrestrial of Star Trek fame) sweater. I don't think Romulans actually wore sweaters, but if you take a sidelong approach to imagination, you kind of get the idea.) I still have the boots, several soles later. Petey once ate through the buckled straps and I had those repaired, too. On the last trip to the cobbler, a strap was lost and they again face sole repair. So I've come to terms with my waning enthusiasm for them. I consider throwing them away, but I haven't been able to bring myself to do it. My perspective on their topline-to-hem relationship has changed over time (or maybe my body has changed), while they have stayed the same. A classic growing-apart.

The so-called ugly sneaker seems to fit the bill for many, but I'm not there. All I see is "trend" in flashing neon. I imagine commuters changing out of these kinds of sneakers once they get to work, a kind of reverse Mr. Rogers. The comfortable shoes get you where you're going, but the right pair is waiting for you when you get there. They're forever relegated as the means in a troubling ends-justify-the-means scenario.

Included in the list of contenders, sitting at the back of my closet: Birkenstock London, Dankso Maria, Clarks Wallabee, a pair of dusty-colored monochrome, Maison Martin Margiela high-top sneakers. A leopard bootie and perhaps surprisingly, a pair of Nike slides are clear front runners. I love my LL Bean winter boots, but the shearling lining makes them prohibitive most times of year. With all of these options, I still struggle to find the right pair on any given day.

In the middle of my search, some friends, Maura Brewer and Abigail Glaum-Lathbury, of the Rational Dress Society, were in New York City to offer a workshop at the Museum of Modern Art. I happened to be writing a post for a popular women's lifestyle blog and decided that they'd make a great interview for the blog's what-does-she-wear-in-a-week column. These artists for years wore little else but their ungendered monogarment, made famous in their Jumpsuit project. When I wrote topically and in the blog's signature style everything seemed to walk a line between parody and political critique of the very elements for which I was purporting enthusiasm. My voice in consideration of fashion was veering, as if compulsively, off the trodden path, despite my longing for the kind of security I thought meant fitting in.

It's of course not that the perspective of these women was irrelevant, the opposite in fact. However, their perspective was self-conscious of the lifestyle blogs' implicit principle that identity resides awfully close, or at the very least, is expressed by the ever-elusive personal style: ". . .my clothes weren't a distraction or a shield, but a mirror instead — a mirror held up to reflect me, just as I am." In another iteration: "I love being the colors girl." Sometimes the correspondence between identity and commodification is made explicit: ". . . people start to develop personal brands – and brands try to become more human." Albeit this certain genre of women's lifestyle blog has a liberal, enlightened, and self-determined affect: "When I find clothes that fit well, I feel more comfortable and confident . . . when someone looks at me now, I know they're seeing the version of me I chose. Not the only version I had access to." They duly take stock of the environment, sustainable manufacturing, avant-garde design, small business ownership, support-local, and support-women. Often items are thrifted, or a mix of high and low (which usually feels to me like a nod to a barely latent class issue.) Finally, they don't forget to keep at least one eye on all of the gazes (call me Man Repeller!) They deftly keep their blog-heads above intersectional waters, while still garnering tangible support from sponsors.

They weren't wrong. I, too, believe critical enthusiasm for self-styling has implications for identity and one's psychic life, although we are not what we wear. Believing that costuming oneself for daily life, as it were, is a worthy task, or at the least, an unavoidable one, it's therefore deserving of our full political engagement and even our informed consent. I followed the lifestyle blogs for their thoughtful musings on the subject. As one who has never fully given herself over to the monogarment (although I highly endorse it), I know (thank you Stacy London and Clinton Kelly) that what I wear reflects something to someone no matter how I might protest or repress. In a market driven culture, not-choosing and choosing are effectively the same. Just think of the billions of dollars in marketing aimed at making those choices for you, while chanting "freedom" in its various forms: free market! free will!

If the dichotomy is false between mind and body then surely, by extension, it is also false between mind, body, clothes, and everything else. Why else does a haircut or parting ways with an item of clothing have the capacity for causing pain like a phantom limb?

Realizing how much my voice was not aligned with the most popular style-blogs, I left my interview with Maura and Abigail parked in google drive only to revisit it upon reading two articles about finding identity through clothes. (There is a murky ontological area in respect to whether identity sits waiting to be discovered through our material choices or something to be created by them – but that point seems less of a concern so long as identity is won in time for cocktail hour.) The quest for distinction, for getting "to wear something that expresses how you feel as a person" allowing that you "never look exactly like someone else" starts to chafe. I was called back to learn from the wisdom of these artists.

One thought in particular from Maura on choosing clothing everyday became the gadfly's voice: "I wasn't getting a huge amount of creative satisfaction out of picking out my outfits every single day because I have other stuff that I do." It gives me pause to consider my life as a style. The world of "other stuff that I do" suddenly expands as it passes through the finite and myopic threshold of individuation. Her seemingly casual remark firmly prioritizes being over expression and marks that being as active, not image.

I finally decided on a new pair of shoes: dark brown, lace-up, classic Doc Martens. I know that, as yet another pair of shoes, they wouldn't have the capacity to end the chronic nature of consumer desire. I wanted to believe in the possibility of fulfilling my list of impossible requirements. What I discovered was a new kind of wager: my new boots could help me be the person I want to be by dressing like I am already her. They would help me support the things I wanted to do, rather than something I wanted to express. If it's wise to dress for the job you want, "like the boss" as it were, then I'd like to think of my best self as that boss. In my case, the boss is a world-wary, ascetic-loving, Inner-Worldly mystic living in the awareness of abundance. She doesn't think about shoes—she's moved on to doing other stuff.

29. House Hunting

After a three year search that spanned hundreds of miles, Cameron and I found a 1940s cape in an idyllic neighborhood with pedestrian pathways winding past old growth oaks, roads passable by only one car at a time, and hills where tiny gothic cottages are nestled tightly on former tent-sites. Despite how beautiful it is in this hilltop village, it would have been hard for me to see without first letting go of the expectations I had for what my life was going to look like. I had to let go of losing my beloved Bell School. To let go of my gardens, full of plants each with its own provenance and story. Rose of Sharon from my grandfather, irises from my father, lilies from Karen and Kassie. Just to name the tiniest few. Letting go of the narratives of the past makes way for the future. First in the mind. I would need to bring into awareness the truth of my relationship with the things around me, as they were, not as I wished they could be. Despite how far I'd come, and how deeply I believe that all work orbits process not product, I'm always somewhat surprised when I reach a new stumbling block. I find that the need for further surrender, for further healing merges when we are confronted with changes and new circumstances, with the perpetually renewed mystery that attends living. Things we thought were gone or healed seem to show up, tempting or taunting us to return to the past.

In December of 2019, I finally found and was moving into a little house just outside of the city. Home is deeply entangled with my sense of identity. The image of what that home should look like, the ideal, it changed for me over time. The images I had of a home in Boston, a cozy, but urban apartment in the North End, was so different from the modest and magical Bell School in the middle of nowhere. Both of these images were not like the pristine, new colonial on the hilltop in the suburbs of New York City. I was carrying stories from before I could remember, before my parents could remember, after all, we were all somewhere before we had the inkling that we might be able to choose. Each home for me became like consciousness itself, my lens. I was immersed, entangled in values, many of which were not my own. What would stepping outside, gaining a better vantage look like? How could I gain perspective on what it meant to be home? The search for these answers looked like touring countless houses over the span of three years. In that time, I was slowly accepting some portion of the death of who I was in the Bell School. This new house had to begin, first with that death, then, with a dream, a vision: inspiration.

My ideal was never the white picket fence, in fact that image always struck me with its terrifying placidity. The pristine uniformity felt compromising. My gut rebelled against submitting to the homogeneity, against being enclosed. I had unconsciously created a litmus test in each house we toured: Standing alone at the kitchen sink, I would look out the window and try to feel the quality of aloneness stirred by the house, the sink, the view. In one house I saw sprawling lawn after lawn, side by side in neat rectilinear shapes, punctuated by the usual plantings: Alberta spruce, azalea, blue star juniper, forsythia, boxwood. That ubiquitous purple rhododendron, a shade that appears lit by fluorescence. Little flags that purport to welcome with images of bees and butterflies, the message subverted by another set of little green and white flags: "beware pets and children, pesticide treated area." These cheery images of flora and fauna no longer truly welcomed by the lushly fertilized and pesticide treated lawns, perhaps the signs have become stand-ins for the creatures themselves. Bubbly plastic menageries branded "play," each within its own fence, little disposable empires for children who would soon outgrow them. Each day of the week a truck and trailer comes, deploying a crew armed with petro-chemicals, roaring engines, and toxic potions in order to affect peacefulness and create the illusion of control. Kitchen window after kitchen window, I would test the pit in my stomach, "Do you feel alive?" The sunnier days only seemed to exaggerate any dissonance, glare blighting the senses.

I looked further west. Old farmhouses nestled into hillsides, creating jaunty angles with crumbling stone walls marking a different time, a different space. Trees stood keeping the tempo between these histories, an accountability. The increasing distance from the city, from work, meant more time on the train. More time getting to the train. A car to get to the train. These rural spaces sometimes allowed a more humane equilibrium between plants, animals, and human designs and that felt like breathing room. Yet isolation persisted. There is no parallel morning coffee drinking with the neighbor in the building next door on the fourth floor. No "good morning" to Shirley as I pass by her resting spot on the third floor windowsill on my way to my apartment on the fifth floor. The teenager living with her mother, practicing her show tunes behind tie-dyed sheets serving as ad hoc curtains. Each apartment window, a portal into another life story.

Politics shifts from urban to rural areas as the shift from living intimately with others, shared playgrounds and stairwells, trains, buses, and bodegas. The occasional wayward Nike sport sock from someone else's family stowing away in my freshly dried sheets from the laundry room. Exploring these increasingly rural towns north, south, and west of New York City, I noticed gates popping up across driveways, and later, born as a retort, more signs: "We support our police." Flags stripped of red fly now, blue and darker blue. The little green and white Chemlawn signs shift their rhetoric slightly out here: "Yard Armour Tick Control." The further we drove the further the houses from one another and the more afraid we appear to become, the more militant.

I started referring to my kitchen-sink litmus test, silently in my head, as the "Revolutionary Road" test, after the 2008 movie about deadly suburban ennui. This test became a more important metric than the number of bedrooms or bathrooms, amount of closet space, or whether or not there was a garage. Were these towns made of bridges or moats? Did they embody luxury or excess? My gut always knew. Alone feels like the body. It feels like being whole. Loneliness, on the other hand, is disembodied, fragmented. Broken.

In the suburbs of New York City, you would be hard pressed to find another Bell School, and if you did, the price tag would look much different. In Maine, I spent no small amount of time purchasing and renovating rental properties. I tried, in vain, to recreate that anywhere within 100 miles of the city. The elaborate specificity of the material landscape was different. It was different enough to make replicating the dream I was still holding onto, impossible. I regularly drove to new cities, worked with new real estate agents from Kingston, New York to Philadelphia. I researched loan options. I ran the numbers in every possible permutation, trading in and out all of the pieces I could conceptualize as variable. It was a dead end. That dead end revealed to me the deep dread behind the failure: I did not believe my artwork would ever be enough. I was always looking for some other thing to support my practice. I realized that inspiration was actually quite advanced. I had a lifetime of mistaking the way I was drawn to the people and things in the world. The quality of that movement, that attraction, is not always the same. I never learned to listen. It was one of those navigation tools I didn't know I was missing. I often moved towards things and repeated patterns that moved me further from that glimmering seed of truth. What was I trying to return to? What was I trying to escape?

To some extent, I'm happy to run on autopilot, to know who I am without having to test every small act. It would be impossible to take account of every fluctuation in my material experience at all times. I imagine driving a car, I certainly react before bringing every movement into conscious awareness. I cling to cause and effect and so I tell myself stories because I fear repeating the pain of my past and I desire things for the future. I repeat familiar patterns because the alternative is being uncertain, is being deadly still, and that feels too vulnerable. This scaffolding allows me to move through the world. However, this movement is often at odds with presence. That malaise seeping into the day to day, seducing me with its promise of safety. Little bits of life here and there, chafing, until they accumulate like one smoked cigarette at time, suddenly demanding attention. Repression, addiction, cancer, divorce, forest fires, floods, pandemic.

Sometimes though, I've simply encountered something new. I left Boston for rural Maine. I began making quilts. I met Cameron and we fell in love. The man I loved and married, to whom I'd committed my life, betrayed me and my entire world collapsed.

It was in these times, for better or worse, that what I'd been doing to move through the world wasn't quite as effective, or, in some cases, no longer worked at all. The stories I'd been telling were no longer corroborated, no longer shared. The habits and patterns of behavior used to maintain certain relationships, or achieve some level of satisfaction in work, now reproduced an untenable status quo.

There are times I've been so lucky, and the exigency for change has come from a place of pure desire, from curiosity, from being present in the flow of my life, from listening to that little red handbag on the floor of my bosses office, listening to the sad, forgotten set pieces in that darkened theater warehouse. I heeded the warning of monotony dulling my body. This is the place inhabited by seekers, entrepreneurs, artists, and innovators. This is the space inhabited by humans because our humanity is nothing if not creative. Despite this, we suffer here in our own element, not understanding it is our true home. We move on instinct perhaps without support, beset by the errors of trial and error, and forgetting to show ourselves compassion.

Sometimes the whole world changes. Our air becomes unsafe to breathe, the water unsafe to drink, our bodies no longer belong to us, but to the state, and disease ravages our communities. These are the symptoms of our fragmentation too; they are the voices of our material experience calling us to our true home.

I couldn't understand my true home until the scaffolding I'd built was replaced with the intimacy of the mundane. I began to listen to the smallest things, lawn signs and fences, kitchen sinks and two-car garages, and it turned out they were the keys.

30. Unpacking

My parents land-line number in my cell phone was labeled "home" despite the many places I'd lived over the previous two decades. They moved from my childhood home the same month that Cameron, our now two-year-old son Lulu, and I were moving into our own house nearby. For forty years, my parents lived in the Tudor-style colonial that sat atop a hill at the end of the cul-de-sac. I helped them pack and sort their things. My mother and I piled the twelve person dining room table with rows of dishes, decorative ceramics, porcelain candlesticks, crystal vases, coffee mugs, cutting boards, table cloths, napkins, cheese knives, platters, a bowl full of lemons that my sister made out of clay in high school, and a small rectangular plastic container perfectly sized to fit packets of artificial sugars undoubtedly gleaned from restaurants. I was touching all the things that, while belonging to my parents, were part of the material landscape of my formative life. At the same time, I began opening the boxes I'd packed in Maine three years earlier, the ones I'd relegated to the purgatory of self-storage on the side of the highway.

Cameron and I packed my boxes that summer in Maine in a panic. We spent a couple of days in a now haunted Bell School, making decisions with no strategy. It smelled different there. It was dirty. Dust and *her* hair tumbled in the corners. There were traces and trails, a bowl of scribbled on papers left over from an apparent game night with friends, other lives being lived in my absence, turning me into shadow, into a ghost in my own house. Rob hosted people, with her, in my house. Little notes between the two of them. She addressed him by his childhood nickname, Robby, something I'd begun calling him in tender moments in the later years of our marriage, "Gabby," he'd respond, a gentle return of sentiment. I experienced these names as terms of endearment between us, and this co-opting stung with such acuteness. I wasn't being replaced, but somehow erased. Alternately, she'd refer to him in her notes by just his last name, like they were a couple of bros. That is something I'd never do and in that I found some satisfaction.

Packing belongings was trying to stem a mortal hemorrhage.

The poison in the house was a fog that descended, making the air inhospitable to the lungs, the colors dull to the eyes. I couldn't sleep inside. Cameron and I slept out on the deck. We had sex without a condom, an attempted antidote to everything decaying around us. The desire for a child was a thread unspooled in the time that long preceded this moment and that would persist steadfast into an otherwise opaque future.

They'd slept in my bed, that pine four poster bed from my childhood. That first time Rob washed the evidence from our sheets and when I returned home after their tryst, he came onto me in that same bed. I wondered if some drug, surreptitiously slipped into a drink had induced my oblivion, my inability to rightfully consent, instead of fresh sheets and my weekend out-of-state, would the violation be apparent? Would the violation and my attendant grief be more sanctioned? Instead it felt dark, like a truth hushed up, denied. Now, after everything had collapsed utterly and completely, there was no need to wash the sheets and it was clear from the state of things they understood this too. The flagrancy and the violence of it all were allowed the light of day, were socialized and given permission. My new reality remained dark, however. I was unable to have sex without flashbacks of the sexual encounters I had with Rob, unaware, and the sex that I had with him under the threat of his leaving me, not knowing the affair persisted even after his claims otherwise. I had flashbacks of the conversations with Nora while she was relentlessly texting with Rob, sharing musings and secrets. I was awash in emotional avoidance, intense dissociation, and plenty of nightmares. To this day, I cannot hear about them without numbness in my arms and legs, shortness of breath, and a racing heart. They conjure, in my body, fear for my life.

As I unpacked the boxes I'd not seen in all of those years, I wondered if I would ever truly be happy again. Even the happy moments were tarnished by a memory of the different happiness that existed before all of the violence. I felt like I was looking at a photo of myself, maybe the picture of Rob and I walking into our wedding reception arm in arm, smiling so large, so unselfconsciously. Or the time we were reunited on campus after a long semester break. I ran over to his dorm, Humphrey's. He met me at the door, eager, smiling ear to ear and fresh off the bus from DC. His hair had grown longer, but he was still wearing the same faded army jacket. When we finally embraced I could feel his body shake. We couldn't stop grinning, still somehow shy around each other. These images now grave in the shadow of what would come. If the whole story had been a movie I would have turned it off. The anticipatory grief and skepticism, a shadow that past trauma casts on future and present joy is not a pleasure for me, no matter how nostalgic it becomes.

I start to think of this shadow as my karma, the reiterations of the past on the present, the itchy compulsion to use the gun that appears in the first act. After all, my memory lays this gun, these stories, out in front of me, like in movies when the assassin unrolls weapons from a black cloth, laying them out like a buffet. It doesn't really occur to look elsewhere when these tools have been so neatly arranged and offered up for use. Accessibility and convenience are all the seduction needed, but moreover, what do we do with a memory that lingers like the remainder in an equation? I wanted to make sense of things by making them whole, by making them commensurate. A primal antipathy to uncertainty wells up inside. I'd rather perpetuate violence than leave something unsolved and as I look around, it seems I'm not alone in that. The only question, "Should I direct that violence inward or outward?"

As I began to rebuild a home, more than three years after leaving Maine, I listened to the stories, the hopes, and the attitudes that lingered in all of my things. I revived and restored damaged chairs and discarded certain artworks and dishes. I wondered at my impulses for preservation at the time I packed, and simultaneously mourned the loss of things that, for whatever reason, didn't make the cut during that fitful August weekend when I tried to scrape bits of my life from the ghost ship that once was my home.

I peeled away the Bangor Daily newspapers dated three years prior. Rob left them in the house for me to use when I returned to Maine to pack. I pictured him getting them from the recycling pile in his mother's laundry room, an unremarkable place where I'd spent much time and would never return. What was she thinking when she watched her son grab the papers? He also left a stack of boxes that once held various plumbing supplies that had been delivered to his father's warehouse. Unlike his mother, I imagine his father taking no notice. I'd wrapped fragile tea cups and art works with these supplies.

Now parts that had been numb and forgotten began the painful flush of feeling again. These were not necessarily parts I wanted to carry forward, but with no image to replace them, I needed them, like an armature, to hold things together. They were parts of the person I'd been in Maine and in my marriage. They were the person that renovated an old schoolhouse and wanted to live in the middle of the woods. The person content with a solitary art practice, sustained mostly by years of waiting tables. The person who'd fallen in love at eighteen years old over countless hours of intellectual debate and chain smoking on the brick-lined campus of our tiny liberal arts college. The person that used the mind to avoid, and even to negate, the body.

I resurrected the terrariums I buried alive. I'd packed them in the freshness of terror. I was so absent from my body it shook and went numb, rendering my limbs capable only of gross and general gestures. It broke my heart to take them from their sunlit home on the shelves that I'd commissioned a friend and artist, Orson, to build at the top of the stairs under the skylight. I'd painted them white, Benjamin Moore Mayonnaise actually, to match the rest of the trim in the house, slightly warming this space nestled coolly in the trees. I shrouded them whole in quilts I'd made, only to place them into darkened boxes that wouldn't be opened again until they were surely dead. I thought of these shriveled and rotting creatures, closed up in the dark, sitting lonely in a bleak, anonymous storage unit. Suddenly, without explanation, suffocated and betrayed by their caretaker. I wonder at how easy it is to be hard on myself for not having recovered from the pain of this wreck when the reverberations throughout my material existence remain so real. Why do I expect to heal faster than the simple material elements, ostensibly so much more amenable to the mandates of will that would have them fixed overnight? Perhaps this is the very crux: our healing is not independent of our material existence, but one and the same. I longed to be whole.

Time and time again, I was disappointed that I hadn't come further. Opening those boxes to discover such sadness and longing for the person I'd been, felt like a regression. It seemed that simply healing the wounds I'd been nursing, replacing them with scar tissue, was not sufficient. The things I was carrying with me, the objects, tools, and clothing of my daily experience, seemed to enter again through the very pathways of those scars, just opening everything up again. Like springtime rains rushing through time-worn beds year after year. I hadn't yet created new patterns, new paths and images. My present simply flows through the channels of my past. I was disheartened. I was impatient at the resurgence of grief.

I needed to accept my own metabolism, my own timetable. I had to move away from rational, linear thinking that I'd been using to navigate my life, to cope with pain into what was wholly uncharted territory for me: non-linear and embodied practices. I had to move from thinking itself to being. In part, this movement meant the need to accept my own death, even if that left only the darkness of unknown space. Sometimes darkness is the truth and no amount of wishful thinking can prop up the ghosts of our past to sufficiently animate our present.

If things stay packed, what happens to the deep parts of ourselves that emerge only if they reappear? The parts kindled, inspired, by the elaborate specificity, the irreproducible magic, of the material world? The small pink eraser shaped like a dolphin that somehow survived countless years and as many spaces. A bronze colored pencil sharpener shaped like a slot machine, complete with a tiny working lever to try your luck at matching three panels of spinning fruits. An old box of Yves St. Laurent cigarettes from Dubai, a gift, white with gold lettering pressed into the textured paper. Spools of brittle thread in jewel tones wound onto wooden spools that once belonged to my grandmother. Multiple small sculptures of nail clippers covered in peeling gold leaf. Scraps of paper listing the colors of cotton yardage for future quilting projects with character names, Plumm Lazlo, and Eroe - a name that persists in memory from a tombstone near the gravesite of my best friend who died in a car accident when we were fourteen, scribbled in its own, idiosyncratic column. Always some old fortunes from cookies with the ink worn to illegibility. Wooden folding rulers, a broken pink umbrella with a wooden horse-head handle and some tangled pieces of crab trap from summer vacations on Long Beach Island. The particular shape and color of the sadness that re-emerges when I hear *I'm Still Your Fag* and remember meeting Cameron all those years ago, or *Brothers on Hotel Bed* . . .

Those parts stay in the shadows. In a storage unit miles away or in the back of the closet. Outside of our conscious attention. They grow dark within until they erupt in disease, wildfires, tsunamis, and riots. Yet some would still deny these effects.

31. Transitions

Cameron and I were still trying to adjust to our new lives, struggling to make art, to make ends meet, with a baby and four dogs in our fifth floor Harlem walk-up when the news channels began intimating that the Coronavirus might not be just a problem in China. I decided to keep my plans to meet my high school friends, Monica, Lisa, and Lori, for dinner at a restaurant in the east village. Monica picked the place. She is the one who organizes those things and I always care more about the getting-together part and less about the what-I-might-eat part, so I ignored the pit in my stomach about this particular choice, a vegan place, Plant Food. The restaurant was the project of a guy named Matthew Kenney who grew up on the coast of Maine and hovered around the restaurant where I worked, Chase's Daily, in Belfast. He started a cooking school and a restaurant across the street and in his down time, he frequented Chase's.

I knew when he was coming in before I saw him, his cologne strong and unmistakable. He'd often come late on a Friday night, a kind of insider's time really. Everyone is pretty much an insider as a local in a small town, especially a small town that sees such an influx of seasonal out-of-towners, but there's also a special kind of inside when you work in the restaurant industry. I suspect even more so when you are the owner and chef of a quite successful, niche kind of place like Kenney and the owners of Chase's.

Kenney's slogan was "the future of food." I'll remember it for no other reason than the decent laugh Cameron, Rob, and I had when Rob remarked that, as a plumber, his business was also the future of food.

Matthew Kenney's Belfast projects shut down under some financial duress. At the same time, Rob had an affair with my friend. I hate to write her name, but I will. It is too difficult, from a practical standpoint, to tell you the rest of the story without it. Frankly, I hate to write Rob's name, too. Their names have become too distinct for things that have faded from actors into textures. There was a time though, when their names were quite and properly dense and antagonistic to my senses.

I worked with Nora at Chase's Daily. She was in her early twenties, about the same age as my relationship with Rob. "So you've heard?" she announced to a mutual friend, Anna, in the local food co-op the morning after my husband confessed to their sleeping in my bed while I was out of town. No, she hadn't heard. Anna had been picking up the morning copy of the Times for Chase's while I manned the counter that early summer morning. It had been too late to find shift coverage, so, despite having effectively learned my life had ended, I got up at 5:00 AM, got into my car, and drove the twenty-five miles to open the bakery counter. The vertiginous clashing of scale hit like a rollercoaster plunging downward on rickety old tracks. On the one hand, two decades of a love affair and marriage steeped in coming of age, spanning geography and psychogeography alike, condensed in the utter casual and nonsensical rendering to small town gossip through the myopic lens of the last six months in the life of a twenty-something just out of college. "Do you know what Nora was talking about?" Anna asked me, the back screen door of the restaurant creaking closed behind her as she returned from her errand. "No idea." I lied. Then I threw up in the bathroom.

I lost many things and I remember the big ones. I kept track as if they were juggling balls ripped from my hands, and then, adding insult to injury, caught up in a tornado. I catalogued the balls: rental properties, garden, job, art practice, home. How would I find them again after the storm had passed? I suppose that's why I attended to them so in my imagination. Don't get me wrong, I didn't think I'd actually survive all of this. It was reflex, like a drowning body gasping for air to the horror of lungs bursting with water. My gasping was not hope. I was all nerves and veins sputtering their last energies. Is this the "putting one's life back together" people talk about?

Rob and I owned multiple rental properties. I imagined those were what would keep us making art. They were great givers of time. I also got no small degree of satisfaction from renovating the old buildings into beautiful spaces.

A guy named Jared owned a gallery called Asymmetrick Arts on the coast in Rockland and he represented my work. Jared was storing several of my larger pieces in the basement where he also had a workshop for his framing business. A nine-foot, hand-pleated, hand-embroidered textile piece called Scattered Field and two huge canvases, collages with tiny pencil drawings, thousands of lines, layered and layered again. Maybe other things, I lost track. It all floated away, beyond my means to save.

Around the corner from Jared was the home of the brand new Center for Maine Contemporary Art, recently having moved from its long-standing home in Rockport to a prominent building commissioned from award-winning architect Toshiko Mori. Suzette McAvoy, the curator, championed my work. She exhibited it. She nominated it for awards. The Center for Maine Contemporary Art exhibits the work of Maine artists. A distinction that would no longer be mine.

I want to call my house my *beloved house*, and for now, you'll have to trust me that it was so. Rob and I gutted the 1870s one-room schoolhouse and transformed The Bell School into my dream home, studio, and acres of gardens. Its walls governed and manifested the life we'd been living for the last decade. It was the incarnation of the spirit that had us leave Boston and with the expectations for a sanctioned life we'd chosen to leave behind.

In the month leading up to my husband's second confession, that he continued his affair after his initial disclosure and subsequent duplicitous commitment to our marriage, glass shattered all around me. There was the front door of one of our rental properties. I got a call that it shattered. It seemed like bad luck, but certainly not existential or supernatural. A few days later, a call from another tenant, in a different house. The door shattered. More bad luck. Rob and I went to lunch at Chase's. We sat at one of the tables in the middle, it being summer tables were hard to come by, let alone one I would've preferred, a booth or something along the wall. Lunch that day didn't feel good. I don't remember what we talked about, if anything. In the summer the restaurant was so full, hundreds of people would wait, sometimes for over an hour, just to sit at a table during the three hour lunch service. If I happened to come in to eat during one of those times, usually when someone was visiting from out of town, it was all I could do to eat in that kind of crowd. That day, I was additionally tasked with the weight of a secret I didn't want to know that I knew. We left the restaurant that afternoon. The floor-to-ceiling plate glass window, the one facing the street, came crashing down after us. The world was falling apart.

"There's something wrong, " I told Rob. My grandmother had just died a month earlier. This glass was a message from her. "Three times is not an accident. It's not a coincidence." I insisted.

After the initial attempts to question my sanity (to call it gaslighting seems like one more element in the too-banal psychodrama to which I never thought I could succumb), Rob admitted the details and timelines of the continued affair. He walked in the door after work, shoved two bottles of wine at me hoping if I anesthetized myself sufficiently it would spare him any interaction. "I refuse to deal with your ego," would have to suffice for "goodbye" as he walked out of our relationship forever. I can't tell you if I ever saw him again, but if I did, I have no memory of it.

There is a story I heard once at a Vipassana silent retreat. It tells of four types of people and their relationship to light and darkness. The first type is in the light moving toward the light, the second are in the dark moving toward the light, the third are in the dark moving toward the dark, and finally, there are those in the dark that move further into the dark. Aunt Jeannette's decades-long marriage ended in a divorce catalyzed by my Uncle's relationship to another woman. I was young at the time, in high school I believe. I wasn't privy to details, but what I did know is that she never remarried. She drank. She smoked long after most. She was in a terrible car accident, rendering her already frail body even more precarious. She bought a new home. It burned down. My mom's best friend Janet got a call, her son hanged himself in some anonymous apartment thousands of miles away. Over the next months Janet disappeared in a cloud of anger and despair. That's it, just gone; she'd not been heard from since and it's been years. Surely hopelessness pervades the spiritual and emotional quality of our lives, but when it makes that transubstantiation into the functional landscape of the material future, stories get all mixed up.

"When people are unemployed for more than six months and knocked off their life path, yes, it's very harmful, but it takes a long time to die a death of despair. It's long term, over years, largely because of the social effects — the difficulty of having a stable home life and the loss of ties to your community. We might see it in the mortality figures in five years." I read this in The New York Times Magazine juxtaposed with the more immediate Coronavirus threat to human life and it stopped me in my tracks. In some way, I felt seen, taken seriously in the deleterious effects of my circumstances. Circumstances which are so unfortunately commonplace they seem to call into question the legitimacy of any grief or complaint. Somehow these metrics confirmed and tethered what I already knew: there is no body without spirit, no spirit without body.

"The future of food," I laughed to myself as I headed down the block to the 125th street subway station to meet my friends at Plant Food. The joke still seemed funny, only of course now I wasn't quite sharing it with anyone and I didn't know Rob anymore. A plumber without a proper name no longer holds so much interest for me as a protagonist in a joke. No longer situated in a booth on a Friday night at Chase's to make the witty observation, there'd really be no retelling of the joke that would keep any humor intact. All of that resided in me, alone, and I wasn't feeling in

217

good spirits about the whole thing. I wondered if I'd smell Matthew Kenney's cologne in this new restaurant. I wasn't ready for that. I was also feeling a bit under the weather. Did I have this Coronavirus? I kept testing the back of my throat for soreness. I found a seat on the subway and pressed my fingers against my sinuses.

The next morning I canceled my meetings for the rest of the week. As things unfolded, these meetings were not rescheduled. In fact, all of my work was put on hold as my fledgling business entered the metabolic hole of Coronavirus and political tumult. Communal crisis tripped on the heels of my personal crisis and my precariously placed feet were swept out from under me once again.

As the world around me closed down, anxiety rippled through any open channel. The news reports, social media, memos handed down from Cameron's employers, second and third hand stories about current and predicted closures, stay at home orders, and all the stories. Yes, old people were dying, but also "There's this guy, he was only in his forties, he had two young kids. Dead." Monica reported from her town in Connecticut.

In March my parents were to take regular care of Lulu, who was now two years old, so that I could finally give some undivided attention to working. Instead, I quarantined, having ridden the subway only to sit elbow to elbow at Plant Food. Coronavirus emerged for me not as a tidal wave, but as another ripple in what was an ongoing event. This rift that had opened up between myself and the material experiences of my life had happened back in Maine that summer three years before. I was already living in the uncertainty everyone around me seemed to just discover. However terrible the uncertainty, there was solace in feeling commensurate with the world around me for the first time in so long.

"Permanently Closed," is what it reads now under the Plant Food restaurant listing. One of countless Coronavirus casualties. In the absence of answers, outside the safety of dinner at Chase's Daily with Cameron and Rob, outside of my marriage to a plumber, the so-called future of food no longer has references. It's left to its own present reality, the simple ebb and flow of the material elements. My body, untethered for so long, is acutely aware of its full and precarious interdependence. There is no inside, no outside, no future, no past.

32. Kiln

At the time of my divorce, I dreamed of a kiln, burning away excess and debris, while alchemizing what remained into new things, stronger and more beautiful. Through darkened space I headed towards glowing light. People worked keeping the fire alive, the floor was concrete and the expanse of space seemingly limitless. The fire's glow could not illuminate the outer reaches of sight, perhaps that was because we were outside. Perhaps in the woods. This fire was contained in an anagama the size of a long hut. The anagama is an ancient type of single chamber pottery kiln. The single chamber, built in a sloping tunnel shape, means there is no separation between the pottery and the firebox. A continuous supply of firewood is thrown into the hot kiln and consumed very rapidly. Stoking occurs around the clock. The process produces fly ash. It produces volatile salts. Wood ash settles on the pieces during the firing, and the complex interaction between flame, ash, and the minerals of the clay body forms a natural ash glaze. This shows a great variation in color, texture, and thickness, ranging from smooth and glossy to rough and sharp.

Pieces closer to the firebox may receive heavy coats of ash, or even be immersed in embers, while others deeper in the kiln may only be softly touched by ash effects. The way pieces are placed near each other affects the flame path. The appearance of pieces

within localized zones of the kiln can vary as well, taking on simi-
larities based on region.

The potter must imagine the flame path as it rushes through
the kiln and use this sense to paint the pieces with fire.

The length of the firing may take anywhere from 48 hours to
12 or more days. The kiln takes the same amount of time to cool
down. Records of historic firings in large kilns shared by several
village potters describe several weeks of steady stoking per firing.

A lot can go wrong. Potters work for months, leaving their
pieces to wait, in precarious fragility, for the en masse, communal
firing. A bit of residual moisture or a slight aberrance in arrangement could create an explosion with reverberations throughout
the kiln. Months of work could be lost. Livelihood can depend on
a single firing.

I could see people tending this fire. They threw huge rolls of
cotton batting on top of the wood. I worked with textiles, not ceramics, so I could recognize this type of fuel. Although in my
work, it was generally used as insulation, layered between other
pieces of stitched fabric. Next, the people themselves started falling into the fire. I saw them go in, they were perhaps friends of
mine. And maybe they went in, insofar as they were my friends. I
imagined the flame path rushing the kiln, and could see who
would become beautiful and who would perish.

The Coronavirus rekindled the sentiment: *we are in a cruci-
ble.* The phrase replayed in my mind as I tried to metabolize the
space that used to derive meaning from being called days. Images

of dead bodies piled up in Central Park, police-sanctioned murders, mass protests day after day, and democratic elections irrevocably undermined for everyone to see. I closed my eyes and imagined these effects as waves on a lake, originating in the form and spirit of the smallest, most seemingly private gestures we perform, often absently, in our most intimate and mundane lives. I left Maine as the 2016 election season ramped up and Brexit passed. I obsessively listened to the news. Somehow the only thing that could calm me was the relative consonance of Brexit with my most private life.

I know people say that those who have experienced trauma often look to recreate the heightened state of their nervous system with which they are most familiar. Perhaps it's not so much that we love the familiar, but it's literally all we know. Just as Rob and I arrived all those years ago in Maine from Boston and continued to navigate our new glimmer of truth with our old tools, expectations, and ideas. It is the stuff of self-fulfilling prophecies. It strikes me as a kind of evidence of how truly difficult we find change, even above suffering.

I was doing my best to imagine the flame path, knowing that whatever the outcome, the potter must also tend to the vessels that emerge.

PART 3: The Monarch

The Monarch is an artist, a creator. When still a caterpillar, she chooses a safe place to spin a silk pad, like a button, and fastens her body to a leaf or a twig. She enters this pupa stage and after a period of time, she will suddenly straighten out her body splitting her skin, first at the back of her head. Over a period of a few more minutes, she sheds the rest of her skin revealing a green chrysalis. At first, the chrysalis is long, soft, and somewhat amorphous, but over a few hours it compacts into its distinct shape – an opaque, pale-green chrysalis with small golden dots near the bottom, and a gold-and-black rim around the dorsal side near the top.

Generally, the form "cocoon" that protects the chrysalis may be tough or soft, opaque or translucent, solid or meshlike, of various colors, or composed of multiple layers. Many moth caterpillars even shed hairs and incorporate them into the cocoon; this can make the cocoon irritating to the touch. Some larvae attach small twigs, fecal pellets or pieces of vegetation to the outside of their cocoon. Some spin their cocoon in a concealed location. In any case, the silk textile is a death shroud honoring her former self and a womb to nurture and form her future.

Although the sudden and rapid change from pupa to imago is often called metamorphosis, metamorphosis is really the ceaseless series of changes that she undergoes from egg to adult. The cells are the same, just rearranged, repurposed.

33. Mary

My grandmother gave me the pink and candy colored blanket folded in her cedar chest. The one she'd gotten from her grandmother. This gift felt like an ancestral recognition of magical things. As if my grandmother could see me, could see my work, and she placed it in a tradition of matrilineage. In 2014, I began contemplating this blanket by starting a new artwork. I found thirty yards of pale, dusty pink cotton sateen, forty-two inches wide. I overlaid the majority of it onto one backing layer of about eighteen feet. Over the next couple of years, I sat at my quilting frame and began, first embroidering and then hand-pleating fifty-three feet of cotton across the surface of the backing. This piece, Pink Background For Perimeter, was first installed at Perimeter Gallery in Belfast, Maine. It followed one wall, around a corner onto another. The candy-colored embroidery erupting in irregular forms as a hand might move over the course of years. Hiding, too, in the organic pleats. The sateen, sensitive to changes in light, reflective, mutable. A women's version of Alighiero e Boetti's eight by eighteen foot tapestry, The Thousand Longest Rivers of the World. From 1976 to 1982, the Italian artist created this critique of systems of classification. The project took him more than seven years researching the lengths of rivers. He was determined to arrive at a convincingly accurate hierarchy, despite the impossibility of absolute measurements. This work presents the findings in a straightforward list in descending order of length, giving no clue to the inexact and contradictory information underlying it. Like all of Boetti's tapestries, it was not made by him; he sent the design to craftswomen in Pakistan to embroider. Unlike Boetti's black and white, text-based, and outsourced masterpiece, mine was invisible, illegible. It was created as a background, to surround in organic gestures of hand. If you stand far enough from this piece to try to take it in, the details all disappear, either around a corner or too small for the eye to apprehend. If you stand close, you become lost inside. To photograph this work requires at least four shots, one wall, then another, close-ups of folded ebullitions of cotton and embroidery, an overall contextual shot for scale and to get the sense of it turning the corner of the room. None of these images entirely convincing. It is hard to find a space to exhibit the work. It doesn't fit into the architecture of our daily lives or even most galleries. This is women. This piece anchored so much of my artwork at the time, a collection I came to call Female Background. It was marked by meditative hand work across large expanses of space, aggregations of fabric layered in all directions and overwrought with spontaneous clusters of material, french knots, scraps of cotton, exposed batting, fabric revealing more fabric. Or paper, or bits of detritus. This work implicated the body. As a maker and as a viewer. It was a translation of abstract time into material and metabolic space. This translation alone was capable of changing all stories. It changed the epicenter of faith.

My grandmother, a generally unsentimental woman who loved the material world, especially food, oversized jewelry, and flamboyant clothing, felt no compulsion to keep things that outlived their purpose either functionally or aesthetically. Despite this, she kept a meticulously folded and never-used blanket in her cedar chest. The pink textile was woven through with a candy rainbow of other colors and the entire surface reflected light, changing its appearance with movement and in folds. Her grand-mother sent it to her from Avellino, Italy, the mountain town her father, Gaetano, left so many years ago, never to return. My grand-mother, Maria Josephina Clementina DeSimone Giangrande, was named after her grandmother. They were called Mary.

My grandmother sewed. She altered her clothes. She pos-sessed a deep respect for craft and hand work, always describing the provenance of a dish or pair of shoes and always reserving unique and unparalleled pride in anything that came from Italy. She loved the made world. She pursued a vision in clothing, in home, in food. Her face would light up when describing an outfit she wore 50 years prior. She held onto every material detail from her life, the shape of a collar, the texture of a coat, the length of a hemline. She remembered dollar amounts to the penny with un-canny precision. If ever she couldn't find something she wanted, she had it made. Her brother, a carpenter, built the furniture she imagined, the cabinetry. Her younger sister, my Aunt Josie, had a friend Amelia. Amelia was a master seamstress with a thick Italian accent, short mousy hair and oversized glasses. She would manifest many incarnations of my grandmother's imagination. (For my eighth grade dance, the culmination of junior high, I, too, found myself unable to find the dress I wanted, everything seemed to have a wayward bow or ruffle (we were only just out of the eight-ies!) I brought Amelia a piece of dark green iridescent taffeta and described a simple sleeveless, knee-length shift with a square collar. Grace Jones meets Cyndi Lauper, interpreted by Calvin Klien. It was perfect.)

My grandmother made sure the brick house that my grand-father built was to her specifications. They lived on the first floor of the triplex for most of my life and it is a place I visit often in my dreams to this day. One wall in her kitchen was tiled, floor to ceiling, in one inch square, orange ceramic from Italy. She was so proud of that wall, I think in some ways it might have been the most difficult part to leave behind when my grandparents moved to a townhouse requiring less maintenance in their older years. I still have one twelve-inch square sheet of those tiles tucked safely in a drawer until the right space appears for their use.

My grandmother wore low-cut blouses, always proud of her endowments. She was a heavy woman, and when she died at 95 years old, the very summer my life was collapsing, she stood barely 5 feet tall. She seemed much taller and anyone who knew her would probably be surprised at the number. She wore size 10 shoes, something we shared, although she always wore heels (I, standing considerably taller and thinner at 5' 9", did not), until of course she couldn't anymore. She wore satin and sequins and wispy angora. She loved black. Her naturally chestnut brown hair was a slightly faded, out-of-a-box vermillion for as long as knew her. Her jewelry was thick and gold, encrusted with diamonds. "Your mother is so conservative," she'd laugh. One day, somewhere in her seventies, she had my grandfather take photographs of her, apropos of nothing special, except an occasion to wear her black lace teddy lingerie under her mink coat with a pair of heels and some diamond jewelry. She printed the images and had them assembled into greeting cards.

She wasn't shy. She took what she wanted.

"Write it in my check," she responded to her boss, Ben Aarons, a lawyer in New York City, after he thanked her for her work. "I don't need your words. Thank you for a job means numbers on a check." One Christmas, as a child, she received only coal.

She described it with apparent good humor, although it was no joke. She talked for hours on the telephone with her cousin Lynn who lived in Pennsylvania, they'd stay up all night and my grandmother would tell me how they would laugh and how she could hear Lynn chain smoking all the while. She loved to throw parties and would do all the cooking. She would hire someone to serve and clean on the special night to ensure she would be able to enjoy herself alongside her guests. I think she remembered every meal she'd ever eaten and every restaurant she'd ever been to. She could recount for hours each plate of seafood that took Aunt Judy, her sister-in-law, weeks to prepare in advance of Christmas Eve. Aunt Judy would take time off work to do so, often spending over a thousand dollars on fish and seafood, enough to make sure she could send everyone, sometimes dozens of guests, home with a plate. My grandmother would relive the experience while sharing the leftovers. Fried shrimp, stuffed lobster tails, calamari, clams oreganata, bacalao salad . . . She loved television and diet soda. Her house smelled like strong black coffee and ammonia. Every object had a story, a proper place, and a reason for being. She read the newspaper, but she had no books.

I have no photographs of my grandmother displayed in my house, no photographs of anyone. I do have her things, though. I live with them and through them.

A small wooden buffet Uncle Billy built with a marble top my grandfather salvaged from a municipal building renovation in Newark.

A red lacquered bookcase in my son's room, designed and painted by my grandmother and built by her brother.

A red ceramic pitcher from Italy.

A large oval mirror over the mantel, framed in layers of rectangular metal, silver cut out in floral motifs to reveal brass underneath.

Cocktail glasses embellished with gold and white mushrooms.

A cherry dresser and bed that were in my mother's bedroom when she was five years old.

Two wool rugs she hooked herself. One, round and orange with a burst of cream and black streaks through the center. The other, a deep pink oval with blue and green floral motifs in regular arrangement.

My grandparents' bedroom furniture. A tall dresser and a long dresser with ornate swirling carvings.

An enormously heavy, pendant lantern hanging from a large brass chain. It's composed of so many thick chunks of colored glass, a mosaic globe.

A white, ceramic sculpture of a monkey, a foot tall, from France.

A large aqua, chinoiserie fruit bowl.

A printed dish towel, orange with colorful mushrooms.

A wooden Windsor chair she used to call her library chair.

A white velvet, tall-backed armchair.

A pink ceramic bowl with a matching lid decorated in a Florentine pattern. It once held powder she applied to her face.

A red and gold Florentine pepper mill and matching salt shaker.

An oversized red bath towel with tassels.

A fuchsia wool bedspread from India.

A pale yellow, cotton tablecloth embroidered with white flowers.

Pink bed sheets with colored embroidery, vignettes of a Chinese countryside.

A vegetable peeler.

A knife sharpener.

A white ceramic baking dish.

A vessel shaped like a golden pineapple, the lid handle, turquoise fronds.

A black and silver knit sweater with white mohair trim.

A silver knit sweater with white mohair shoulders.

An orange satin nightgown and its matching robe.

The long beige dress she wore at my parents' February wedding and its matching jacket with fur trimmed cuffs.

A beige lace sheath dress.

An ostrich handbag.

A white leather clutch with snakeskin.

A pink velvet jacket.

We see only through things. They show us invisible worlds.

34. Inheritance

Sunday afternoons my mother, father, younger sister, and I drove the seemingly interminable thirty minutes from our suburban home in Morristown to my grandmother's in urban Newark. Her home was a sanctuary for me in an otherwise poor city that provoked my vigilance. These regular visits promised a leisurely mid-afternoon meal, pasta, I hoped for rigatoni, and a large pot of tomato sauce with sausage, pork, and meatballs simmering on the stove.

My memories of the trip to her house flash in images from my particular vantage, a small person peering through the backseat window of the family car, my mother's boat the Chevrolet Caprice Classic - picture the old cop cars from the 80s, a huge blue steering wheel and bench seats. The drive seemed long as a kid. First, we had to get on the highway, a telltale sign of a longer journey. The seatbelt began to chafe and sitting upright and still taxed my childhood metabolism. I saw an intermediary world in the grasses and rocks on the side of the busy highway and this was distraction enough from my physical restlessness and characteristic imaginative retreat. What strange nowhere place this side-of-the-highway! I was sure things that managed to enter this threshold space were forever lost to the rest of the world and that I, too, could happily disappear there.

However, on this particular trip, we didn't take the family car. My father had just bought a shiny, gold-colored Acura Legend with beige leather interior. It was a cocoon of suburban warmth transporting us through that highway threshold space, transporting us between worlds. My father's new car was a midsize luxury sedan, which, although modest by luxury car standards was a far cry from its predecessor in our lives: the no-frills, manual-everything, compact Mercury Topaz that my father commuted with for years. The Topaz felt like a tin can, a kind of perviousness to the elements, less like a cocoon, more like a windbreaker. The Acura was no Mercedes, with its almost-peace-sign bauble sitting atop the hood. It was certainly not the glamorous Jaguar marked with the small sculpture of the leaping animal, curves mimicked in the inimitable shape of the car itself. Certainly the rich kids were picked up and dropped off in cars like those. The Acura had no icons or animals announcing itself. But for me, it ever so slightly changed the character of the security I'd always felt growing up. It added a hint of glamor, of luxury. Was it possible for such embellishments to create a feeling of *more safe*?

"Don't slam the doors!" my father would warn, even preemptively scold, guarding his new possession. I didn't have to, they had a way of heavily falling into place, effortless and sealed against the world, precise, firm. Inside, swirling walnut wood lined the doors and the console. "It's really wood?!" I asked my father, incredulous. It had a sunroof. The sound coming through the speakers was louder and clearer than the thin, static trimmed trails that, by comparison, came through any of the radios or boomboxes in the house. It was the first time I'd even considered that something other than clothes or cars might be branded, *Bose,* I knew that remembering the name might be a kind of cultural capital and filed it in my memory.

On this Sunday, we exited the highway and crossed the portal into Newark. The light, the sound, and the landscape changed from green to gray, from soft to hard. People, too, were part of this elemental shift. At the first stoplight, men pressed in on the car, washing the windshield or pushing bouquets of flowers towards the window. Sometimes they would just ask for money, skipping the performance of exchange. This re-entry to the world breaking my highway reverie; I'd watch from the backseat, edging away from the windows.

As my father navigated the city, I still kept watch from the backseat, but not from the vantage of imagination, instead, I was on alert. It couldn't have been more than a couple of miles from the highway exit to my grandparents' house on North 12th Street. In that time, we passed a corner lined with fantastical dresses for sale, all vibrant colors of pink, yellow, red, and orange. Sequins and polyester satin catching even the grayest light. These colors struggled to breathe life against the backdrop of this busy, treeless intersection. The disparity between their aspiration and the desolation of this landscape, the din of cars puffing exhaust, was just too great for them to be credible. The dresses seemed, instead of objects of hope, like objects of desperation, straying too far from the truth of this place to gain traction, to pull from the reality into the vision of something else. As if hope must only be measured in small, humble increments.

Then there were the chain link fences, often woven through with plastic, black or green and white stripes. These fences confused me, simultaneously aggressive and permeable. Were they offensive or defensive? I didn't know, however either option seemed to suggest there was something here to fear.

Several houses were painted in a particular scheme I'd never seen outside of the city, the top half dark green and the bottom white. I can't explain why this particular combination disturbed me so much. It felt foreboding. Gloomy, like clouds passing overhead and lingering on an otherwise sunny day.

Packs of abandoned and now wild dogs roved. I had such deep love for animals, maybe especially dogs, and seeing them skinny, dull, and hunting struck both fear and despair into my child heart. Above all else, this was evidence that the world was hostile.

Finally we pulled into the off-street parking spot framed by a tall, brick, planter my grandfather built. This long planter formed the fourth wall of a small courtyard. We would arrive always through this yard and through the backdoor, into the small, blue-tiled laundry room that adjoined the kitchen. Immediately the smells of food, olive oil and tomato, meatballs frying, would greet me, sweet reward for the journey.

This Sunday, we all sat together eating and talking, as we always did, when suddenly, my grandfather leapt from his seat. He was like an animal alerted to a disturbance beyond the sensory purview of the rest of us. He bolted through the front door, leaving it open in his wake.

The rest of us startled, somewhat confused, but as hurriedly as possible, got up from our chairs and followed him. I just caught sight of him running after a car, yelling. He had chased would-be car thieves from the new Acura. They'd just managed to *punch a hole* under the lock. Those words, *punch a hole*, stays in my mind because it suggests a mechanics that has always taken a moment for my imagination to conjure. It felt like a turn of phrase specific to these kinds of incidents, another kind of culture capital: to *punch a hole* under a lock. Noted. My mother, sister, and grandparents returned shortly to the kitchen, apparently nonplussed, while my father and I stayed, sitting on the wide brick steps for a while.

I needed to stay outside, sitting on the stoop, because nothing felt normal. There could be no simple return to the kitchen table. I needed this physical space, outside, nowhere, to process what had happened and that space wasn't the inside of a warm house, full of delicious food.

This attempted robbery felt like an attack on my father, on his story, what little I knew of it. My face flushed as rage surged, before I could account for it. What was worse, was the growing knot, a strange and incomprehensible sense of betrayal. After all, if theft was born of poverty, didn't they know that my father was poor? In this moment, this unexpected mix of emotions revealed a precarious place in between worlds. This precarious place between rich and poor, safe and unsafe, this was the unreal threshold where I lived. Perhaps that hell strip along the highway was not as much fantasy as an image that made sense of the territory to which I felt I belonged, when the material circumstances of my life were not capturing the truth. The story of our things was not available to the eye alone.

I couldn't understand at the time that these visits to Newark were travels back in time and class, prodigal returns whose metabolism hadn't been all sorted out. Driving into Newark wasn't disconcerting because it was other, it was so because it was darkly familiar: desperate, worn out, lonely, pressing on windshields. It was the still present seed of striving. I was, in fear and urgency, yes, but also in gentle hopes and unflagging curiosity, peering into places that I didn't belong. More than that, my desire for any of the fully formed spaces I experienced was equivocal. I certainly had no fetish for squalor, (which was not the case for many of my suburban punk rock friends with penchants for art and drugs), but nor did I envy fancy cars.

I was quite aware, at a young age, of a topography of *too expensive*. This included certain toys, like one-to-many Breyer plastic horses and all manner of Barbie accouterments, but naturally progressed to clothing, cars, and colleges. Many of my classmates wore designer labels, the little Polo figure prominent on their crisp, pale yellow, button downs, or the Guess triangle signaling on a denim back pocket. I understood these things were not for me. I would request a particular t-shirt and my mother would get one for me, only it wasn't the one I'd asked for; there was a pocket on the front and some off-brand insignia embroidered on it, yet she'd insist it was *just like* the one I'd requested. Collections of similar instances expanded for me the territory of alienation, both from my parents (could they really not see the difference, or were they deeply indifferent?) and from my classmates. In high school, I was happy living in Hanes men's crew neck undershirts from a plastic packaged three pack at the drugstore. *Too expensive* was partly an expression of economics, of what my parents' income would permit, but it was also an expression of ethical disavowal. Although I don't think my parents used these words, brand name items were deemed shallow and excessive.

It is not that my parents didn't love beautiful things, solid wood furniture, wool oriental rugs, silk ties and blouses, wool three-piece suits, because that they very much did and invested in such for themselves and for our home. It was the puffed up space between brands and materiality that chafed. That airy pocket of dissonance was dishonest, narcissistic. The things in our house somehow seemed tethered to the narrative infrastructure of our lives: things were serious, perhaps even grave. Attention was paid to the way things were made and the materials used. Perhaps they, too, shared my sadness of *looking in*, and they solved it with their particular material strategy. They held onto their identity, their dignity, in independent choices through eclectic inspirations. They could somehow *solve* that threshold of alienation by connecting to the material things around them. Travel and art. They curated a vision for their lives in a creative space that I could not yet fully see. I hadn't developed my own lexicon.

I imagined that if the thieves had known my father's story, they would have recognized a shared vantage, a mutual *looking in*. It would change their inclination to take the car because my father would no longer be other, no longer a site to take *from*, but instead a site to be *with*.

My father grew up in a house just twenty-five feet wide and not much longer, with his young mother, Anne, his older siblings Arthur and Kate, and his grandparents, Rosolino and Rosa DePeri (his youngest sister, also Anne, would be born seventeen years after my father). Rosalino had come from Sicily to work as a tenant farmer in Louisiana a short decade after the lynching of eleven Italian Americans in New Orleans. Life in Louisiana falling somewhat short of a so-called dream, they planned a return to Sicily when a layover to visit Rosolino's sister brought them to a section of Garfield, New Jersey known as "Guinea Heights." Home to mostly poor Italian immigrants, many from Rosolino's hometown of Marineo, Garfield was only a handful of miles from factory work and New York City.

It remains a mystery how in 1922, this couple would come to adopt Anne. Anne, born Mary to a family of seven children, proved one too many upon her mother's untimely postpartum death. Anne grew tall, lanky, somehow both languid and statuesque, her Austro-Hungarian heritage idiosyncratic against her adoptive family who appeared sturdier, shorter, earthier, darker. Anne would give birth to Arthur at just sixteen years old. Her trajectory became one of scraping together a living doing what she could, mostly cutting and styling people's hair out of her home.

My father was born on a Sunday in 1945, Mother's Day. On that very day, his father left for California, not to return for over three years.

"My father's coming home, my father's coming home!" I'm not sure how he knew that his father was returning, but on that day, he rode his tricycle up and down the street singing. My father shared this memory, somberly, one night as he sat with me in the dark before I fell asleep, as was our tradition throughout my childhood. This is the only memory my father ever shared with me about his father, one of his hope before it was destroyed by the reality.

As it turns out, his absence had been a blessing, a brief reprieve. When he returned, he wreaked a reign of terror and trauma destined to endure multiple lifetimes and span multiple lives. I only hear of these things third-hand, bits and fragments from cousins who know more than I. Sometimes my mother knows things, although she says my father does not share memories with her either, even when pressed. "Your grandfather Arthur died when he was forty-five. Your father was only seventeen at the time you know. And do you know what he told me? He said he was *relieved*. Can you imagine that?" My mother recounted the exchange. It was meant as an illustration of my grandfather's character and as an indication and indictment of the abuse. It was also meant to describe my father's trauma.

Perhaps my father was able to live in that relief enough to move forward, if not fully beyond. He reflected instead on his mother and teared up as he thought about her who, still a child herself, read to his older brother. "Why did she read him Shakespeare?"

There is a small black and white photo of my grandmother framed in silver, which sat for years in my parents' house. She is standing outside with her Sicilian parents. She is tall, 5' 10", and long-limbed. Her bony elbows protrude from under short sleeves. I know this because when I was in high school, I stared at the photo for hours, drawing her. The shadow of her hat over the delicate features of her face, the way that shadow played across the patterns and folds of her printed dress. She smiles and squints in the glare of a sunny day, her parents stand only to her shoulders, disappearing to my memory. I don't even know their names. She never told me stories, so in high school, I spent time trying to draw her from photographs, to trace a resemblance, a family narrative in image if not in word. I told her about the project, although I have no memory of her response. These drawings always left off somewhere in the middle, none of them finished. I never knew quite how to resolve her story. She always seemed just floating in a space to which she didn't quite belong.

Perhaps my father was chasing the same invisible space I abandoned in those portraits. The space where stories disappear, where if you act wisely, you can replace memory with beauty. Growing up, I never saw any photographs of my father's father. My grandmother never told family stories, she never told me stories at all, but, as a single, poor, teen mother she did pick up Shakespeare and read it to her son. That was a story my father chose to tell me.

My father joined the air force and was able to attend law school on the GI bill. "I wanted to be around smart people," he told me when I was quite young, as he sat with me while I fell asleep. Part of our nightly routine also included reading. Night after night he read: Little Women, The Adventures of Sherlock Holmes, White Fang, Uncle Tom's Cabin, Robinson Crusoe, The Adventures of Tom Sawyer, and countless others. When I went to college years later at a school that prized primary texts over text-books, I barely needed to buy any books because my father had them all: John Locke, Adam Smith, Hegel, Kant, Heidegger, Plato, Aristotle. This education was part of the strategy for *becoming*. It was part of my parents' curated life. It would be perhaps easy to mistake their subtle craft for simple immigrant and class striving. While these books were aspirations to a certain kind of culture and class, white and wealthy, they also aimed at honing the imagination towards something just beyond that culture. It was creative work. My father seemed to approach these books and beautiful things as lenses, as clues more than ends. They were liberating. Not only because upward mobility meant increased opportunities, but also because my father is capable of luxury. He can experience both emotion and presence in the space of food, art, literature, and music. This renders the material world a place of catharsis and sublimation. A spiritual place.

When I was just an infant, my parents wanted to buy a little house on Lincoln Street in Verona, New Jersey. They needed to borrow money for the down payment. They thought first to ask my mother's parents. Although not affluent, my mother's parents had that money to spare. Yet, they refused the loan. That grand-mother, Mary, cultivated as a virtue the kind of extreme independence often born of trauma. She behaved as if she wanted to prepare her children for hardship by creating it, often enacting scenarios, like this one, that would fulfill the prophecy of her conviction: life is hard. It is through the contrast between my mother and father that I can see my father more clearly.

Anne, however, to whom that money was meaningful, made them the loan.

"Poor people can't afford sentiment," my father mused as I recounted a conversation with my grandmother Mary. She told the story of shopping with her father for her mother's casket. He balked at the prices: "I don't care what it looks like," he joked. "I'm not going to dig her up!" My grandmother laughed as she reminisced. At the time, I, too, adopted the spirit in which the story was delivered. It seemed funny and clever, wise even. I was taken aback at my father's different perspective, and as was usual, I felt resonance with my father's insight: the emotions we experience through the material world, their extension into our psychic space, are no small part of truth. Although my father was also poor, it was sentiment that he pointed to as an attribute, maybe even a foothold, to another place. *If only there was enough money, feelings wouldn't be so hard to bear.* Affluence is *more safe.* Maybe we could reorder the events: Perhaps if we could feel the feelings, wealth would follow.

Nothing remains from my father's household growing up. Everything was used up, worn out, thrown out. There's no fifty-year-old waffle irons and tablecloths still in their original packaging, as in my mother's family. There was a hard realism to my mother's family, an appreciation of beautiful things as bulwarks against fear and loss. There was great attention paid to endless preservation, an obsessive cleanliness, plastic covers on white upholstered couches, and elaborate rules of engagement for interacting with household items. Particular ways one must touch things and sit to avoid undue wear and tear. This ethic was waged at the cost of other things.

These material relationships marked their politics as well. Each woman passing the ethics of these relationships to her children. My mother and her brother, conservative. My father and his three siblings, more progressive. Staying the same on the one hand, evolving on the other.

When I was about seven years old, my father caught sight of me walking down the carpeted hallway of our house wearing socks with holes in the heels. "Take them off and throw them out immediately," he commanded. I could only just glimpse the traces of poverty pressing down in those moments. A repudiation of countless painful memories. He scolded me harshly when I finished doing the dishes leaving a solitary unclean spoon: "Life happens in the margins. No one cares if you do 98%, only if you do 102%." He told me stories about athletes who practiced for hours even after practice had officially ended. Transformation could be achieved as simply as a pair of new socks, by not only drying that last spoon and returning it to its drawer, but then scouring the sink. However, these material details must be attended with vigilance.

My father and I played catch in the backyard and basketball in the driveway. He also introduced me to yoga and to meditation. He sought out dance lessons, piano lessons, horseback riding lessons, art museums, Michelen rated restaurants, ballet in New York City, opera in Rome, hikes in the woods along the Delaware Water Gap. He never failed to point out the most insignificant experience of beauty, whether the Bach playing in the car on the way to nursery school, a flower in the garden, or a small ceramic object in the house. He and my mother fought, sometimes violently. She was protecting the house and its contents from the innate destructiveness of my childhood, and he wanted to let me touch and play with the fragile objects under her watch. A chip in the lid of a small, blue enameled brass bowl barely keeps the secret of one such episode.

He taught me dissent. I called him from college when a fellow student explained to me the countless ways in which women were inferior to men and had a different role to play in society; he used a king and queen metaphor at some point. "The mother isn't going to help a child with math homework," he predicted. "And don't give me any of that Marie Curie shit," he argued for the historical evidence of men's intellectual supremacy, and warned me against using what was surely an anomalous case. I knew to call my father because I knew he would, with the sharp viciousness of elegant rhetoric, triumph with aplomb. He would both support and arm me against these attacks. He described the systemic roots of sexism and racism, rendering this classmate small and impotent. "This perspicacity, this incisive wit would keep me safe," I processed the experience, one of many with my father.

Unfortunately, it wasn't wit alone that protected me, it was the will to use it to protect what he most cared for, and that I took so deeply for granted that I didn't notice its absence in a partner until it was too late.

That Sunday at my grandparents' house, we sat on the front steps and looked at his damaged car. Managing not to cry was a familiar contraction, a retreat of everything in my body to someplace as far inside as possible, securing a hard knot, impervious.

"It's just a thing," my father comforted. He was truly equanimous, unfazed. His body was large and calm, unhurried, languid
and statuesque like Anne. He looked out through his glasses at the
empty, now quiet street in front of us. Perhaps we both reflected
on his life in whatever ways we had access to at the time. If he felt
a fraction of the stories that seemed to well up within me, he didn't
betray it. Or perhaps he did, passing on the deep lesson that we
are not our things, nor are we subject to them. We collaborate
with them to transform our worlds. He was capable of giving rise
to endless expression, nothing could truly be taken. Each thing
was full of potential, simply waiting for vision.

Beauty could transform, could change the character of the
past, could digest and then birth a new truth. This would be a
truth liberated from all the noise of personal stories we were
handed before we could chart our own destiny. Stacks of old photos framed in someone else's imagination, but co-opted images,
indiscriminately, none-the-less. The key to resurrection would be
twofold: creating our own beauty and accepting the unknown.

Several years after the incident at my grandparents' house, my
father's Acura was stolen out of a parking lot in Morristown. Lines
had blurred over time, the city and the suburbs. I drove now,
rarely occupying that place of back seat reverie. The Acura was no
longer new and I was no longer new to the world it contained.
The dissonance was dissolving. This time, the loss of the car was
unremarkable.

35. Desk

I wish I had the perfect desk at which to sit and try to tell you about my relationship to God. There's so much setting the scene that has to be done, or in this case, sitting at my monstrously heavy, white (-ish) Pottery Barn desk, a remnant of my former life, so much that has to be undone. Like dimming the lights or even lighting a candle for a date, "slipping into something a bit more comfortable," as it were. We're so familiar with these gestures and routines, but when you stop to think about it, how far reaching the implications! How much harder would we have to work for those ineffable moments if we didn't engage our surroundings, extend ourselves into that thick material ether we navigate daily? Sometimes stubbing a toe or bumping a shin. Other times, moving through our lives as fluidly as full-extension, soft-close drawers, as luxuriously as curved shower rods. I'm not saying for everyone whatever this scene is must be the same, in fact, in many cases the hard work is accepting that what really turns us on, or, the voice of God, is not at all what we were told and sold it would be. Sometimes we can't quite evict the long-stemmed, red roses or a booming, male baritone from our imagination. That is our impoverished life. Meanwhile, all this furniture populates our lives! Always impediments, or, alternatively, boons to some scene that plays out whether or not we're fully situated in the director's seat.

To tell you about God, I want a room that is a bit darker than the one I have. I can't seem to find the easy way to tell you, to broach certain topics, when my body isn't oriented to the earth correctly. I couldn't map it out for you, probably because as we live and breathe, it's a moving target, but I know it when I feel it. All too often I sit to write and the energy is diverted, like running into some unexpected road construction on the drive home, maybe even right outside my house. This *diversion* feels like restless legs, or like "Did I leave the kettle on the stove?" Maybe the temperature is wrong or the chair is positioned at odds with the latitude and longitude. Which desk could be my companion in this, could possibly be up to the task? Maybe it's not even a desk at all.

Today, though, I sit at this old, Pottery Barn beast. Not truly old for furniture, only about fifteen years, but old in the life of fashionable things made from fiber board instead of wood and easily showing the evidence of time. It's huge, half of it for writing and then another entire desk, attached, for sewing. The tops are propped up by filing cabinets filled with sketchbooks and collages, records of art exhibitions long past, an old copy of my graduate thesis. These traces of an art practice have no trouble sharing space with folders marked "property taxes," "health 2017", "dog vet records", "car", and "insurance." There are stacks of pamphlets telling me how to insert batteries into various appliances or what kind of water I should and should not pour into my iron. I have never once turned to this information, but am afraid of throwing it out. Perhaps not because I'll need it, but because if I do need it, I will be the kind of irresponsible person that can't keep control of things as simple as paper brochures. This piece of furniture has no trouble holding all of this at once. I tried to make separate categories. I marked flimsy manilla folders with bold Sharpie ink. I often reuse the folders, turning them around or scribbling out one title and replacing it with another. I try to keep things straight, so that I'll always know my concessions from my cares. Discernment lies in these arrangements.

My desk is a concession, and even still, my desire to write persists. I want to find a way to tell you about sitting at the front door of the house I grew up in on Jardine Court in Morristown, New Jersey, the five bedroom, Tudor-style colonial at the top of the hill. My mother urging me to go out and play with the kids I watched running around down the street. I felt my entire body stiffen, a hard "no." Yet, she persisted, insisting. I was more comfortable watching, perhaps a bit lonely, but more just alone. "Yes" I wanted to be behind that glass in the shadow of the porch roof. I didn't want to run around with the other kids. The foyer was dark, the sun never really penetrated the porch or through the door. The floor was tiled with gray and brown glossy ceramic, patterned with flowers and flourishing loops, like garlands. The tiles were always cold. The house was always cold.

I want to sit in that dark now, not at this stained white desk. I can still imagine the pictures in the glossy Pottery Barn catalog that seduced me all those years ago. I think the desk was part of a collection named Bedford, so puritanical - how aspirational for a working piece of furniture! I wanted to buy that kind of life where my work was bright and orderly, somehow intensely productive, but carefree as a trust fund from Westchester County. This desk held a false promise of presence in work, a lightness of being. As soon as I ordered the desk, the surface began to mar. The glossy white promise gave way to a rough, gray, papery substance just underneath. Any drop of coffee would stain, almost immediately, and any blight on the surface would suck in moisture and bubble up. It scratched easily, cleaned poorly, and very quickly lost the semblance of that happy-work it promised. It revealed itself as an imposter once used.

I have a desk that's better, but I've never actually used it as a desk. My friend Lisa found it when we were both living in Maine. She noticed the listing in a little paper booklet, a statewide publication of classified advertisements considered with some reverence in the state. Uncle Henry's, as it's called, sold for $4, an alchemist's guide for trash to treasure. This particular desk was solid oak and wide, like from a school administrative office a long time ago. It came in parts, which always fit together a bit awkwardly. In the manic frenzy of my exodus from the state, I ended up with just the top. When, after several layovers, I finally got it up the five flights of stairs to my Harlem apartment, I purchased hairpin legs to replace the heavy oak drawers that used to support it. The apartment was so small, the oak slab soon became piled with old plastic takeout containers holding paint brushes and tubes of acrylic paint, a sewing machine, and clothing in some stage of the laundry cycle. Underneath, baskets filled with shoes, extra foot pedals and power cords for sewing machines, and old magazines featuring my artwork indiscriminately collected dust.

In addition to finding this desk, Lisa protects me from the simple things I'm afraid to do like talking to strangers and getting on buses. She spells out directions, writes them down on a scrap of paper and puts it in my pocket, loads them in my phone in multiple ways and places. She never asks me to *get over* anything.

Lisa and I grew up together in New Jersey. When we were in junior high, we would ride our bikes through trails in the woods after school. She never betrayed fatigue at my chronic and obsessive interrogation: "Are my tires getting flat?" I had this image of my bicycle just falling apart as I rode, half-panicked, over gravel and dirt. This every day. She tacitly acquiesced to keeping watch over me, letting me know if the wheels were coming off. All the while making me laugh.

Lisa's mother remarried when we first started high school. She met a man with two sons, who were our age. His wife had cancer and he'd been recently widowed. Lisa would be moving to the neighboring town. I was afraid we'd grow apart if she was that much farther away and especially if she had to attend another school. Thankfully, her mother taught Spanish at Morristown High, where we attended, and that meant she got to choose. Her new town was affluent and mostly, if not all, white, so while our high school was observing Martin Luther King Day, Chatham High was in session. We both understood that was a bad sign, but took that day in January to tour their school. I went along for moral support. I remember little of the tour except for our shared glances to communicate so many hard no's. They knew we didn't belong as much as we did. Several awkward remarks about the holiday were directed our way. "So soon!" One teacher openly shared her judgment about the speed with which Lisa's mother was marrying this recently widowed man. This provoked another knowing glance between the two of us, "this woman is terrible."

We survived Tiffany's death together.

Lisa went to college in Virginia while I was in Maryland. She would visit and we'd share my twin bed, head to foot. Once she brought the guy she was dating. Still we shared the bed. We laughed quietly while he slept on the floor. I didn't have a car and Lisa picked me up at the start of holidays and summer breaks so we could head back to New Jersey together. On one of these trips, her teal Ford Bronco overheated, smoke rising from the hood. We fed it bottles of Evian before the gas station worker figured out what we were doing and offered us the hose. I don't remember how we got home but was equally impressed and not surprised that Lisa knew what to do, like the time she ran straight into an angry bees' nest to save a small child from its swarming frenzy.

A decade later, we sat in her parents' dark basement, back in Chatham. We listened to song after song and she made the playlist for my wedding, burning everything onto CDs. Only later to have the DJ go rogue replacing Radiohead with Gloria Estafan, closing the whole affair with *Another One Bites The Dust*. "This is my real life right now," I remarked aloud from the bar with some appreciation for the tacky absurdity. At least Lisa and I agreed on what songs were for love.

I took the oak desktop when I left Maine. Lisa had just moved to another part of the state. We'd shuffled all our stuff around and I ended up with it. She helped me pack the trailer that had been detached from a large truck and dropped heavily on the gravel drive of the Bell School. The desktop was too beautiful and heavy to leave. Its vintage, its solidity, harkened back to someplace safer, to a place where things were as they seemed. It was scratched, but only to reveal more of the same, heavy, grained wood. It supported my fantasy, one where I was a detective or private investigator, perhaps sometime in the early 70's. That seemed like it might be an appropriate heyday for the desk, and being just before my birth, it was easy to romanticize, having had no real acquaintance with the time period. In this scenario, my office would have a heavy wooden door, the privacy glass window would be marked with the name of my agency (I never quite figured out what that would be) in a golden stencil, outlined in black. Some font that doesn't even exist anymore because if it did, it would seem too self aware, like a costume, sentimental, a Wes Anderson brand of twee, instead of just itself. The desk magically embodied this very particular territory. Its peeling varnish and chipped corners were too earnestly ratty to suffer these pitfalls. It managed its own presence, just sweet enough with no cloying aftertaste.

Finally, I moved the desktop, back down the five flights of stairs into a rented van and brought it to my new house in New Jersey. I replaced the desk-height hairpin legs with a 16" version. It sits in my living room in front of the fireplace, no longer a desk. Instead, it's a coffee table, home to the green and blue marble chess board I bought in Athens when I was seventeen years old. I'd saved up money from walking neighborhood dogs and bought the $800 round trip ticket to travel to Greece with Monica to visit her family in the seaside village of Nea Makri. Stacked next to the chessboard are two ceramic tiles marked with impressions of Maple seed pods that I had custom made for Cameron by a potter friend in Maine. It seems only right now that this piece of oak resides in good company among friends, lest it find itself painfully incongruous, an energetic pearls-before-swine-predicament.

I imagine if I were sitting at the oak desk, I might find that bit of darkness, the kind that I felt when watching those kids play from my place in solitude inside the cold foyer. Or glancing over to meet Lisa's eyes on Martin Luther King Day, or on my wedding night when Radiohead was supplanted by Gloria Estefan. Pottery Barn doesn't really allow those stories. It's an unassailable and pristine image, a trap of unattainability, built to fail just in time for a newer, "better" version to be purchased. A disposable culture.

Yet, it is the dark, assailable stories that fill my memory. It feels like an impasse sitting here, a discontinuity between my interior space and my exterior space. I am watching from shadow, my memory rife with preternatural extractions from this twilight. I meet these disruptions, instinctually, with hard no's but those are mostly cajoled, provoked, seduced with long-stemmed roses, reprimanded in booming baritone, curbed, and educated into pained and begrudging yes's. Sometimes there weren't yes's at all, just the tatters of no's transgressed. A fragile twilight dissolved by klieg lights. The glossy advertisement image persists and prevails, despite all evidence of material degradation.

When writing, it's important to set the scene. To orient the spiritual space of writing to the material world. The maxim: "Show don't tell." What does this really mean? *The meaning is in the stuff.* The doing and the tables and the clothes and the conversations. Not just writing, but living, is not in the meaning skimmed from the surface, brought to light as it were. The meaning is so specific that it adheres to and within only something commensurately specific: elaborate, irreducible materialism. It bears deep scratches to the surface. It can be penetrated, but remains the same throughout, integral, solid oak. How could I tell you about this small, dark, expansive watchtower that I've lived in from the time I can remember while sitting at this piece of whitewashed, particle board fiction?

I'm going to dim the lights a little bit so that I can tell you what's inside: When I was young I would fly.

I would walk, in the middle of the night after my parents had long been asleep, to the top of the stairs, my left hand outstretched, a winged animal. I would place my right hand on the banister. I plunged downward, effortlessly. My hand would glide, frictionless, but still sensibly, along the smooth wood of the banister until reaching the end, which curved into curled punctuation, finitude. I would then evaporate. Only to return to the top of the stairs the next night, looking down calmly towards the blue-gray moonlight streaming through the front door and reflecting back from the glossy tile, again taking flight.

I remember myself as a child, or not so much as a child as *being* a child, looking out from behind the glass door from the cold darkness of the foyer at the other children playing in the street. I remember flying in the darkness. Even when speaking I was watching. The words I said always answered, not the question posed, but instead: "What is the answer they are looking for?" This served me quite well in school.

I took comfort in the woods because they were also dark, even during the day.

I sunk into the water of the bath, closing the curtain tightly against the light, closing my eyes and letting the water fill my ears.

I felt the irresistible fright of the particular dark that attends crisp, cold air on a starry night while walking the dogs. A rush of chills comes over me and I urge the dogs to hurry, while trying to peer beyond the purview of yellow streetlights, just in case.

Waking up before dawn words fall, letter by letter, onto my keyboard and to the digital page, as if emerging more easily from this dark, their natural home, than from the brightness of stale yesterdays and someone else's tomorrows that always exist in day-light.

I return to darkness for solace. It is the source of flight. It is the source of friendship. It is the source of desire, of *yes*. Darkness cloaks the desk, the world, enough for the truth to materialize beyond the image. In a world that preaches light, I am an atheist. Sitting here, tracing my history in darkness, in the unmistakable integrity of material things, I remember a different kind of story. God was there all along.

36. Soul

"I looked at my grandmother's dead body and I just knew it wasn't her anymore," my mother mused about the soul. We sat in her bedroom and she looked into the distance as she recalled the experience.

My mother and I weren't particularly close when I was growing up. My memories of her are of someone distracted, her back turned, engaged in some other task. "Mom, watch me!" I would call from the diving boards at the pool or from the living room practicing some dance routine. Inevitably, she would miss the dive, the performance. I didn't particularly begrudge her disinterest in children, quite frankly it is something we share.

My grandmother, Mary, looked at my father holding me as a baby and remarked, "All he needs is a pair of tits." Her observation summed up a certain reversal of traditional expectations and roles.

My father is an atheist, and I was aligned with him. Not through sheer allegiance but in a shared disposition and bearing in the world, something that appeared in the way we moved, the way we spoke and thought. I certainly noticed, even as a young person, the disconnect between purported Christian values and the behavior of the Christians I knew who seemed more focused on condemning people than embracing them. I was repelled by the loose language that informed such consequential political and environmental beliefs. The Christian faith often seemed not to guide reason, but to wage war against it.

I eschewed Catholicism, especially as I grew into my teen years and found their myopic campaigns against bodily sovereignty just another not-so-subtle patriarchal violence. My mother went to mass each Sunday. She enrolled me in CCD (Sunday school for Catholics) at St. Virgil's Church. The classes were held in the small school adjoining the church. I used to sit staring out at the mulch-covered playground and wondered about the kids that actually attended the school full time. I sat through the classes, mostly bored and sometimes frustrated by the tactics. A priest once substituted for the class and regaled us with personal anecdotes and his practices in the world as one of Jesus' disciples: "If someone honks their car horn at me when a red traffic light turns green because they feel I haven't pulled out quickly enough, I just sit there through another light. I make them wait."

"What an asshole," was my father's reaction to my retelling of the story.

Once, the church held an overnight retreat at the school for those enrolled in CCD. They played a movie where several teens were in a fatal car accident. Some of these teens went to Heaven and some to Hell. The ones that went to Hell were shown descending into fire, each in an industrial looking elevator, crying out in pain and despair. After the movie, I argued, "If you are so confident in your beliefs, why use such horror and scare tactics? Why subject us to this kind of fictional propaganda?" I was sent home.

When I was sixteen years old, confirmation approached. Instead of CCD classes held in the school, various adults in the church community volunteered to host small groups of teens in their homes and teach the curriculum leading up to the sacrament. I remember walking in the evenings to the classes held in a small house less than a mile from my own. As I walked west in the twilight I thought: "If God truly existed, in all the glory and power they say, then I would surely know of him without all of the church's noise. No one would need to *tell* me." I watched an enormous sun set pinkly on the horizon and concluded, "there is no god."

When the time came, I refused to receive the sacrament of confirmation. My mother, frustrated, sent me to talk to Sister Linda, a heavy-set woman with glasses, a particularly harsh and disciplinarian nun who was generally feared. I walked into her office and her gentleness surprised me. I told her frankly: "It would be disingenuous for me to proclaim a faith I do not possess. Further, it wouldn't be respectful of the church community. I don't believe in God." She kindly agreed. I don't remember her words, but she seemed to offer that I spend the time I needed in the world. She offered me respect and compassion.

I think my mother was disappointed that Sister Linda had not lived up to her authoritarian reputation. However, there was nothing more to be done. It wasn't until I left college and began slowly making my way towards other ways of knowing that I slowly made my way back into kinship with my mother.

My thesis in college had been on the futility and failure of the mind as our guide and leader. I used Dostoevksy's <u>Notes From</u>

<u>Underground</u> to talk about the main character as a modern anti-hero. This character was crippled in various manifestations by a disproportionate reliance on reason. I understood him as a scathing critique of enlightenment values. I wanted to find the antidote.

My first intuition was to move toward image, toward art making. When I moved to Boston in the year following graduation, I enrolled in painting classes at the School of the Museum of Fine Arts. I painted from life. I thought more about how it must be for the models to hold still for so long, to choreograph their poses. Some were more skilled than others, quickly able to move from one sustainable position to another. The women seemed more at ease than the men, who all behaved as if they lost some kind of bet and expected it to be easier than it was. I painted piles of fruits and vegetables. I painted the little green and white stickers on the red and yellow bell peppers to the surprise of the instructor and the rest of the class who had omitted the stickers in their renderings.

I had in mind that I would create a portfolio and apply to graduate school, somehow picking up where I'd left off after high school. My creative life evolved from painting. My art-making practice slowly allowed me to connect body and intuition. It was my gateway to investigating other fringe pursuits like mediumship, dream tending, and shamanic practice. It would take me nearly a decade of this work to finally attend graduate school.

My mother became the person in my family with whom I could share my experiences. My relationship with her strengthened in direct proportion to my acceptance and recognition of an always-latent mysticism that I could now glimpse in the shadows of my memories. Solitary walks in the woods. Sleepless nights.

Prayers cloaked as meditations. Serendipity denied as coincidence. Sunsets denied my full company because I'd trivialized the material world by amputating it from the spiritual world.

I spent a lot of time at my grandmother's house in Newark as a kid. It was the house my mother grew up in. I loved sleeping over there; it meant a steady stream of homemade pizza and television. In the morning, Grandpa would go to Calandra's Bakery and bring home a box of fresh Boston Cream donuts for breakfast. On one weekend visit, they took me down the shore to Long Branch where there was a huge saltwater pool fed by the ocean. As I sat at the edge, a kid ran by, knocking me to the ground. I hit my head on the cement and my grandparents took me to the hospital. My mother, miles away at home, heard me cry.

My mother gifted me a deck of tarot cards she kept wrapped in a silk scarf in her dresser for years. We invited a psychic to come to her home and meet with us; we compared stories of what my deceased grandmother, Mary, had told each of us. My mother and I found an ability to connect here, in a world of spirit, of faith, in the space of the mystical. After Luciano was born, my mother found the paper the psychic had given her, my son's name had been scrawled at the top a year before his birth.

I asked my mother, when I was in my late twenties, "Why do you believe in a soul?" I don't know what I wanted from her, but I suspected she was the right place to go for this kind of inquiry. She would in fact take it seriously and I trusted that she had experience of other worlds. It was then that she told me of her experience of her grandmother's dead body. I believed her and for perhaps the first time, I knew what she meant.

37. Cloud Cover

As an artist I spent a long time thinking about process as opposed to product. I know how to work in the moment, letting layers accumulate and intuition guide the way. I know which color to use and when a painting is finished. I can embroider for hours and apply sheer layers of paint endlessly to reveal new accumulations, aggregates of shade and line.

I created a book of images called <u>Time Test, True Story</u>. Cameron and I were on a hike outside of Durango, Colorado. We arrived at a clear and still alpine lake reflecting a near perfect image of fat cumulus clouds perched above. I took a photograph and used it to create a black and white image of the clouds.

I bought a brand new ink cartridge for my little Hewlett Packard printer and a stack of translucent vellum paper. I proceeded to print the cloud image hundreds of times, 584 times to be exact, until the ink cartridge sputtered and ran dry. Each image was a bit different. Sometimes the vellum got stuck in the printer. Sometimes the machine sucked two pages in at a time and printed a bit of the image on both sheets. Sometimes it made errant marks or skipped spots; I can't really account for it. Do machines tire? Do they lose focus? Were the papers loaded just a bit differently from one another? The ink changed color slightly from print to print. Slowly the cartridge emptied, expired.

I used silver ink to "correct" each image that bore increasingly less resemblance to the original. I colored in faded bits of clouds and highlighted the misprinted areas. I studied these images. I layered them, letting the time show through the vellum sheets stacked one on top of the other. I collected each image in a two volume book, documenting this journey. Its truth, its story, the way we move through time: Irregular. Unaccounted for. Small. Which image tells the truth? How much time does it take to get to the story we want to tell? Should we leave out the parts that don't quite fit, the mistakes? Those off moments, the ones out of step with the rest, are they ugly? They are certainly queer. I find these fleeting pages exhilarating with hope and rife with possibility. Each errant mark a brave glimpse of a path yet unseen.

I often put myself in vulnerable positions, especially in my art practice. It is my mode of operations, whether in the making of one piece where I allow the steps to lead the journey, or in the trajectory of my work, piece after piece, where somehow stitching fabric into a quilt turns into editing video. I like to learn and to grow, to keep moving. I don't often stop to savor success. In fact, I sometimes fail to account for success altogether because I'm already on to the next challenge. For example, how could I be a great quilter if now I made video art?

Each step could seem, from the outside, to undermine, repudiate, or even just transcend the past in a way that might invalidate it. To the contrary, all of the moments press in simultaneously. They are inextricable from one another and reverberate back and forth.

On the one hand, this way of being in the world is a form of growth, an orientation always towards growth. It is a certain facility in the darkness and the unknown. A trust of process. On the other hand, it is a failure to take on the full power and responsibility of my voice and my wisdom at any given moment.

In 2019 I'd arrived in a place where I could name this intersection of forces and interests. My intellectual and spiritual curiosity met my material intimacy and I began to regularly work with women asking questions about their clothing in a deep and meaningful way. We put together the fabrics and the shapes, but we also told stories from a new source of channeled power.

I created a very special business, called Mirror & Lens. I was no longer relegated to one world or the other, but living meaningfully with the question that has driven everything. What does it mean to be an embodied spirit, or in other words, to see in the dark? I had the immense privilege of taking others gently by the hand into this question and helping them discover that they, too, no longer have to lose parts of themselves.

Abundance took on a new meaning. I was in the energy of the question, in the energy of desire. What I want to manifest is always more life, more desire. Although this always feels fresh, it is built on so many desires that came to fruition before it. It is the desire born of a lifetime of manifestations, a lifetime of beauty created and lived.

38. Gratitude

Before I open my eyes each morning, I stay in my dreams. I wander through them a bit longer, looking in the rooms, peeking around corners. I ask questions of the people and creatures that show up, or I just take a moment to observe them a little longer.

I hear Cameron and Lulu talking in the kitchen. Lulu sits on the counter telling stories and eating a small bowl of cheerios, walnuts, raisins and one date (his precise instructions.) Cameron makes coffee. Soon they bring me a glass mug, full, and set it down still steaming on the clay tile on my nightstand. The tile has an image of maple seeds pressed into the top of it. Years ago, at Haystack, Cameron said he loved the little helicopter-shaped pods. At the time, he considered getting the image tattooed. When he returned to Chicago the sight of them would spark painful longing, sadness, and sex all at once. I was friends with a potter in Maine who worked with leaves, mushrooms, and tree bark. I asked her if she'd make these tiles, for Cameron. We live with them still.

Cameron opens the curtains.

At this point our dogs have already found their way into the bed and under the covers. They adjust to curl next to me as I sit up, coffee in hand. I look at the dogwood tree outside the window and the light falling across the pink walls of our bedroom and onto the wool rug.

I made the rug years ago, and its companion that sits next to Cameron's side of the bed. (The pink and red wool rug that my grandmother made decades before lives at the foot of the bed.) They were part of an installation that also included two wooden platforms on wheels, each painted in a damask pattern. Two layer cakes, slices cut from them. Rows of chalk. Each platform is almost identical, but not quite. Layers and patterns of gray and white, rows of planks and stitches and cake, splitting up and marking space, marking time, measuring, moving, slipping away. The same. Not the same.

I'd driven many miles to a woman's farm to get the wool for these two rugs. We sat in her kitchen and talked a long while before I followed her into the barn. I entered the stall with the sheep, each a different color, if only slightly. When I left, she handed me two large, clear plastic bags of wool. Both gray, one a little lighter and one a little darker. She showed me how to hook small sections of the fine strands through a gridded mesh panel in order to create the thing I imagined.

I open my laptop and I begin to write.

39. Portraits

I was nineteen years old in 1996 when the Museum of Modern Art mounted an exhibition: Picasso and Portraiture: Representation and Transformation. About to leave the museum, I wasn't ready to let go of the images and I purchased the exhibition book for more than I'd ever spent on a book before and maybe since. I've moved more than a dozen times since then and the quite large book has come with me each time. Although, I haven't picked it up to read it for decades, until now, writing this book.

I begin reading this morning and I feel a wave in my abdomen, only it's a wave that doesn't travel, it just sits large, energized, and fully formed, urging me to turn the pages. The book begins: "In this "century of abstraction," no genre of painting might have been expected to fare worse than the portrait."

"Yes," my mind whispers, deep resonance, quietly, it almost feels like fear. I knew this exhibition affected me. I visited it with my father. He shared a love of art, but maybe moreso, he wanted to give me the experience of it and he, at every turn, made that a possibility, an opportunity. We would visit museums, not just in New York City because it was only thirty miles from our home, but it was the focus of all our traveling. We went to art museums across France and in Italy. He could barely stand sitting on a beach for a week. The times we did travel to Long Beach Island as a family are recorded in images of him, shaded by hat and t-shirt, reading books, highlighter in hand, while my mother enjoyed swimming in the ocean and sitting in the sun.

I knew upon opening this book, just now this morning that I was being drawn to it for a reason. The book was a clue, a piece of my mystery. "Yes," abstraction does seem at odds with portraiture, with an image of a human being. We've become measured and conceptualized, dragged from our elaborate specificity into IQ, EQ, BMI, gender, race, jobs, diagnoses, bank accounts, sexuality, political affiliation. The relentless onslaught of identities, bought and sold at the expense of our humanity.

In surveying Picasso's portraits of the women with whom he had intimate relationships, they depict changing and changed images of these subjects. The women are transformed, as the title of the exhibition describes, perhaps depending on the quality of the affair at that time, perhaps the mood of that month, or even just that morning. One image appears beautiful and serene, another harsh and almost grotesque. These paintings described an intersection between the one who sees and the one being seen and all of the rich space in between. Namely, they described the relationships themselves. In fact, it did not surprise me that one of Picasso's subjects, who sat for him when she was just nineteen years old, Suzette, was publishing her life story: I Was Suzette. Now, eighty-one years old, she didn't even go by the name Suzette, she went by the name Lydia Corbett. Yet, this process of portraiture had changed the way she saw herself. Enough that she saw fit to title, to frame and direct, her life's story with the name of who she was in that portrait. The portrait, like a Schrodinger's cat proposition, shows the subject becoming what it is, *in relationship*. It becomes what it is when it's seen. Interconnection and interdependence revealed as the nature of being.

The transformation does not end there, however. It is not a metamorphosis relegated to the so-called subject. In this mutualistic exchange, the artist also changes. Robert Rosenblaum writes: "But today, almost fifty years later, the visible connection between Picasso's art and love life is so taken for granted that when, for example, his works of the early 1930s are talked about, the growingly useful phrase "the Marie-Therese period" evokes something far more visually specific than, say, "the Surrealist period."" This is the crux of style. It is not the general, the abstract, the trend, let's call that Surrealism, instead, it is the elaborately specific personal and material truth of the artist. It is love that drives vision from the inside out. Picasso's style transforms his subjects as he is transformed by them. His style is both a reflection of himself and the way he sees the world, his mirror and lens.

I didn't want my holistic styling clients to follow trends, or try to figure out which things match or are so-called flattering. These things exist just in the mind, fragmented, like Surrealism as a category for Picasso. What does exist is a practice that keeps us in touch with both love and connection and that tethers those two elements to material experience.

When the human mind balks at the camera's eye view, it knows there is still more to the story, more than the purported truth of verisimilitude. No artist has ever drawn with her hands, only with her eyes, and the eyes are never the eyes, but the whole complex human sensory body, stories and attitudes, pressing through our limbs, expressed in our myriad creations through this uniquely specific embodied apparatus.

"Yes." To have style means to learn to see. Picasso's portraits aren't astounding because of photorealistic verisimilitude. They are astounding because they create new vision, they change the way we see the subjects and the way the subjects see themselves. They transform the world.

When I first began working with clients, we'd see each other about six times, each visit was a couple of hours. During our first session, we review an in-depth questionnaire I provide: "What is the item of clothing you've kept the longest? What are you wearing in your memory of feeling your best? What is your favorite texture, your favorite animal? What are your spiritual practices? What are the activities you currently do? What are the activities you want to be doing?"

The next meeting is in their home, usually the bedroom, and very hands on. "Please empty your drawers and closet of all of your clothes before I get there," I instructed each client. Would you believe this instruction has never been followed? Each client has done so more or less. They leave out a season that is still in storage, they go through their closet and pull things out one by one, but don't empty it all. They pull out 90%, but for whatever reasons, it doesn't all come out.

Sometimes I think it is too hard to bear witness to our full extension into space, the anxiety of our diffusion. Sometimes I think we just don't believe it matters. We find it hard to see these things, like an old sweatshirt from college or a drawer overflowing with socks. We minimize the importance of things we've predetermined inconsequential to the story. We already have a story in our minds and we rarely want to start at the beginning, it's too daunting. Like reading a book and getting lost in reverie, only to find you've passed through several pages not having registered a word, but instead of going back to where you left off, you go back just some of the way. We have foundations, limits, places we just don't want to go.

My clients and I sit together in piles of things and I listen. I listen to stories that women tell not knowing they are about to tell them. They are stories pieced together as word is born from word. We discover them as item after item is held up, touched, considered, felt in the body.

I return home after our second or third session and I journey. I ask my guides for a style guide to offer each client. For one it is a snake, shedding skin and keeping low to the ground, unencumbered, vulnerable, and ready for new growth. For another, it is a flying fish, at home in multiple worlds. Julia has the power and grace of a gazelle. Gigi, the goose, is rooted in her community. Ashley, no animal at all, instead a serene lake, pure reflection. Her inner calm allows her to serve and guide others.

At the end of our time together, I create a magazine. A portrait. A collage. Like the Picasso portraits, it is a record of our journey together, a mood board and a mantra. It is an image in time of the past bearing down on the present and offering specific hopes for the future. It is an alchemical process, not unlike the one that transformed Lydia Corbett into Suzette. This book is more poem than prescription. It is holding space, but the space isn't empty, it's a loving and beautiful space.

The reason artists can paint, can create, is because their sense of beauty in the world bears down and presses through the body into the heart, into the gut, into the hands. There is a flood inside of clues and love and I feel this flood, this wave, every time I work with someone. It is a flood of resonance, like the feeling I had opening Picasso's portraiture book this morning, that "yes." We are creating a portrait. Restoring complex humanity, beauty and compassion to perception. I can do that for my clients because I see them as beautiful, as whole.

Is my vision missing from the sartorial images we create together? No. It is the mutualistic journey that produces a benevolent and powerful new truth. Is my skill mixing patterns and colors? Knowledge of trends? Of sustainable fabrics and retailers? Facility with shapes? I can do those things, but no, my skill is empathy. Empathy is the spiritual bridge.

This work is about intimacy and the wisdom of connection. It grew out of a dissolution with craft, on the one hand, and art on the other. This mirror and lens is how we see. It is how we reflect that back and forth to each other and in the world around us. This tender work infuses that connection with beauty, mystery, and love.

It should not be surprising then, that I soon realized I could not do so many of these portraits. I couldn't do more than one at a time, certainly. For each client I was immersed in a vision of their world. I was tapping into my creative and spiritual resources and this required research and analysis from the mind, time from the body, empathic investment, and emotional collateral. For each client, I listened, I wrote, I envisioned, I journeyed, divined, and created.

My earliest clients helped me to develop this profound practice. My clients are not subjects relegated to static material, paint on a canvas or stone on a plinth. They are breath fueled by desire, fueled by breath. With each story told and retold and each item of clothing worn, they expand the notion of their own humanity. Those small acts of individuation offer some bit of sanctuary for the rest of us.

Picasso's portraits are revolutionary not because they look like what we already know, but because when they speak, some voice within us assents: "Yes." Albeit trepidatious in the face of the unknown, but unable to resist none-the-less, desiring, *inspired*.

Working with clients I found a place I longed to practice, the place where embodied spirits meet in trust and compassion to create a new vision altogether.

Style is how we see.

40. Layers

I sit for hours looking out the windows at my garden. I wander outside in the garden. I walk up the hill and look back down at the garden from the top. I look in the morning. I mark the light at noon. I walk outside the perimeter of the fence at 3pm. In the morning I carry a cup of hot coffee, in the afternoon tea. A glass of wine or maybe even a cocktail in the evening. I watch the dirt, the rocks, the leaves, the rise and fall of the compost heap. The scattered bits of debris animals casually leave while going about their day. Small holes appear and disappear under the porch stairs, under the fence, upending a couple of bulbs or a recently transplanted echinacea.

The small yellow evergreen leaves of the illicium, anise-scented with small fruits in the fall, will create a five-foot hedgerow marking the far side of a small, terraced patio area I created by collecting and stacking stones from other parts of the yard. It will find the dappled shade it likes under the leaves of the coral bark maple, which in turn is protected by the hundred-year-old oak in the front yard. The garden archway frames the chartreuse-leaved maple which mostly disappears in the winter leaving layered hedgerows of dark shiny azalea and the yellow illicium. In the spring, these textures and colors shift and are joined with lilyturf, orange, white, and yellow daffodils, and purple crocuses. Followed by hostas, mint and thyme and a small bit of Irish Moss spilling over the edges onto the buttery yellow pea gravel of the patio and pathway leading to the rest of the yard. Shade in the summer giving way to sunlight in the winter, colors ebb and flow, brighten, then brittle and pale. They move through the days, the seasons, the years. This space of the garden extends in so many directions at once, viewed from the peaks and the lows, the present, memories of the past, of gardens past, and imagined from a future.

I think about Cameron at Haystack, his relationship with the natural world and his creative aspirations. His resistance to broach the topic of nature or even of beauty in his work. We talk about the garden together. "You make our world beautiful," he says.

I can see my high school art teacher's house from my garden. I had no idea she lived here until a couple of months after we'd moved in. Her memory is now sadly fading and sometimes when I catch a glimpse of her through the shade of her private courtyard, I simply pass by in deep fondness. Her house sits on the hilltop above us. She once wrote in my college applications, "She has among the rarest potential of any student I've ever had." It might be the most encouraging thing anyone has ever said to me. She had given me the gift of space and time to grow and this I remember each time I look up towards her house. A monument to possibility, to love, to art. Material mantra.

41. Gates

I've been dreaming of huge lions lately. Not just regular-huge, but mythic huge. They keep telling me I need to use my voice. I think it's more than that, though. I think they want me to own my voice. To celebrate my success. I've gotten so comfortable striving. So comfortable in the unknown of transition, in the Heron's twilight, that I think I've developed a bit of an aversion to actually seeing the sun full in the sky or the darkness complete.

I took a photograph of my garden the other day. More precisely it was an image of the newly laid gravel path leading through the cedar arch and under a star-shaped lantern made of colored glass. The path is lined with flowering hostas and creeping junipers. Through the gate the grass is dappled with sunlight and the scalloped edge of the far side of the fence creates the backdrop for fresh beds dotted with small coneflowers, more hostas, and Japanese painted ferns. Soon, an aronia bush and a package of white tulips will arrive and find their place, too.

A couple of days after taking the photograph, I came across another picture. It was a cedar arch over a garden gate, covered in vines dying back at the end of the fall. Only in this image, I couldn't glimpse into the garden beyond, the gate was closed. I'd taken this picture almost exactly one year before I took the one of my own garden, and several months before even finding the house where I now live.

Cameron and I were driving around in New Jersey and feeling a bit hopeless. We'd been looking for a home for almost four years. "Pull over!" I was excited as we nearly drove past the gate. I got out and took the image. That is what I wanted. A garden. A gate. It was an aspirational photo. It was a wish. The gate seemed like a beautiful invitation to the unknown beyond, an invitation to mystery. Its beauty promised more beauty. It framed a yet unseen future.

When I first moved to New York City I had a vision in a journey about a series of garden gates. Paths winding through lushly green spaces, dappled with sun, leading only to more gates. I thought these gates were more questions. That they held future mysteries, exciting and full of promise. While that's true, what I didn't realize is that the beauty behind each gate was not a question to be answered, but instead it was more desire to be lived, a wish for endless gardens and gates.

It is a wonderful thing to be able to visualize and manifest one's dreams. More still, to recognize all of the dreams manifested and our magical ability to bring to material fruition from the vastness of our imaginations.

When we bought our house, less than a year ago, the yard was bare. There were no paths, no garden gates, just a couple of waning shrubs grown awry and leafless with neglect and a couple of wayward patches of pachysandra dotted with weeds and poison ivy. Some cinder blocks lay outside the porch door, perhaps once serving as an adhoc station for a small grill.

I look at the photo from a couple of days ago and I remember to see all of the mirrors of my imagination, materialized around me. In love, in work, in things. So many wishes fulfilled.

I am grateful to be home. I am grateful that home means I'm not finished yet. Like a gate, or a good marriage, home is just the shape of the beginning.

42. Mirror and Lens

My styling clients come to me when they have a nagging sense. When they're in the throes of their own mystery, but perhaps haven't quite accepted it. They want to dress their part of the story. Sometimes they want to dress their way out, like Wile E Coyote painting a fake road at the edge of a cliff. They are looking for a portrait, for me to see them in their beauty and to reflect it back to them.

I would, of course, love to oblige, if I thought it would last. But the trick is not showing them a picture, an image of themselves. If a true picture existed, if it were possible, it would be easy. A quick polaroid like those washed out images of models they re-arrange to plot fashion shows, or maybe it would look more like an MRI or some spun out double helix pinned and splayed on a dissecting pan. Perhaps if I dressed them up just so, arranging the colors and shapes. Maybe I could select rich textures and luminous colors to match the seasonal light and for a moment they'd be quite pleased until they returned home, to feel that bit of space that creeps in between body and spirit. That special dysmorphic terrain that exists as a river moves beyond the vacation snapshot you've taken to preserve that special moment of unity, when all sentiment coincides perfectly with the material elements, the moment that is nothing if not fleeting.

It is all I can do to teach people to use the lenses I use in order to see, to believe that there are lenses at all. (The myth of objectivity is awfully intractable.) Then they will always know to follow the river, instead of trying to stop it. To stay in step with themselves, or rather, in some eccentric, syncopated skip. To relish those dissonant moments when, upon looking into the mirror, a stranger peers back. In those hiccups, in that skipping tempo, a heartbeat more wayward even than a small inkjet printer delivering page after page of shifting clouds, a world of clues appears as an invitation. An imperfect breadcrumb trail.

When I first started developing practices and working with clients, I was concerned about devoting more creative energy to styling without clarity about a greater purpose. After all, I had worked as a professional stylist for a major women's retailer and it was a shockingly bad experience considering how much it should have aligned with my interests and talents. Retail is a place that wants to give answers, to create certainty, and at it's worst, to create false, self-serving stories. As antithetical to resolving pain-points as it might appear, I am interested in the questions. If uncertainty is our element, then, paradoxically, the truth lies in those questions. Quick and superficial answers like a new blouse that promises happiness, sex-appeal, or a carefree spirit, cuts off the blood supply to those vital questions. Those kinds of answers move us out of presence. I was ultimately not interested in simply telling people what to wear or encouraging them to buy more things. Styling in that context was one of myriad channels for capitalist and consumerist values to operate. I decided to use shamanic journeying practices for clarity around this new work.

In a shamanic vision, I asked my guide, a young doe, for insight into the purpose of guiding people in relationship to their things. She quickly brought me to the edge of a small lake, and I could see through a clearing in tall grasses, a white crane, pristine, standing at the far bank. I then began to see clothing appear, camouflaged in the brush around the perimeter of this lake, mostly hidden in the trees. Then appeared certain red, diaphanous silhouettes. The crane chose one of these brightly colored garments and draped it over his head and eyes: "The purpose of this work is shape-shifting. It is to give new sight."

I call myself first an artist, because I need to *make* in order to see. Making is a way of living with things, just like getting dressed each day. I need to know my knowing. I must continue to learn the texture and temperature of my boundaries, my yes's and my no's. The hard stops and the soft, imploring whispers bound to fluctuations of light. I need to practice staying in relationship to that wisdom in soft oil sticks, on the cotton rag page, hard inflections of graphite, thin trails of ink, washes of watery pigment resisting smears of colored wax. All of my gestures met with grace in this visceral abundance: ecstatic compromise.

We are taught this meeting, flesh and spirit, media and imagination, lessens our power, when in fact it is the release of ego in exchange for the wisdom of presence. It is the jumping-in of double Dutch. This so-called compromise is the glory of connection in the ether of mystery.

43. Monarch

The summer Cameron and I met, there were turtles everywhere. Every time I would drive down the interstate, giant snapping turtles would cross the road. Walking in the woods: box turtles. Nearly everyday an encounter.

"Turtles all the way down," he and I said simultaneously in one of our very first conversations. We were crocheting sculptures at a gray wooden table in a studio overlooking the ocean. We were both referring to the cosmological proposition that the world sat on the back of a giant turtle. This giant turtle sat on another turtle and so on, all the way down. We laughed, delighting in connection.

The turtle story is about how we know things. It is a story I've encountered again and again. I've held onto it in all its forms. One of my favorites, Dostoevsky's <u>Notes from Underground</u>: "For in order to begin to act, one must first be completely at ease, so that no more doubts remain. Well, and how am I, for example, to set myself at ease? Where are the primary causes on which I can rest, where are my bases? Where am I going to get them? I exercise thinking, and, consequently, for me every primary cause immediately drags with it yet another, still more primary one, and so on ad infinitum. Such is precisely the essence of all consciousness and thought." I recognized this plight within me, this endlessness. I was locked in my head and like Dostoevky's Underground Man, I was always ill-at-ease. Wracked with doubt. These turtles were just bases and causes stacked forever. I was trying desperately to get out of the system.

The turtles and the Underground Man's so-called *bases* are the demonstrable truths we feel free and confident communicating with one another. The connection that Cameron and I had, uttering this phrase, was the way out. It was connection which inspired a kind of faith, the knowing that resides outside of the world. It was a leap into the abyss, into the darkness. It was sacred. I encountered the part of myself that didn't demand proof. It simply was.

I drove Cameron to the Bangor airport when our time on Deer Isle came to an end. Every turtle I saw for the rest of the summer reminded me, a mantra: *you know the truth; you know love.*

When Nora lived with us, I saw blue herons. The turtles lasted only that one summer in 2005, but now, it was 2013. I drove to work and two Herons swooped down from a hillside towards the water and passed within 20 feet above my windshield. I went for a run, a blue heron accompanied me for a brief stretch down the road, just above and ahead, leading the way. Nora and I sat at the edge of an inlet on the coast in Belfast. We'd followed a little path through some brush behind a school that was no longer in session. A blue heron landed opposite us on the bank. Again, and again the heron showed up for me. I understood at the time that this bird marked a transition. The blue heron is a twilight hunter, a liminal creature. I'd hoped at the time that she was affirming a transitional period in my art practice, in my spiritual development. I thought she was affirming this movement deeper into the knowing of dreams, of connectivity. Perhaps she was, but what I see now is a deeper and more profound change was brewing. The upending of my life as I'd known it.

When I founded Mirror & Lens to practice holistic styling, I used the heron as the symbol. After all, it was the heron guide that came to me and assured me that shape shifting was the path forward. I created a silhouette of the flying bird and placed her next to the same silhouette in a mirror image.

Now, I walk through the narrow, one lane streets of my little neighborhood. I marvel at each zinnia, dahlia, peony, and cosmos reaching out over into the road. I've noticed a new animal. A new messenger: the monarch butterfly. The body of this creature is a mirror unto herself, two elaborately patterned wings her signature.

The monarch butterfly begins life as a caterpillar. The caterpillar eats. She eats more, and then even more. She is metabolizing the world around her, taking it into her body, transforming this experience into herself until the time comes to build a cocoon. Inside this hard shell the obliteration of the caterpillar body is violent and complete. The larval brain stimulates the release of enzymes which dissolve most of her tissues into their constituent proteins. The broken-down caterpillar body, within this self-created cocoon, is reconstructed into a new being entirely.

The color of the newly formed wings is created from the world the caterpillar absorbed. Through its food, its nutrients, its material experience. Caterpillars deprived of food for just one day develop into butterflies with stunted, pale, and more yellow wings. Those who are allowed free access to food retain darker orange colors and larger wings. The color influences flight durations, mating patterns, and the ability to signal warning to would-be predators. The butterfly expresses the truth of her material experience and this expression changes the quality and path of her life.

The monarch butterfly has a strong inner compass that allows her to migrate thousands of miles, and yet, her migration is not a life's work. Instead it is a journey she makes with her ancestors and progeny, a relay, taking up to five generations to complete the full path. She has a circannual clock and a solar compass, adhering to the mandates and rhythms of her own body in deep interconnection with both the environment and her heritage. She only lays eggs if the conditions are just right; this requires the milkweed plant. Her clock is the very same inner and outer clock of the double Dutch jumper.

Almost everyday, the monarch passes through my garden. I see her, deep orange and black, alight on a patch of vibrant petals. She has emerged fully integrated, fully integral, a mirror unto herself. She bears witness only to her fraction of a larger journey, and yet she is sovereign in the mystery that is not without purpose.

Even after her death, the memories of the caterpillar remain with the butterfly.

Acknowledgments

Whenever I consider the deep well of gratitude that springs from this book, one thought persists above the others: The list of people is either too long or too short to be credible.

There's the only one: Cameron.

This book would simply not exist without Alexandra.

It is with unmitigated pride that I am from my parents. My experience is of them, through me. They made this way for me. To my baby, my mirror and my lens. To my sister, who drove with me to Chicago when everyone thought I was crazy.

Choosing to follow the inevitably idiosyncratic clues of one's vision is lonely stuff, but I have the most ingenious and kindred friends on earth, whose courageous selves make it safe for others, especially for me, and I admire and take solace in their existence: Monica, Lori, Christine, Lisa, Rachel, Kate, Amy, Kathryn, Dan, Mindy, and Melissa.

To Rob, who helped me realize the freedom to do whatever the fuck I wanted, which is how art is born.

To Cameron's family, who supported us from the beginning.

To Pony, Petey, Buster, and Flash.

Art is nothing if not faith and there are those along the way who affirm that faith, who give courage and hope, who in fact make that their vocation: the people that are Chase's Daily, for creating beauty, art, and magic from this material life and sharing it with so, so many. Suzette McAvoy, Dan Kany, Britta Konau, the late Owen Smith, Sheridan Kelley Adams, Kirsten Jacobson, Randy Regier, Jared Cowan, and Bethany Engstrom. And to all of those who've collected my work over the years: powerful whispers to *keep going*.

To my Tabor neighbors, stewards of this wonderland. Especially to our trees and those who protect them, Shauna and Meg.

To those who go beyond in search of truth in practice and helped guide me through a most difficult transition of my lifetime: Jane Burns of Journeys to the Soul, Susan Bakaley Marshall and Chris Marshall of the Thirteenth Moon Center, the Mid-Atlantic and New York Vipassana Associations, and Julia Frodahl.

To Sarah Cottrell, who told me I had a memoir and generously shared her experience and resources, and likewise to Rogan Kelly who offered leads and encouragement along the way. To Jenny Dalton for reading and giving feedback on my draft. To Summer Stewart and Unsolicited Press for seeing and supporting this book.

About the Author

Gabriella D'Italia (she/her) is an interdisciplinary, award-winning fine artist. Her work explores home, nature, female identity and the contributions of these environments to our human wisdom and sustenance. She is best known for her highly inquisitive, pro-craft, feminist fiber works and multimedia collage. Her work has been exhibited at biennials, salons, embassies, and galleries internationally.

Gabriella grew up in Morristown, NJ. After receiving her BA in Philosophy and the History of Science and Mathematics through the Great Books program at St. John's College, she moved to Boston and then Maine, where for two decades she immersed herself in costume design, quilting, leadership roles in nationally recognized fine craft organizations, and teaching courses on creativity. She holds an MFA in Intermedia from the University of Maine, Orono.

Gabriella lives and works outside of New York City with her family.

About the Press

Unsolicited Press is based out of Portland, Oregon and focuses on the works of the unsung and underrepresented. As a womxn-owned, all-volunteer small publisher that doesn't worry about profits as much as championing exceptional literature, we have the privilege of partnering with authors skirting the fringes of the lit world. We've worked with emerging and award-winning authors such as Amy Shimshon-Santo, Brook Bhagat, Elisa Carlsen, Tara Stillions Whitehead, and Anne Leigh Parrish.

Learn more at unsolicitedpress.com. Find us on Instagram, X, Facebook, Pinterest, Bsky, Threads, YouTube, and LinkedIn. Unsolicited Press also writes a snarky newsletter on Substack.